QUARTET IN HEAVEN

By the same author

THE CHILDREN'S SUMMER
EMBER LANE
THE END OF THE HOUSE OF ALARD
GREEN APPLE HARVEST
THE HIDDEN SON
JOANNA GODDEN
THE PLOUGHMAN'S PROGRESS
SUPERSTITION CORNER
SUSAN SPRAY
SUSSEX GORSE★
TAMARISK TOWN
TAMBOURINE, TRUMPET AND DRUM
THE VALIANT WOMAN
THE LARDNERS AND THE LAURELWOODS
THE TREASURES OF THE SNOW
MRS. GAILEY

★ By arrangement with James Nisbet and Co., Ltd.

SHEILA KAYE-SMITH

★

Quartet in Heaven

★
★ ★
★

CASSELL & CO LTD

LONDON

CASSELL & CO. LTD.
37/38 St. Andrews Hill
Queen Victoria Street
London, E.C. 4.

and at

210 Queen Street, Melbourne
26/30 Clarence Street, Sydney
P.O. Box 9, Lower Hutt, N.Z.
263/7 Adelaide Street West, Toronto
P.O. Box 275, Cape Town
P.O. Box 1386, Salisbury, S. Rhodesia
122 East 55th Street, New York 22
15 Graham Road, Ballard Estate, Bombay 1
Islands Brygge 5, Copenhagen
Gartenstrasse 53, Dusseldorf
Avenida 9 de Julho 1138, São Paulo
P.O. Box 959, Accra, Gold Coast
Galeria Güemes, Escritorio 518/520 Florida
165 Buenos Aires
Calcada Do Carmo 55-20, Lisbon
25, Rue Henri Barbusse, Paris 5e

First published 1952

Set in 12 pt. Bembo type and
printed in Great Britain by
J. W. Arrowsmith Ltd., Quay Street and Small Street, Bristol.
F. 452

CONTENTS

FOREWORD

THESE studies in sanctity do not profess to make any special contribution to the life histories of their subjects. St. Catherine of Genoa has been dealt with exhaustively by Baron Friedrich von Hügel in his great work *The Mystical Element of Religion*, Cornelia Connelly's life has been fully written by a religious of her order, while on St. Rose of Lima the hagiographers have worked for centuries, and a new book on St. Thérèse of Lisieux must appear almost every month.

My object is psychological rather than biographical. I want to see these four women as human beings before I attempt to examine them as saints. The tendency of religious biographers has so often been to enlarge on the spiritual side of their subjects, while smoothing away or even rubbing out the marks of our common humanity, that the supernatural has been deprived of its sacramental base in the natural, and appears in consequence tenuous and uninspiring. Jacob Boehme asks: "How can I, being in nature, attain the supersensual ground without forsaking nature?" I believe that the saints have found the answer to this question, but that the hagiographers have in many instances deprived their answer of half its meaning.

In some ways my quartet is more like a *pas de quatre*, for there is among them a constant movement and change of partners. Two of them, St. Catherine of Genoa and St. Rose of Lima, belong to history, while St. Thérèse of Lisieux and Cornelia Connelly belong to modern times. A fresh combination is that of Cornelia Connelly and St. Rose of Lima, who both spring from the New World, from North and South America respectively, while St. Catherine and St. Thérèse were born and bred in Europe. St. Catherine combines with Cornelia Connelly in the married state, while St. Thérèse and St. Rose are both unmarried, though only the first is a nun. Finally all return to their original partners, for St. Catherine and St. Rose are saints in the grand manner, complete with visions, ecstasies, miracles and almost inhuman penances, while Cornelia Connelly unites with St. Thérèse in the more ordinary ways of prayer and work and suffering.

The word saint, of course, has different meanings on different levels. On one, which is the sense in which St. Paul uses it in his correspondence with the young churches, it belongs to all the baptised—"the saints who are in Corinth"—in Ephesus, in Philippi. On another level it is applied to those whose goodness is impressively above the average; but on the highest level and in the technical and formal sense, it depends on the rite of canonisation. Cornelia Connelly is the only member of my quartet who has not been canonised, and if I should use the noun and its attendant adjective in connection with her, I wish to make it clear that I use them in the second sense only and that I accept unreservedly the judgment of the Apostolic See, which alone has the authority to pronounce to whom belongs the character and title of Saint.

The author is indebted to Messrs. Longmans, Green for permission to reprint extracts from letters published in The Life of Cornelia Connelly.

THE
MATRONS

Caterina Fiesca Adorna

I

THE plague was in Genoa. That was nothing new or even unusual. The city lay open on all sides to its visitations. There was probably always some infection at the docks, and the traffic of the roads, pouring in to meet the traffic of the sea, brought the disease from Naples, Rome, Venice, Pisa or wherever it happened to be raging. The weather and seasons seemed to make no difference to the place's vulnerability. Those who were fleeing or fighting the pest in this stifling summer of 1524 could remember or had heard their parents tell how one of its worst visitations had been just after the abnormally cold winter of 1493, when the harbour basin was frozen over and the roads were blocked by the strange and terrifying snow.

The usual history repeated itself. Those who could go, went, the merchants, the bankers, all the rich—their families if not themselves—clutching their posies and their pomanders in the frail belief that it is not so easy to breathe death from a perfumed air. Only the poor remained, as always, and those who helped to nurse the poor—the Lombard doctors, the priests, the Franciscan tertiaries. And many of these were afraid.

Ettore Vernazza was afraid, though he had nursed the plague-stricken before. In the epidemic of '93 he had worked in the open-air hospital at the back of the city, in the canvas street which the Lady Caterina had caused to be erected, under the conviction that fresh air would not only reduce the danger of infection but would benefit her patients. He had been a very young man then, twenty-three years younger than the Lady

[3]

Caterina, but their friendship had ripened into a very nearly perfect thing, which had further enlarged itself to include not only himself, but, after his marriage, his wife and three daughters. They were all her friends, her disciples, treasuring her goodness and her wisdom, and though she had been dead fourteen years he could feel her with him now. Indeed it was she, the thought of her, that had brought him to Genoa to nurse the plague-stricken poor in the lazaretto which he himself had built and endowed.

His wife had died some years ago, but his daughter Battista was a nun in the city. He decided to go to her and ask her advice on a matter he was unable to decide for himself.

"What do you think I had better do? I am determined not to forsake the poor. But do you think I had better go about on horseback or on foot? In which way am I most likely to avoid infection?"

This touching fear of disease and death in the midst of all his heroism had kept him both practical and humble. He must for others' sake, for the sake of the poor themselves, take no avoidable risks, and he must also envisage the consequences of such risks as were unavoidable and provide for his work having to go on without him. He was a lawyer, and his careful, elaborate, fully-thought-out will—a true lawyer's will—had been drawn up to ensure that his lazaretto should survive the death it might inflict upon him.

At the same time he was humble, for he felt that his fears were unworthy of the friend who used to work beside him, for she herself had had none. As he asked his daughter that very innocent question there may have been in his heart a reproachful prick of memory. Had he not once seen the Lady Caterina stoop and kiss the mouth of a plague-stricken woman in the Hospital of Pammatone? The woman, dying, had tried to utter the name of Jesus, "and Caterina when she saw the mouth filled as it were with Jesus could not refrain from kissing it with great and tender affection". She had in consequence caught

[4]

the plague, but had not died of it. Perhaps if he caught it he would not die. . . .

His daughter was speaking.

"Oh, Father, we are drawing near to the feast of St. John the Baptist, and are at the worst of the heat. Yet you are determined to go among the plague-stricken."

But by this reference to the Baptist she had unwittingly destroyed the force of her pleading, or rather had diverted it to other ends. For it was Vernazza himself who had founded the Society of St. John the Baptist for work in the prisons of Naples, Rome, Genoa and other cities, with those condemned to die. He had shared with many their last night on earth, bringing them comfort and courage to meet their end. Could he possibly use his patron's Nativity as an excuse for himself evading death?

So he answered—

"Must I hear such things from *you*? How truly happy I should be if I were to die for the poor."

Then she could only say—

"Father, go."

He went, but his sacrifice did not preserve him. He caught the plague and died of it in a few days. During those last days in the Lazar House I think he must have lost the last of his fear. We can picture him lying there, withdrawn from the heat and smells and turmoil of the ward, wrapped closely in the love of God—the love which his friend Caterina had taught him was equally the light of heaven and the fire of hell. Now that death was close and accepted there was nothing to terrify the man who died a martyr to the plague-stricken poor. He belonged to an age when hell-fire threatened and frightened even the devout. But La Fiesca had taught him that only the willed rejection of God's love could turn it from creating light to searing flame. It is true that its fire burned also in purgatory, but there it burned not the man but his sins. It was a consummation that the soul itself asked for, longing above all things for its own purification as it plunged—that had been her exact word—from the awful purity of the sight of God to cleanse itself at whatever cost.

On the Eve of St. John the Baptist he received his viaticum: "and in three days," writes his daughter, "he fell quietly asleep in the Lord."

2

Caterina Fiesca Adorna. It is a lovely name—it sings. Yet it proclaims a tragedy similar, though in reverse, to that of Romeo and Juliet. Those lovers were separated by the strife of their families, but though the warfare between the Fieschi and the Adorni had been as bitter as that between Montague and Capulet—the Fieschi were Guelphs and the Adorni Ghibellines —it was not their strife but their reconciliation which brought wretchedness to two young lives.

Caterina Fiesca and Giuliano Adorno were temperamentally unsuited to each other: he was reckless, extravagant, dissipated, selfish and bad-tempered, she was shy, silent, thoughtful and devout. Yet they were married in the Cathedral of San Lorenzo early in 1463, when Catherine was only sixteen and her husband a few years older. It was purely a marriage of social and political convenience and bound, one would say, to turn out badly even in times when in marriage much less was expected and much more accepted than is the case today.

It might perhaps be thought that Catherine was not only temperamentally unsuited to Giuliano but to marriage itself. She was of a solitary, introverted nature, and when no older than thirteen had begged in vain to be allowed to follow her elder sister Limbuana into the convent of Augustinian canonesses which at the time stood next to the Church of Santa Maria in Passione. This desire cannot be regarded as the proof of a religious vocation. If it had been so, surely she would later have taken advantage of her long widowhood to enter either that convent or some other. This would have been considered a very right and proper thing for a widow to do, but there is no evidence of her having made the smallest attempt to do it, nor did she so much as join a Third Order, though tertiaries were in fashion.

It seems possible that her desire for convent life was unconsciously a desire to escape marriage, to which in those days the cloister was the only alternative. Certain of her biographers have read in it the signs of an exceptional early piety, but in view of what follows it is difficult to believe that this was so. Catherine was undoubtedly good and devout. She lived in times when you were not likely to be one without the other. There was only one religion and no high-minded infidelity. But if her girlhood had been one of outstanding holiness and she had really been given to the practice of interior prayer, as some have suggested, it is difficult to account for her behaviour during the years that immediately followed her marriage.

Those years, there is no doubt whatever, were terribly unhappy. There were no children, and Giuliano neglected and humiliated her from the first, leaving her alone for months on end, either at her mother's house (her father died before her marriage) or at one or another of his own palaces. She seems during this period to have been without any resources of prayer and comfort. Either she moped by herself or tried in vain to find distraction in blameless but boring social activities.

So she drifted on until she came very naturally to the edge of a nervous breakdown. She was in a state of utter misery, unable to bear either the slight human contacts she had established or her own sad company. To the growing sickness of her mind physical illness would have been a relief, and on the eve of the feast of St. Benedict in 1473 she uttered this strange prayer: "St. Benedict, ask God to make me stay three months ill in bed."

Two days later she went to see her sister Limbuana at the

convent, and to her she either confided or betrayed her miserable condition, for the good nun, as any nun would do in such a case, advised her to go to confession. But Catherine did not want to go to confession, her reluctance no doubt being due to the natural reticence of an introvert as well as the disordered state of her mind. She could not bear to speak even to a priest of her sorrows and her sins; but she agreed to go into the convent chapel and ask the chaplain's blessing. It was not going nearly as far as her sister wanted, but it was far enough for God's hand to reach her and snatch her out of all her miseries.

As she knelt before the priest she suddenly saw herself in the light of the love of God. It was a light like fire, not only revealing but consuming. It consumed all her hopelessness and wretchedness, and in the heart where they had been only love remained, crying out—"No more world! No more sin!" She need no longer fear either of them—or loneliness or neglect or resentment or Giuliano or herself. "No more world! No more sin!" She was a free woman, walking out of the prison where she had been locked up for ten years. She was saved.

"No more world! No more sin!" That cry was forced from her by the sudden overflow of eternity into the few seconds ticked out by the clock as she knelt before the convent chaplain. In those few seconds she had lived through one of the most startling and exciting experiences possible to a human soul.

Conversion, of course, is not an exclusively religious phenomenon, and even in cases where its causes and effects are supernatural, its mechanisms belong to nature rather than to grace. Normally—for as a process of change and adaptation it is normal—it works peacefully at the level of consciousness. We all of us frequently change our opinions and even our habits —not to do so would indicate a mind afflicted by paralysis if not by rigor mortis—but such changes can as a rule be observed in all their stages and seldom cause any disturbance in the depths beneath. It is only when the process involves the deeper, unconscious springs of our will that the earthquake happens.

The earthquake in Catherine's case was not the same as that which had shaken St. Paul and St. Augustine, though some of its manifestations were not unlike. Her conversion did not involve, as did theirs, a complete change of direction—to truth from error, to good from evil. It was rather a sinking of goodness and truth into a deeper layer of the personality than that on which they had operated hitherto.

In her case there could be no question of turning from error. She rose from her knees in the convent chapel believing what she had always believed—the full Catholic creed. Nor was there any running away from vice to virtue. Her disposition had always been melancholy (and her life had done nothing to make it otherwise), but it had never been bad, and though her sins were to exact from her some years of penance they were not such as the world at large would take much notice of, nor she herself, perhaps, but for this new sudden light of love.

She had gone through an experience by which the religion that had hitherto been superficial and external became vital and fundamental. Superficial does not in this case mean insincere but pertaining to that shallow surface cradle where too many of us nurse too much of our lives. Religion to be fully operative must possess the whole being, penetrating all levels of consciousness and finally obtaining dominion over the dark territories of the unconscious self. "For, lo! thou requirest truth in the inward parts and shalt make me to understand wisdom secretly." But with many good and pious people it never seems to leave that poor little surface cradle, though for many also there is at one time or another a rebirth in what Baron von Hügel calls the Second Consciousness. This rebirth can be painful and even dangerous, though only exceptionally does it produce such an upheaval as that experienced by Catherine.

3

Curiously enough, parallel cases to hers are more easily to be found in the annals of Protestantism than of Catholicism, the reason probably being that certain Protestant sects have required their adherents to pass through the ordeal of conversion in much the same way as the adherents of the old mystery religions had to pass through the ordeal of initiation. These adherents in the majority of cases are respectable, good-living men and women already attending the chapel or meeting-house, but not admitted to full membership, even in some cults to baptism, for want of a personal experience in which they obtain an individual assurance of salvation. This experience, especially when it is expected or even required of its subjects, can be entirely subjective. On the other hand, it is often real enough, and in such classic instances as have been reported, it is not at all unlike what happened to Catherine.

John Bunyan's conversion, as described by him in *Grace Abounding*, shows the same preliminary state of wretchedness, releasing itself suddenly into an experience of joy and safety in the love of God. The wretchedness in his case was deeply coloured (if such a word can be used in such a dismal connection) by Calvinism. Like many good men of his period he feared that his soul was lost and that all his longings and strivings after God would end in hell among the reprobate. Calvin did not work on virgin soil but on a persisting travesty of the Augustinian teaching on predestination. Nevertheless we may be sure that Catherine's fear and melancholy were due to other causes than John Bunyan's, as the sins for which she afterwards did penance must have been of a different order from the innocent game of tip-cat for which he reproached himself to the end of his life. But though causes were different, states were remarkably alike. Bunyan's initial stage of misery followed a course very similar to Catherine's, for in his case as in hers there was no gradual lightening of the sky, nor even a quick break of tropic dawn. The dark night of his soul broke without sunrise into a full and blinding day.

Again, the change in his character, though of a different quality, was of the same nature as the change in hers. He was not a bad man suddenly turned to God. He had never been a bad man; he had always been decent, kindly, well-disposed, though for a long time spiritually unawakened. It was the inspiration rather than the direction of his life that had changed. He lived in a new intensity for God and the things of God as he understood them. He could have echoed Catherine's silent cry of release and exultation, though in his heart the words might have been changed—"No more hell! No more tip-cat!"

Another, less widely-known, example of this type of conversation is that of James Weller, a travelling preacher on the Kent and Sussex borders in the early years of the last century. His account of it may be read in an odd little book called *The Wonders of Free Grace*, printed at Battle, Sussex, in 1834. Weller was born at Smarden in Kent, a wretched poor-law child, prenticed out on a farm and from his boyhood alternately urged and baffled by the religious demands of his nature, which he failed to satisfy in what he calls "the steeples of the crown of England". As he grew up and attempted, in spite of poor health and a confused intellect, to earn his living in the starvation years following the Napoleonic Wars, his life became a muddle of religion and shiftless poverty, the former sinking ever deeper and deeper into the shadows of Calvinism and the fear of hell.

Though nominally a member of the Church of England he had come at an early age under Nonconformist influences and on growing up joined one of those many small sects which misery, starvation and spiritual neglect caused to spring up among the struggling farm-workers of the Weald. He could not however feel sure that he was saved. On the contrary, as time passed, he felt an ever-increasing conviction of his eternal loss. Monstrously coupled with this conviction was the growing intensity of his love for God, until in the end all thoughts of himself, body or soul, were lost in one of the most profound surrenders man surely ever made. Convinced that God's will, even if it took the form of his own eternity in hell, must be good and right and just, "I said Amen to my own damnation".

It is hardly surprising that on this peak of self-abnegation the light should shine at last—in this case verily a snow-light, he calls it "a silver light", which bathed him and blessed him as he knelt at prayer in his poor little room, where privacy could be obtained (since he was married) only by wrapping himself in the bed-curtains. Like Bunyan, like Catherine, he had found release, though it took a form more like Bunyan's than like Catherine's, since like Bunyan's it was primarily a release from the fear of hell. The thought of sin seems to have troubled him less than it troubled either Bunyan or Catherine. It was not for his sins that he was to suffer eternally but for a sort of general appeasement of the Divine Justice. Throughout the book he accuses himself of no worse failing than a tendency to run into debt—a tendency hardly surprising if one considers the hard facts of his existence. Indeed he regards his debts less an as offence than an infliction and they are as insistent at the end of the book as at the beginning. The final scene and crowning triumph of his evangelistic life—the opening of the Calvinist chapel at Salehurst—is spoilt for him by the dreary consciousness that it will only lead him more deeply into debt . . . But James Weller is too tempting a subject for digression.

There is something truly touching in these two stories of uncovenanted mercies, these wonders of free grace abounding so far from their accustomed springs. But both Bunyan and Weller show the limitations of their own systems, especially when we come to compare their post-conversion lives with Catherine's. The preliminaries are very much alike and the crises almost the same, but later on we find neither the same depths nor the same heights. Weller, particularly, is not very

different after his conversion from what he was before it. Both
he and Bunyan devoted the rest of their lives to preaching and
writing, and Bunyan was great enough to endure the loss of
freedom for his faith. But it is obvious that in both the main
release was a release from the fears engendered by their own
particular brand of religion, a release which enabled them to go
forward in the ways of God without the hobbling, crippling,
paralysing thought that even these might lead to hell.

4

For Catherine, too, free grace abounded, but her release was
mainly from herself. Also in her case the positive side of conversion heavily outweighed the negative. "Oh, Love," she
prayed, stumbling from her knees with a murmured apology
to the priest who was only dimly aware of her deliverance,
"Oh, Love, can it be that thou hast called me with so much
love and revealed to me at one view what no tongue can
describe?"

With the compression of a dream the thing had happened
and with some of the confusion of a dream. Yet as an experience it was not complete. Two days later, in a room of the
Adorna palace, she had a vision of Love himself. She saw "in
spirit" Our Lord with his cross upon his shoulder, dripping
with blood, and at the sight was so filled with self-reproach
that the life-long defences of her nature broke down and she
cried: "Oh, Love, if it be necessary I am ready to confess my
sins in public."

This vision is described by her first biographers, who were
not inclined to reduce the marvellous aspect of their subject,
expressly as being "in the spirit". Of course no "vision"
physically affects the optic nerve, but quite often it is definitely
"seen", as were the visions of St. Rose of Lima, St. Bernadette
of Lourdes and many others. Catherine's vision, however,

[13]

though objective in the sense that her mind and faculties were entirely passive in its perception, was plainly not "seen", for the description of it in the *Vita et Dottrina* adds that "the entire house seemed full of streams of that Blood which she saw to have been shed because of love alone". It is actually the only objective vision recorded in her life, except one or two doubtful experiences in her last illness, and it is her only contemplation of the Passion, a subject with which none of her later intuitions were concerned.

Being thus in a double sense unique, it made almost as deep an impression as her conversion itself. As before, the revelation of God's love had been accompanied by the revelation of her own sinfulness. Throughout her life she was to see Love as light, and in that light her sins were black indeed. We have seen that she had never been a sinner in the conventional sense of the word, but she could not look back on the last ten years, or rather see them suddenly exposed in that blazing flash of reality, without acknowledging her own failure to respond to Love's demands. She saw all the unfaithfulness of those ten unhappy years, she saw herself refusing to accept and will her sufferings as Love intended, thus throwing herself as an obstacle across the divine purpose. She could have cried with the prophet Job: "I have heard thee with the hearing of my ears but now my eye seeth thee. Therefore I abhor myself and repent in dust and ashes." Catherine repented indeed in the dust; "Oh, Love," she had cried in the first flash of vision, "I am ready if it be necessary to confess my sins in public." It was not necessary to do that, but the shyness and reticence of her sensitive nature must have been nearly as deeply mortified by the general confession that she made four days later.

Catherine's attitude to confession is a special and unusual characteristic of her sanctity. In most lives of the saints the confessor is of great importance and sometimes almost of as much interest as his penitent. St. Teresa of Avila had a famous director in St. John of the Cross, St. Margaret Mary consulted St. John Eudes, St. Rose of Lima had no less than eleven confessors. But it was not till Catherine was an old woman that she had anyone who could be called a director, and then it might be said that she directed him as much as he directed her. Don Cattaneo Marabotto, as we shall see later, had an almost uncritical reverence for his penitent, and was apparently unable to discriminate between the genuinely supernatural and the merely neurotic manifestations of her psycho-physical state, though she herself was never to confuse them.

During the earlier part of her life she had gone regularly to confession, though she does not seem to have found in it the comfort and psychological release that it brings to many or she would have been more ready to avail herself of it at the crisis of her life. After her vision of the Passion she at once made a general confession, and she frequented the sacrament at regular intervals for three or four years afterwards. Then she appears to have dropped it entirely for a very long time.

This, to put it mildly, is most unusual and no doubt excited comment, especially as during this period she had, as we shall see, aroused it in another way by becoming a daily communicant. The Church's law does not require confession oftener than once a year if there is no grave sin; and it is practically certain that Catherine made this annual confession or at least conformed to the ruling of St. Thomas Aquinas that "he that has not committed any mortal sins is not bound to confess venial sins, but it is sufficient for the fulfilling of the Church's precept for him to present himself to the priest and declare himself free from the consciousness of mortal sin." But from, roughly, 1476 to 1499 "she was guided and taught interiorly by her tender Love alone". It is her director, Don Marabotto himself, who writes this account of her and fully understands the idiosyncracy—for one must call it that—of his penitent. "If she attempted to lean upon anyone, Love immediately caused her such great mental suffering that she was forced to

[15]

desist, saying, 'Oh, Love, I understand thee.' And when she was told that it would be safer if she put herself under obedience to another and while she hesitated as to what to do her Lord spoke to her within her mind: 'Trust in me and do not doubt.'"

Conversion had not changed Catherine's nature but had made of it a rare vessel of grace. A shy, silent introverted saint may not be so attractive to humanity in general as a lively, gracious, expansive one. But there is a place and a function even for silence and reticence in the kingdom of God, and though within its walls the lion may lie down with the lamb the leopard is not always asked to change his spots. Catherine was not required to mortify her natural reticence beyond the penitential period that immediately followed her conversion. For her the sacrament of penance was penance indeed and we have seen that she made a general confession almost at once. This was followed by the regular use of the sacrament for four years. She dropped it only when she dropped the many other penitential practices of this period.

She indeed did penance during those four years. And here we have one more interesting contrast between her and those two other converts we have studied. For both John Bunyan and James Weller the main release had not been from sin but from hell, and when the fear of the latter was removed the former went with it. Though Bunyan was more conscious of himself as a sinner than was the little man of Smarden, neither of them would have dreamed of doing penance for sins which they believed to have been utterly and everlastingly blotted out. As they were safe from hell, so were they safe from sin and clothed for ever in imputed righteousness.

But not so Catherine. "She saw the Offended One to be supremely good and the offender just the opposite. Therefore she could not bear to see any part of herself that was not subject to Divine Justice, with a view to being thoroughly chastised." Hence "she did not hesitate to pronounce this sentence: 'I would not have grace and mercy but justice and vengeance shown me.'" This is very like James Weller saying amen to his own damnation, though with Catherine it is amen to purgatory instead of hell. Love had first shone as light, revealing her sins, and now as fire it must consume them. She was anticipating her own doctrine of purgatory and voluntarily plunging into it after that vision of the Offended One.

We are told furthermore by the compilers of her Life that she refused ever to try to gain a plenary indulgence. "Not that she did not hold them in great reverence and devotion. . . . but that she would have wished that her own self-seeking should be chastised and punished as it deserved than . . . . by means of such satisfaction set free in the sight of God." She also abstained from asking the prayers of others, "so as ever to be subject to every punishment and condemned as she deserved".

To our modern careless and good-natured attitude towards sin in general and our own in particular all this sounds highly exaggerated and extreme. Poor Catherine, we might say—as had we been in her place we should have said Poor Me—she was more sinned against than sinning. All said and done, her sins cannot have amounted to much. She never did anyone any harm. Accidie? . . . . Well, who shall blame her, considering the way she was treated?

But to argue thus would be to forget that she had had a simultaneous vision of God and her own soul, an experience similar to that of Cardinal Newman's *Gerontius* who, on being brought after death in to the presence of the Offended One, could only cry—

"Take me away, and in the lowest deep
There let me be."

Being both realistic and virile in her reactions, she determined to seek her purgatory here and now, so that when at last Love called her to his house there should be no further delay.

[17]

Apart from such unusual heroisms as we have mentioned, she followed most of the penitential practices of her time—she wore a hair shirt, she renounced both meat and fruit, she put thorns in her bed, she spent six hours a day in prayer and went about with her eyes fixed on the ground. And all the time she felt a fire burning in her heart, a fire that was partly spiritual, consuming her guilt, and partly physical, consuming her body with dryness. To those around it seemed to consume the very food she ate, for she digested it so quickly "that it looked as if she could have digested iron".

But her acts during this period were not all penitential. Side by side with her works of reparation went a practice of a very different nature and one that was at that period exceedingly rare—the practice of daily communion. Shortly after her conversion "her Lord gave her the desire for Holy Communion, a desire which never failed her throughout the whole course of her remaining life. And he arranged things so that communion was given her." During her ten years of brooding, her attitude towards the Blessed Sacrament had no doubt been lukewarm, as there is nothing more destructive of spiritual hunger than self-preoccupation. But from, at latest, the May of 1474, she went daily to the altar.

This must have demanded great courage, as well as great devotion, as it would daily have called attention to her shrinking, diffident self, and in times when even nuns in enclosed convents were not allowed to communicate oftener than twice or thrice a week, it might easily have been thought presumptuous. Indeed, it is plain that she was aware of this and suffered in her shyness, for she once acknowledged that she was envious of priests because they could say Mass and communicate daily without arousing comment. She even suspended her communions for a time when a Franciscan friar of whose opinion she thought highly suggested that there might be something wrong in such very great frequency. But she suffered such distress in consequence that when the friar (afterwards beatified as Blessed

Angelo of Chiavasso) heard of it he sent her a message that he had spoken only to test the purity of her intention and that she was to return to her daily practice—which she did at once.

5

We are so used to seeing the saints standing alone in their stained-glass windows that we forget that they too had their families and perhaps more than a usual share of all the usual family complications. For those of them who did not join religious orders the way to heaven must have been jostling with fathers, mothers, brothers, sisters, husbands, wives— above all husbands and wives.

A saint's husband. Much could be written about a saint's husband—about the husbands of St. Frances of Rome, St. Elizabeth of Hungary, St. Margaret of Scotland, and a great many more who are described in the Missal as widows. Here we have St. Catherine of Genoa's husband and we should like to know very much more about him than we are actually told.

We can only guess from his treatment of her that he had been as reluctant to marry her as she to marry him, and was in his contrasting way as unsuited to marriage. No doubt he blamed her for all the unhappiness of their married life. He would have told his friends that she was melancholy, awkward, frigid—that she had driven him to find his pleasures elsewhere and to spend his money on those with greater appreciation of the things it would buy. So when in the summer of 1473 he comes home humble and penitent, we are almost as much surprised as his neglected wife.

True, it is a broken, battered, bankrupt Giuliano who comes home. But those were not the days when an erring, spendthrift husband might return to live on the charity of a rich wife. Giuliano had as much legal right to Catherine's money as his own and had no doubt spent it with his own. It was his free, unforced choice to return to her and live with her in poverty to the end of his life.

What memories had the prodigal carried of her into the "far country"? Was she beautiful? We do not know, for no contemporary portrait of her exists, and we who have seen how the authenticity of even the photograph of a modern saint can be destroyed by "touching up", would not expect a truthful likeness in those painted at the time of her canonisation, two hundred years after she was dead. But certainly he took away enough of her to bring him back again.

He must have found her changed, but then he himself was changed. His troubles had shaken him and set his feet on a way that was not unlike her own. A conversion brought about by troubles we have brought upon ourselves is not likely to be of the best or most enduring quality, and the fact that Giuliano's endured until his death can be mainly attributed to Catherine, and to the kindness and generosity with which she received him and invited him to share her new life.

Giuliano was fortunate to be a saint's husband, as none but a saint would have welcomed him so kindly, so utterly without reproach, after he had neglected her for ten years in the course of which he had wasted their joint inheritance. There was yet another circumstance, which must have given at least as much pain to the childless wife as his extravagance and his neglect. Giuliano was the father of a little girl.

This child had not been casually begotten, as seems clear from his giving her his mother's name, Thobia, and from his making regular provision for her throughout his life from his own exiguous funds; and Catherine showed the true gold of her heart by the readiness with which she swept aside all regrets and jealousies and became herself the kind friend and protector of the poor little girl. All her life she took an affectionate interest in her welfare, and when Giuliano died and she was left as the executrix of his will, she administered not only his bequest to his daughter but another to an unnamed woman who was almost certainly that daughter's mother. In her own will there is a touching bequest to the now grown-up Thobia of Catherine's best silk gown.

Giuliano's first concern on coming home was to save what he could out of the wreck of his fortune. No doubt Catherine helped him, for in striking contrast to her mysticism goes throughout her convert life what can be described only as a good head for business. This is shown again and again by her organisation of the charitable works she engaged in—we are told that her accounts were never wrong by a single farthing— and by the number of wills she made in succession, all of which display her grasp of complicated finance and a clear judgment of commercial values. No character is easier to see in the flat than the mystic, who is commonly labelled an unpractical dreamer and dismissed to the other world he inhabits while still living in this. But it is a fact that many of the best-known "mystical" saints were great administrators and in money matters more than a little tough. To find examples one has only to think of St. Catherine of Siena and St. Teresa of Avila.

Catherine was no exception. Indeed, ever since her conversion there is something essentially virile and manlike in her character which feeds the mystical element and is fed by it. She had been unable to prevent Giuliano leaving her when she was an unawakened girl, but now she is awake in two worlds as it were, so she immediately takes charge of the new Adorna household. It may have been Giuliano's plan to sell his palaces —the winter palace in Genoa and the summer palace out at Pra—but Catherine is the more likely urger of the next step which was a move not simply to a smaller house, but to a house in a slum.

The Hospital of the Pammatone was in one of the very poorest parts of the city, and to a little house quite close to it Catherine and Giuliano removed in the autumn of 1473. It would, however, be a mistake to think of them as driven by poverty into these surroundings. Enough had been saved of Giuliano's fortune to provide a much better house and more than the one servant they took with them. Their choice of a home was due to a voluntary decision to live on as little as possible, so that they could devote what remained of their estate to the good of others.

Giuliano had become a Franciscan tertiary and had agreed with his wife to a life of perpetual continence. The change in him is almost as startling as the change in her, who no doubt had helped by her generous forgiveness and fine example to deepen its reality and to make of the proud, spoilt, spendthrift, self-indulgent aristocrat the humble servant of the unfortunate. To be a tertiary was in those days to be more openly a religious than it is now. Giuliano would almost certainly have worn the habit as he worked with other tertiaries and the friars of the Franciscan order in the hospital which was under their control. The maid Benedetta also was a tertiary. But Catherine, the saint of that little household, felt no desire or call to join the order. She went her lone way of prayer and penance to which she had now added the pursuit of good works.

6

These centred round the hospital, which was a big, flourishing institution, founded some sixty years earlier by one of Genoa's merchant princes, Bartolomeo Bosco. In Catherine's time it contained a hundred and thirty beds, and attached to it was an orphanage for a hundred girls, who learned to weave and work the silks for which the city was famous. The whole undertaking was in the hands of the Observant Friars of the Franciscan order, but most of the nurses were lay-folk, some of them, like Catherine and Giuliano, among the highest in the land.

For in those days it was considered a noble work to nurse the sick. We have come to stress so heavily the cruelty and darkness of the later Middle Ages that it is easy to forget the other side of the picture—the flourishing state of institutions that in these days of enlightenment have either to bribe a staff and beg for subscriptions or else be taken over by the state. All that the state does in modern times for the relief of suffering was done in Catherine's time by Christian compassion, by men and women who did not merely provide money and sit on committees, but personally waited on the sick and destitute with their own hands.

Of course these people were what Mr. Arnold Lunn calls "divinitarians". They helped humanity not so much because they loved humanity as because they loved God. Moreover, unlike the humanitarians, they did not concern themselves with the causes of the suffering they relieved. It is typical of them that they would risk their lives nursing those who had the plague, but never think of destroying the harbour rats; and in the same way they ignored social injustices and economic evils. But their ministrations must have had about them a savour and a sweetness that it would be difficult to find in social services today. Nor was there any nonsense then about the "deserving poor". The poor were to be relieved because they needed it, not because they deserved it—or rather they were all deserving, since every one of them wore the halo of the Son of Man—"ye have done it unto Me".

Besides the care of the poor in hospital there was the care of them in their own homes. The ladies of Genoa had formed themselves into a guild for visiting all the poorer quarters of the city—somewhat after the manner of district visitors, except that their visits were not so much of supervision and inquiry as of personal service, often of the most menial kind. Catherine became one of these Ladies of Compassion, and as such visited homes in the very foulest slums, sweeping and scrubbing and cleaning, even taking away the filthy verminous garments of the inhabitants to wash and repair in her own home. This must have been an act of real heroism on her part, for she had always been fastidious and hated all that was dirty and ugly.

Thus penance and works of mercy went side by side for some years, but already she was approaching the end of the Purgative Way and entering on a new stage of her spiritual life. She had not been working in the hospital more than a year when she started the practice of daily communion, and two years later there was another change and the beginning of another practice of a yet more unusual and infinitely more startling nature.

We are told in the *Vita et Dottrina* that "her Love said he wanted her to keep the Forty Days of Lent in his company in the desert. And then she began to be unable to eat." It was then Lady Day, 1476, and Lent was nearly over, but after a break of three days at Easter she resumed her fasting and ate nothing till the forty days had been observed. Similarly she fasted throughout Advent, which was then observed much more rigorously than it is now. She continued these fasts for more than twenty years, long after she had abandoned her other penitential practices. Indeed she did not regard them as a part of penance, for she was literally unable to eat, and if she attempted to do so the food immediately made her sick. Moreover, during her fasts she was always in better health, stronger and more active, than at other times.

There is no need to regard these accounts as exaggerated. Human beings have repeatedly shown themselves capable of going without food for much longer periods than is commonly thought possible. It is merely a question of the mind or soul getting firmly into the saddle of that body which St. Francis of Assisi so expressively calls Brother Ass. Besides, in Catherine's case, the fast was not absolute. She received Holy Communion daily—and that alone is known to have kept a man alive for over six weeks—and probably after it she drank the glass of wine which in Genoa was taken as a sort of ablution by the faithful. Further, she drank from time to time a glass of vinegar and water with pounded rock salt. This beverage corresponds to the potion of bitter herbs drunk during her fasts by St. Rose of Lima and may have been chosen for the same unconscious reason—the production of an alkaline reaction, thus avoiding the acute acidity which blows out an empty stomach into a mockery of good cheer. Similarly in modern times the regular drinking of orange juice has formed part of those "fasting cures" which were fashionable before the war.

But though there is no reason to call Catherine's fasts miraculous they were undoubtedly supernatural. Not only was she more active and vigorous than when eating normally, but her own attitude towards them was entirely spiritual in its wisdom and its humility. Indeed her natural diffidence made them at first the cause of scruples. Could they possibly be a snare of the devil—provoking her to pride or eccentricity? She would sometimes force herself to eat, "considering that Nature required it", and her characteristic shrinking from anything that made her appear conspicuous would urge her to eat when at table with others. But her fasting came from deeper springs than her own will and if she took food she was unable to retain it. As she explained to her friends, "This inability to eat is the work of God, with which my own will has nothing to do. So I cannot glory in it." Then perhaps in gentle rebuke of their religious sensationalism she added: "There is no need to marvel at it, since in the eyes of God this is a mere nothing."

Catherine never failed to distinguish the significant from the insignificant, the interior from the exterior, in her spiritual life. In this she was wiser than her friends, who were inclined to be equally impressed by her religious ecstacies and the neurotic psycho-physical states which intruded later. She had now passed out of the penitential stage of her life and had entered on its longest, richest phase. One by one she had dropped her penances (for we have seen that she did not regard her fasts as being in the nature of penance) and had entered into more or less normal relations with those around her. During the four penitential years she had fled human company except that of her husband and of the poor and destitute, but once they were left behind her she began to gather round herself a little group of friends and disciples, and it is to these good people and their successors that we owe our knowledge of her life and doctrine, for she herself left not a single written word.

7

The most important and interesting of Catherine's friends, the one who was also most like herself and therefore the one most likely to understand her, was a young man, young enough to be her son, called Ettore Vernazza. They met in dramatic circumstances. The plague had broken out in Genoa —by no means for the first or last time, but this was one of its worst visitations. Everyone who could do so fled from the city, but Catherine had recently been appointed Matron at the hospital, and even if she had not we cannot believe that she would have deserted her post.

The causes of the epidemic were still unknown to the medical science of that day, and no doubt its treatment was primitive and confused, hence the very high death-rate of four-fifths of the population. But Catherine, with a practical intuition ahead of her times set to work to organise open-air ambulances and semi-open-air wards, covering the great space at the back of the hospital with tents made of sailcloth and relying on fresh air at least to check the spread of infection if it could not actually work a cure. Medicine was still a superstition rather than a science, but there was no limit to the devotion of those who worked with and under Catherine—the self-sacrificing religious, the heroic doctors and nurses, who remained in a city they might have fled from, to nurse the plague-stricken poor at the risk of their own lives.

Among these "divinitarians" was young Ettore Vernazza,

the son of a Genoese lawyer, who himself was just setting up his practice of the law. He came of a good family and circumstances and might easily have left the town, but he chose instead to devote himself to those who were forced to stay behind and suffer the consequences. He had great faith in a decoction of cassia root, with which, since this was a medical free-for-all, he is said to have achieved some quite remarkable cures.

We do not know exactly how or when he met Catherine. I like to think—though this is only conjecture—that it was when she herself had the plague, having kissed the mouth, or rather the Word in the mouth, of a plague-stricken woman. This poor creature was on the verge of death and struggling with her dimming senses and failing powers to utter the name of Jesus. Catherine had urged her repeatedly to call upon him, but her dry tongue was like a log in her mouth and incapable of speech. Then at last her lips moved, as if the name that her tongue could not speak had filled the mouth behind them and forced them to part. When Catherine saw this happen her love overflowed and she forgot the plague, she forgot infection, she forgot her own danger; she could think of nothing but the Word incarnate as it were in this poor dying mouth. So she stooped and kissed them both.

It was an act of utter holiness and utter madness, and the former was not to exempt Catherine from the consequences of the latter. She was struck by the plague as surely as if she had caught the infection by accident and against her will. She was to know at first hand the horrors she had done so much to relieve. But she did not die—and here is another pleasing, if unsubstantial, conjecture: perhaps she owed her recovery to Ettore Vernazza's cassia preparation. It is certain that recovery was rare in those days when epidemics swept the majority of their victims into the grave.

But no matter when or how they met, their meeting was the prelude to one of those rich, creative friendships which are found so often in the lives of the saints. As St. Francis of Assisi and St. Clare, as St. Francis de Sales and St. Jane Chantale, as St. Vincent de Paul and St. Louise de Marillac, St. Catherine of Genoa and Ettore Vernazza were henceforward to work together for God. It is true that, unlike the others, they both lived in the world. Neither of them founded or even joined a religious order, and not long after meeting Catherine, Vernazza married and became the father of three daughters. As for Catherine, she was the friend not only of Ettore but of Bartolomea, Tommasina, Catetta and Ginevrina. To the eldest girl, Tommasina (afterwards Sister Battista of the Augustinian canonesses), she stood as godmother, and she seems always to have been regarded as the friend and general counsellor of the family.

But her friendship with Ettore was of another, higher nature. The difference in their ages made them more like mother and son—perhaps Catherine had always wanted a son; while the difference in their spiritual stature seemed to demand the relations of master and disciple. Catherine at last had found a soul who could in some degree understand hers, but her attitude towards him, in spite of her natural diffidence, was always that of guide and instructress. She was, moreover, wise enough to recognise a spirituality quite different from her own. Ettore belonged definitely to the active rather than the contemplative side of humanity and Catherine seems to have made no attempt to train him in mysticism, but to have been always ready with encouragement and advice when he sought to break new ground in active good works.

These were to make him in the end only a little less beloved than Catherine. Shortly after he had finished nursing the plague-stricken it occurred to him that there were many poor people who had "seen better days" and therefore might be too proud and sensitive to ask for charity. He devised a scheme for visiting and relieving these privately in their homes, and with a tact and delicacy which suggest Catherine's inspiration

—since she always hated to be noticed when she did good —he arranged that the visitors should be anonymous. Each one was to be disguised by a little veil or mask, hence the foundation was known as the Institute of the Mandiletto. He also founded the Society of St. John the Baptist for work among those condemned to death. Each member had to hold himself in readiness to sit with a condemned man in his cell during the night before his execution, and Ettore himself spent with many a wretched criminal his last night on earth.

In return for Catherine's active interest in all that he did and loved, Ettore became her amanuensis and historian. But for him we might not know as much as we do about her life and teaching, for it was not till some years later that he was joined by Don Marabotto and his own daughter, Sister Battista, in the compilation of that rather confused work, *The Life and Doctrine of St. Catherine of Genoa.*

Catherine herself was probably too busy to write—too busy in the hospital and in her own soul. Besides, we must remember that in those days writing was not a likely fruit of experience. Printing had only just been invented and was in an early, cumbrous stage, so it is most improbable that she ever thought of her teaching being conveyed to others through the medium of the printed word. We may regret that she wrote nothing, for we should like at least a few glimpses of her that are not through the eyes of others. There is no reason to think that Vernazza and Marabotto did not faithfully and accurately record her doctrine, but in the matter of her spiritual life, of her contemplative states and ecstacies, they were both, especially Marabotto, too deeply lost in admiration of their subject to be able to discriminate between what in her was truly supernatural and what was not. It is only by reading between the lines that we can see that such discrimination—marvellous in an age when as little was known about the human mind as about the human body—existed clearly in the mind of Catherine herself.

8

Her spiritual life had now possession of her whole being, unconscious as well as conscious, hence the "given-ness" of certain practices, also of her doctrine, which came to her usually in the form of locutions. "Her Love said. . . ." "Her Love spoke in her mind. . . ." such are the beginnings of many revelations; and it is notable that though she always speaks of God and Christ as Love she never uses the imagery of human passion nor even the language of the Song of Songs. Nor was she one of those saints who have passed through the mystical experience known as the spiritual marriage. There is an impressive dignity and austerity about her Love, who moreover is always light and never fire except in hell.

Nor did she seek for spiritual consolations; indeed she fled from them, fearing that she might rest in them and not in the Reality they both manifested and hid. Nevertheless, and as it were in spite of herself, she tasted abundantly of spiritual joy. She had continual ecstasies, which lasted sometimes for hours, and when recovering from them would try, often in vain, to tell those around her of all she had experienced of joy and knowledge. Sometimes even when she was at work her hands would suddenly fall to her sides, and she would pass into a sort of trance, from which, however, she could always be roused by the call of any duty, which she would then perform with the face of an angel.

Her attitude to these experiences is one of the deepest, most touching humility. She insisted that to be able to enjoy them only two things were necessary—on one side God's grace, on the other an entirely-given human will. This belief brought her into conflict with those who had entered religion, and insisted that the monk or the nun was better fitted for the mystical life than anyone living in the world. On one occasion a famous preacher who was also a Franciscan friar challenged her, insisting that because he had taken religious vows of poverty, chastity and obedience he was more free to love God than a woman who, though she lived in poverty and chastity, was very much her own in the matter of obedience. At this Catherine cried out: "If I thought your habit could gain me just one more spark of love, I should tear it off you," and continued to refute him in ever-growing distress and excitement until in the end her hair came loose and tumbled on her shoulders. "Oh, Love," she cried, with her flushed face and tumbling hair, "who shall stop me loving thee? Even if I were not only in the world but in a camp of soldiers I could not be prevented from loving thee."

Her trances and ecstasies continued to the end of her life, and are truly a part of her conversion, since there is no record of her having had any abnormal experiences before then. In this she is different from many saints, and many who are not saints, for her psycho-physical type generally manifests its chief characteristics in early youth. We cannot accept her trances as being in themselves a proof of holiness. Many who are far from holy can go into trances; indeed some earn their living that way, and it would be as idle to proclaim that all trance conditions are fraudulent as to proclaim that they are all supernatural. The supernatural element in Catherine's trances is not to be found in their external symptoms, which are pathological, but in the spiritual revelations which form their content.

The Holy See itself has proclaimed that she could have been canonised on the strength of her doctrine alone, and nearly all this doctrine was the fruit of trance states or near-trance states. There is, however, this very important difference between her and the purely "natural" medium. The latter is normally quite unconscious and unable to remember what she (or, as she would put it, her "control") has said while in a trance state. But Catherine's difficulty when she came back into this world was not to remember what her Love had said but to make others understand him. She must indeed have been sometimes in the position of trying to translate "words which it is not lawful for man to utter", and even if she had written down her own experiences we probably should never have known the full content of that revelation made in the deeps of her mind.

Such revelations as have come to us through the writings of her friends are intellectual rather than emotional, doctrinal rather than practical. She was not one of those saints to whom later Christians were to owe new pious practices, such as those associated with the "First Fridays", the Miraculas Medal and the gaining of the Sabbatine Indulgence. Her teaching mainly concerns the relations of the soul and body and the hidden worlds of heaven, purgatory and hell. The *Treatise on Purgatory* (which was not of course written by herself but by her disciples from her spoken and remembered word) embodies the most famous and original part of her doctrine. In it we find the doctrine of the Plunge—the action by which the soul brought at the moment of death into the most pure sight of God, as it were judges itself and hurls itself voluntarily into the place of expiation, desiring nothing but to cleanse itself and offer its atonement to the Divine Justice.

"The soul which does not find within itself the purity in which it was created, seeing the stain and realising that this stain cannot be cleansed except in Purgatory, quickly and of its own accord casts itself in."

The whole of her teaching on the Hidden Worlds is indeed a spiritualisation of the rather solid imagery in which those worlds had been clad by medieval speculation. Her hell is remarkably unlike Dante's—"The goodness of God's mercy shines even in Hell, since his justice might have given the souls therein a far greater punishment than he has . . . . even in Hell the soul does not suffer as much as it deserves. . . . If we leave this life in a state of sin, God will take away his goodness from us and leave us to ourselves, and yet not altogether, since . . . if a creature could exist that did not participate in some degree in the divine goodness, that creature would be as evil as God is good."

As for heaven, she could hardly speak of it, though it was with her no future state. She dwelt there already, but was unable to express the wonders of her dwelling-place. "Oh, if only," she cried to her friends, "I could tell you what my heart feels," and when they begged—"Oh, Mother, tell us something," she answered, "I cannot find words. All I say is that if only one drop of what my heart feels were to fall into Hell, Hell itself would be transformed into Eternal Life."

9

The year 1496 is marked by certain changes in Catherine's life, both exterior and interior. She was now nearly fifty and her health began to fail, which is hardly surprising, for she had worked hard nursing the sick for nearly twenty years, and had been once herself at death's door with the plague. As her strength declined it was only natural that she should come to depend more on others. Up till then she had always kept aloof, or at least her complete, self-sufficing independence must have made her appear to do so, in spite of her overflowing kindness. Her friendship with Ettore Vernazza was certainly not one of equality—he looked up to her and depended on her spiritually as her disciple. As for Giuliano, though a reformed character, he can never have been any help or support to his wife. All the evidence points to the contrary, to his leaning on her and being guided by her.

Nevertheless it must have been a shock and grief to her when he died. He became seriously ill at the beginning of 1497 and died in the autumn of that year. His illness had a curious effect on Catherine's normal habits of prayer, or perhaps one should say that it made a normal act out of a curious abstention. Ever since her conversion she had abstained from prayer for others.

It was one of the strangenesses of her very individual and independent type of religion. She neither prayed for others nor asked them for their prayers. She said that she knew God held them as well as herself in his love and knowledge, and she was content to leave them there.

But poor Giuliano had always been a bad-tempered man, and now in his last illness, suffering constant pain, he became so impatient and irascible that she feared he might lose his soul. So, breaking the custom of twenty years, she prayed to her Love, saying: "Love, I demand this soul of thee"—and from that hour she found Giuliano resigned to the will of God.

There is only one other instance of her having used intercessory prayer, and it is very similar to the first, since it was for the dying husband of Argentina del Sale, a humble little woman who for years was her servant. This poor man was dying of cancer of the face, and like Giuliano complained bitterly of his sufferings. His wife begged Catherine for her prayers, and once more they were given and with the same result. It is hard to believe that either of these poor suffering creatures would have gone to hell for their impatience, but Catherine obviously feared for them, since for their sakes alone she broke her established custom, and certainly in each case the result was a happy death. It is notable that for neither did she ask for recovery or even a mitigation of pain. She prayed only for their souls.

She was now quite alone, for though Argentina del Sale was later to make her home with her, that could not be till after the death of her (Argentina's) husband. Moreover, Giuliano's daughter Thobia, in whom Catherine had always interested herself, did not live to inherit that best silk gown but died soon after her father. Catherine was now unable, through failing health, to continue her work as matron, and was for the same reason obliged to take food after communion, so her extraordinary fasts in Lent and Advent were brought to an end. At this time she made another change in her spiritual life, equally drastic and more far-reaching—she sought the help of a director.

For twenty-five years she had gone her own way, sailing her spiritual craft without help from anyone, but now, as her powers declined, "the Lord gave her a priest"—Don Cattaneo Marabotto, a very holy, simple-minded man who had been appointed Rector of the hospital.

10

It is perhaps surprising that when Catherine decided to lean on another human being she did not choose a man who was in any way her intellectual or spiritual equal. Don Marabotto was almost naïve in his simplicity, and he had not in his spiritual make-up the smallest degree of mysticism. He was practical, sensible, kindly, and helped her in matters of health and finance as well as of the soul. Some of her love of solitude must have remained interiorly in her choice of these two men— first Vernazza and then Marabotto—to share the wonders and graces of her soul's life. We can only guess her need of reinforcement from natures complementary to rather than identical with her own. Marabotto was to fill a position quite different from Vernazza's. If the latter was spiritually her son, the former was her father. His mere presence was enough to strengthen and reassure her, giving her the comfort and support her human frailty needed in these latter years.

As for his direction, it seems mainly to have amounted to receiving, admiring and recording her spiritual confidences. He certainly neither taught her nor led her. But he comforted her. Having abstained from regular confession for so long, she found her first confession to Don Marabotto something of an ordeal. She told him frankly that she did not know where she was either in her soul or in her body, and though she wanted to confess she could not remember any sins. When she actually did confess he found her soul "like that of a small boy who might have committed some trifling offence in ignorance". Till the end of her life she was always to find difficulty in producing matter for absolution, though she was never without a humble sense of her own weakness and proneness to evil.

Her exterior life was still lived much as usual in the precincts of the hospital. It was quiet and simple, but not austere—in the sense that the wills she made at intervals during the last years of her life (will-making was fashionable at that time in Genoa, and was not her best friend a lawyer?) mention beautiful objects in silk and damask and silver and she had never thought it unbecoming to holiness to wear a silk gown. Her nursing activities had ceased; she was no longer equal to them—she was wearing out.

Ever since her conversion the relations between her soul and body had been, humanly speaking, abnormal. Perhaps they should be called supernatural, but the tragedy of our fallen nature is that the supernatural has become the abnormal, and a relation between soul and body which God may possibly have intended to be normal for mankind has been turned by sin into something too difficult for "the body of our humiliation" to sustain. Catherine's soul was still firmly in the saddle of Brother Ass, but Brother Ass in old age was no longer equal to being so strongly ridden and had begun to go lame. The illnesses which afflicted Catherine at this time seem definitely to be of a psycho-physical origin—indeed some of her symptoms are a translation into terms of the body of what had formerly been purely spiritual states. The burnings of Divine Love which in her spiritual hey-day had given her so much strength and joy became transmuted into physical heat and distress. She felt consumed, dried up. She also had feelings of intense cold, her whole body shuddering and trembling. At times she would suffer from vomitings and spasms of the throat that made her speechless, also discolorations of the skin and curious symptoms such as the pitting of her flesh, "as if it had been dough," and so great a sensitiveness that it was impossible to touch her. Then suddenly she would be well again, in robust health, these states alternating and lasting several days.

They were accompanied by similar changes in her spiritual equilibrium. Though the fine point of her soul never wavered from its true North, she would have horrible moments of confusion and desolation. Once she cried out that her mind was like a mill, another time she compared herself to a soul taken from paradise and finding the world nothing but hell.

None of this need surprise us. It is only in the stained-glass windows that the saints never grow old. In real life they grow old, grow tired, grow sick like the rest of us, but love God and are loved by him no less for that. Catherine accepted her infirmities in the spirit of perfect conformity with the divine will. No false pride made her struggle to keep up the practices of her mental and physical health. She dropped her fasts, her activities in the hospital, and she turned very simply and humbly to the support of her fellow creatures.

Don Marabotto was the chief of her comforters, though she must sometimes have been wearied by his stolid insistence on seeing the supernatural if not the miraculous in her extraordinary physical states. Black spots, discolorations, morbid hungers and thirsts, vomitings (which he politely called "accidents"), shiverings and burnings were all to him, equally with her trances and ecstasies, marks of divine favour. Von Hügel finds Don Marabotto "slightly comical", whereas I find him slightly pathetic. No doubt the two must be combined in any really human character, as most of our best comedians have realised. To Catherine he was a true friend and comforter—in her desolations she would turn to him as naturally as a child to its father, and "God gave him grace", so that like a father he could soothe the pain away. She also trusted him as much as she loved him, and when her old clarity and business acumen failed, she made over to him the entire management of her worldly affairs.

II

Catherine felt herself to be dying; but when—and it was more than once—she asked Don Marabotto for extreme unction he always refused her. No doubt he was right, since her illness was of psychological rather than physical origin and probably at this time entirely functional. Yet a functional illness if unchecked may become organic. It would be interesting to know how many of our physical illnesses are of mental origin and modern medicine is working on those lines, but in Catherine's day, and indeed much later, her condition was a puzzle to the doctors, or rather it would have been if they had been called in.

As it happened, they were not summoned till within six months of her death, by which time her sickness had taken sufficient organic hold to be no longer susceptible to Don Marabotto's comforting. By then all the portents were that Catherine was suffering from some form of kidney disease— the burning fever, the dry yellow skin, the vomiting and failing sight are all symptoms that would be clearly recognised today. But even the physicians were inclined to regard them as of supernatural origin. They declared that they could find no sign of bodily illness and were therefore unable to provide a remedy.

Catherine longed to die, not with the morbid longing of bitterness and impatience, nor even with the pathological longing of exhaustion, but with a deep spiritual longing to be with her Love, free of the obstacles put up by a sick body. For many years her body had been her servant and had offered no resistance to her soul, but now it was definitely in her way and she longed to be without it. She had always reverenced death, which must have become familiar to her in the course of her work among the sick and plague-stricken in hospital. There is a record of this prayer of hers: "Oh, Love, I wish for nothing but thee, but if it pleases thee, let me go and see others die and be buried, so that I may see in others that great good which it does not please thee should yet be mine."

But that good was not to be denied her long, though before it came there is an interlude which shows Catherine's fundamental sanity and common sense, in contrast to the folly and spiritual vulgarity of those who surrounded her. It also puts the sixteenth-century practice of medicine in a better light. At about this time, the summer of 1510, there returned to Genoa an illustrious doctor, Maestro Giovan Battista Boerio, who for many years had been court physician to King Henry the Seventh of England. A year ago the king had died of an illness which in its course and symptoms was not unlike Catherine's, so on Boerio's return to the city it seemed only natural that he should be called in for consultation.

His attitude to her sickness was very different from that of the other doctors. He immediately advised a treatment and suggested remedies, though what they were we are not told. What we are told, however, is that Catherine was filled with joy at the prospect of a cure and gladly promised to obey all his instructions. It is true that she reproached herself later for having rejoiced in her human self alone, without first trying to find out the will of her Love in this matter. But certainly for a while her soul was ready to mount again on Brother Ass, if only he could be cured of his stumbling.

The remedies failed, and after a few weeks' trial of them she was no better. But Maestro Boerio evidently did not blame her for any lack of co-operation, for to the end of her life he continued to visit her and to hold her in the highest esteem, calling her Mother as if he too were her disciple.

As for Catherine, the knowledge that she now most certainly must die filled her with an overflowing joy. On one occasion, though in great pain, she passed into something like one of her old ecstasies, and lay for about an hour, not speaking, but laughing joyfully. Another time her laughter was so gay that those around her asked what she was thinking of, and she replied that she had seen such beautiful, joyful, merry faces that she could not stop herself from laughing. Her pains grew worse, she was so weak that she could hardly make the sign of the cross, yet every day she was well enough to receive Holy Communion, and spoke such heavenly words to the Blessed Sacrament that those around her were moved to tears.

The little circle round her during those last months included not only an illustrious doctor, a famous lawyer, the Rector of the Hospital and the son of a former Viceroy, but her two little servant maids, Mariola and Argentina, both of whom she dearly loved, especially Argentina, who lived with her now as her daughter. Catherine sought her friends for spiritual values only; hence, by earthly standards, their mixed company. They all loved her and reverenced her, but none of them really understood her, and the two who understood her best were both absent on the day she died.

Ettore Vernazza was far away. He had gone out of the city on one of his errands of mercy. By so doing no doubt he was pleasing Catherine best and showing himself most faithful to her teaching. The absence of Don Marabotto is more difficult to account for, as he was certainly in Genoa at the time. It may have been due at least partly to the fact that he was no longer Rector of the hospital, but had lately been succeeded by a certain Don Carenzio who possibly considered it his right to attend her last moments. Don Marabotto may have agreed to withdraw, seeing that Catherine was no longer conscious or aware of who was at her side. He was certainly with her two days before her death and heard what must have been her last confession.

He was also there on that earlier occasion when, feeling the end was near and perhaps knowing that before it came her mind and senses would be clouded, she asked to have the shutters opened so that she could see the sky. Lying there she watched the daylight fade, and still desiring light asked for candles to be lit around her. Then she lifted up what remained of her voice and sang the *Veni Creator Spiritus*. But she never took her eyes from the sky. The black Italian sky with its great flashing stars hung before her like a spangled curtain veiling heaven when, having finished her hymn, she lifted up her voice again and cried triumphantly: "No more earth! No more earth!"

It is not perhaps what we should cry who have not her eagle gaze and can see heavenly things only through the homely, friendly shapes of the things that are made. But it links her death-bed with that wonderful moment years ago in the convent chapel, the moment of her conversion, when she cried in joy: "No more world! No more sin!" Between her and that moment stretched years of the profoundest experience the human heart can know. She was going to heaven, but she already knew it well, having lived there even in her flesh. She knew purgatory too—the purgatory into which she had plunged herself at her first clear sight of God and of her own sins, and that more subtly cleansing purgatory she lay in now, passive, enduring pains not of her own seeking. But soon she would be free, saved not only from sin—which indeed had now no hold upon her—but all the humiliation and frustration of her human bondage. So she could gladly cry: "No more earth! No more earth!"

12

After this she lingered for another fortnight. Sometimes her mind was clear, and she added a codicil to her will and fixed her burial place, or rather agreed to her friends' suggestion for it. At other times she continued to display all the symptoms of a terrible illness, which however mental and nervous in origin was now rampantly organic. By the middle of September she was delirious and vomiting blood. Yet the friends and physicians gathered round her bed still saw nothing but the supernatural in her state. As for Maestro Giovan Battista Boerio, it is possible that his own failure to cure her had converted him to the idea that she was incurable by any earthly physician.

It is certainly remarkable that in spite of occasional paralyses, vomitings and the most violent symptoms of organic disaster, she never failed to receive and retain the Blessed Sacrament. Two days before her death she had a particularly terrible haemorrhage; nevertheless she communicated at the usual hour. A little later she must have become delirious, for it is surely in delirium that she spoke her last coherent words: "Drive away," she said, "that beast which is looking for food."

She spoke quite calmly and appeared neither agitated nor distressed. It is probable that all she saw, in a sort of dream, was some animal, some pasturing cow perhaps, ridiculously out of place in her bedroom. But her friends, of course, could accept nothing so homely, and decided that she had seen a ravenous demon threatening to devour her soul. In that case it is surprising that she remained calm; moreover, she had never been in the habit of seeing demons. But she must not be allowed to die after words that any non-privileged sufferer might have spoken. Indeed, in time it was decided that even though referring to a daemonic onslaught these last words were not good enough, and in the later editions of her *Life and Doctrine* they are followed by the more edifying: "Lord, into Thy hands I commend my spirit." But as this phrase does not appear until the edition of 1615, a hundred years after her death, Catherine almost certainly did not utter it.

The next morning she lost more blood, but received Holy Communion as usual. It was for the last time. All the rest of the day, which was a Saturday, she lay motionless, almost pulseless, and when, as Sunday dawned, her friends asked her if she would like once more to communicate, she said nothing, but pointed to the sky. A few minutes later her soul passed as peacefully from earth to heaven as the night passed into the day.

13

Caterina Fiesca Adorna = St. Catherine of Genoa.

From the moment of her death her cause, or candidature for canonisation, was in being, but it was not till over two hundred years later that amidst all the dignified splendour of a grand ceremony she was finally raised to the altars of the Universal Church. There is nothing automatic or perfunctory about the process of canonisation. It involves an immense amount of study and research, a most painstaking sifting of the evidence. It therefore moves most swiftly when the candidate has belonged to a religious order, which can in the nature of things devote much time and many minds to the business. But Catherine belonged to no religious order, not even as a tertiary, and though there was a general and immediate desire for her unique type of holiness to receive official recognition, there was, to put it plainly, nobody to do the work.

There were, however, two very strong currents of influence to move the powers. One was her own family—the Fieschi, leaders and rulers in Genoa, with many ecclesiastical connections. The other was the popular cultus that started in the city almost immediately after her death. Though she had been a sick woman for the last few years of her life, her name was still blessed by the poor, by those whom she had nursed in hospital or as a *Donna de la misericordia* visited in their own homes. The decree of Pope Urban VIII, which forbade the public veneration of those whose extraordinary holiness had not been formally recognised by the Church, was not promulgated till more than a hundred years later, and by that time this cultus of Catherine was so firmly established that it was allowed to continue unchecked. It was not, however, till 1675 that the title

Beata, which had been informally hers since her death, was officially bestowed upon her.

The process of her canonisation went forward slowly. By this time her fame had spread, and among those who pressed her cause were the King of Spain and King Louis XIII of France. But before the ceremony could take place her teaching, as received and written down by her faithful friends and disciples, Messer Ettore Vernazza and Don Cattaneo Marabotto, must be carefully studied in order to receive the approbation of the Holy See. In all there were three lines of investigation—her teaching, "the heroicity of her virtues", and the miracles claimed to have been worked by her after her death.

At last the infinitely slow, careful, cautious process was complete, and on Trinity Sunday, 1737, "in order that the faithful in Christ may have in Blessed Catherine a perfect example of the Love of God and their neighbour", Pope Clement XII formally canonised Caterina Fiesca Adorna in the Basilica of St. John Lateran. The function included three beatifications, one of them being that of Vincent de Paul, a "divinitarian" lover of mankind who, though very different from Catherine in temperament, was in his works of mercy, like Ettore Vernazza, her true son and a man after her own heart.

St. Catherine of Genoa—Widow. That is how she appears in the calendar of the Universal Church, and her Mass (which is not universal, but "by special grant in certain places") is based on the common of a holy woman not a martyr, which is sometimes called the Common of Widows. It seems clear, however, that the valiant woman of the lesson is not a widow; indeed she would probably regard it as a stain on her efficiency if her husband pre-deceased her. But throughout the missal the designation of widow is liable to misunderstanding, and after studying the feasts of those holy women who are neither virgins nor martyrs one could not be surprised at any insurance company which should refuse to insure a saint's husband, as not a single one of them seems to have survived his spouse.

The reason for this no doubt is that in most cases the sanctity of the wife has not flowered till the death of her husband removed certain human and earthly obstructions. St. Frances of Rome and St. Bridget of Sweden (for instance, and there are many others) devoted their widowhood to the founding of religious orders. But one must acknowledge that the description sometimes appears arbitrary, as in the case of St. Margaret of Scotland, who survived her husband only two days and probably did not even know of his death, as he was killed in battle at some distance from her. St. Catherine of Genoa certainly survived her Giuliano by a much longer period, thirteen years altogether, but her widowhood does not appear to have made the smallest difference to her way of life either spiritual or material.

She continued to live in the same house, to do the same work, to see the same friends, to follow the same practices of prayer and contemplation. She was neither more nor less a worker, a teacher and a saint. Indeed throughout her life Giuliano seems to have had little or no influence on her, except in so far as the misery of the first years of her marriage stems from his bad treatment and neglect. After their reunion he sinks almost into nonentity, though it is possible that this may be due in part to hagiographical suppressions, and that really Catherine thought and spoke of him more than would appear from the official records. But it seems certain that it was she and not he who ruled their little home, who made the decisions and offered the sacrifices. We never hear of him speaking or acting in any way that would make his presence felt, so when after twenty-three years that presence was withdrawn it can have made very little difference.

Catherine's sanctity stands apart from marriage. Neither her wifehood nor her widowhood marks it in any degree. Detached, independent, self-sufficing (except during the last few tired years) she moves through the distractions of human life as calmly as a strong ship cuts through the waves. There was no need for her to withdraw from the world into some religious order, for from that first cry of "No more world!" that world had lost its power against her, and she had lost her need of it even as an intermediary.

"*Sitivit anima mea ad Deum fortem vivum*" are the first words of the Mass appointed for her feast on March 22nd, the day of her conversion. "O God, my whole soul longs for thee, as a deer for running water. . . ." She had indeed longed, she had indeed drunken at Paradisal waters, till the vessel of her heart was full—"A heart to serve thee, O God, a heart to serve thee. . . ." She had walked in Paradise, but she had also walked the wards of a hospital. She was a great lady both in the city of Genoa and the city of God, but her friends were the poor, the sick, the plague-stricken. She chose them because they were His.

14

Von Hügel says of Catherine: "She became a saint because she had to." If she had not she might have sunk into a psychological abyss in which her character, or even perhaps her reason, would have disintegrated. Her nervous, brooding, introverted nature had in it all the seeds of chaos. We have met her type, we have read of it in volumes of psychology, we have seen and heard of the miseries and abnormalities to which it can become a prey.

But for the grace of God, those first ten unhappy years of her marriage might have set the pattern of her whole life. Already we see the threat of pathological illness—"Oh, God," she prayed, "may I be three months ill in bed." She might have become a standard hysteric case if there had not been in the depths of her being, striving under the dominion of what she calls in her teaching the False Self, a True Self athirst for God. It was that self, rising suddenly out of the deep and sinking its false image, which transformed her in a moment, sending her unusual powers flowing into the right channels, so that hysteria passed into ecstasy, morbidity into mysticism, and introspection became wisdom. The false self was still there, buried in what had been the grave of the true, but its clamour was for ever stilled and never again could it hope to dominate the mind and will which were now both in union with the mind and will of God.

Catherine's type of sanctity is certainly unusual, almost one could say eccentric. The strength of her individuality is shown both by its practices and its abstentions. She went daily to Holy Communion at a time when such frequency was more likely to provoke censure than admiration; yet during the greater part of her convert life she pursued her adventurous way to heaven without what many would have considered the necessary guidance of a director. There were also her unusual reluctances in the use of intercessory prayer and the invocation of saints, balanced by equally unusual compulsions in the matter of fasting.

But though both positively and negatively an eccentric, Catherine was, unlike many eccentrics, neither proud nor obstinate. She did her best to avoid calling attention to herself, forcing herself to eat if others were present during her fasts, abstaining even for a while from Holy Communion when one whom she revered suggested it was a presumption on her part. And when age and infirmity made it difficult for her to maintain her special way of life, she changed it without hesitation, abandoning her fasts and turning to the comfort offered by a director whose powers in all save his priesthood were inferior to her own.

Undoubtedly she had great gifts of mind and intelligence. There was nothing of the "simple saint" about her, yet the simplest, most expansive, friendly saint has nothing to teach her in fundamental tenderness of heart. She combined with the heights of mystical prayer a life of humble service to others, visiting the poor, nursing the sick, at the cost of her health and the risk of her life. There is nothing "withdrawn" about her except in temperament, and even that flowers suddenly into the most beautiful acts of love—Catherine leaving her best silk gown to her husband's illicit child, Catherine so readily forgiving that same husband who had injured her so deeply, and living with him in friendship and kindness to the end of his life, Catherine the kind friend and counsellor of the whole Vernazza family, Catherine who loved and cared for as a daughter her little servant girl, and above all Catherine who kissed the Word on the lips of the dying plague-stricken woman, transforming even death itself into love.

Cornelia Connelly

I

IT is a cold January morning in the Florence of 1880. A thin, sharp wind blows down from the mountains through the brown and yellow streets, and the congregation of the American Episcopal church shudders and huddles down into its furs as it comes out of the steam-heated warmth. It is not a large congregation, for the cold and lovely churches of the city are a temptation even to those of another religion. Only a faithful few, either staunch Protestants, or nostalgic exiles or invalids who require steam-heat, attend eleven o'clock Matins at the American Church.

"Sure, it does one good to hear an American voice in the pulpit," says one of them to her friend. "How long has Mr. Connelly been here?"

"Some twenty years or more, I reckon. Mom used to know him way back in '61. But he doesn't look as if he'd go on much longer now. He's getting old."

"How old is he?"

"I couldn't tell you for sure, Remira, but he's getting on for eighty."

"Does he live alone?"

"Oh, no. His daughter Adeline lives with him. You saw her at the organ—at least you saw her hat. She looks after him and sees to all the church chores."

"Is she the only one?"

"I'm not sure. I believe there's a son over in the States. But Adeline's the only one in Florence. I like her. Folks say she sometimes goes to one of those Italian Popish churches when her father isn't around, but I can't blame her for that, considering all things."

"What things?"

The friend buttons her collar more firmly against the wind as she begins really to talk.

"Would it surprise you, Remira, to hear that her mother was a Roman Catholic nun?"

It certainly has surprised Remira.

"My! You don't say! How could that have happened? How very, very strange!"

"It sure is a strange story, and you'll think it stranger still when I tell you that for more than ten years Mr. Connelly was a Popish priest."

Remira stops in her tracks.

"Lord a' mercy! Then how——"

"I'll tell you how it all happened. You can't live as long as I have in Florence without hearing the story. But let's step out. This wind is searching me."

2

When the beautiful Miss Cornelia Peacock married the Rev. Pierce Connelly, her eldest sister, Mrs. Montgomery, was seriously displeased. She had been her guardian ever since the death of their parents, and had brought her up specially with a view to making a good marriage. The Peacocks were one of the oldest families in Philadelphia, proud of their Yorkshire descent and occupying an important position in the city; while Cornelia herself was a lovely girl, with a skin like magnolia blossom, lively dark eyes and a shining weight of jet-black hair. She was gifted too, and her sister had developed her gifts by engaging some of the best professors in town as her instructors. She could accompany her own fine voice on the guitar, she could draw and paint, speak French—in fact she had all the right female accomplishments, based on a firm grounding of more useful subjects.

She had money, too, not an enormous amount, but enough to give her beauty and talent a fitting dowry. It was dreadful to see her throwing herself away like this on a mere clergyman of no particular family, only a vaguely Irish origin. It is true that the Peacocks had always been Episcopalians, as suited their English descent, and if a bishop had asked for Cornelia. . . . There was no good telling her that Pierce Connelly would one day be a bishop, because she was quite sure that he would not.

It was her sister Mrs. Duval who was always saying that Pierce Connelly would make his mark. The young man had evidently "got round" her, for she liked him very much indeed. He might not be all they could have hoped for Cornelia, but he was a perfectly delightful man, charming and intelligent, and so gifted that he was bound to rise in his profession. His family, too, though nobodies in Philadelphia, had both property and influence in the South.

While the sisters argued, Cornelia quietly took the matter into her own hands. Besides her creamy skin and her dark eyes, she had a peculiarly firm, well-shaped mouth, a little too large, perhaps, for the simpering fashions of the day, but beautifully drawn, expressive and determined. When Mrs. Montgomery scolded her about Pierce her eyelids might droop, but her mouth remained firmly set, and as soon as she was twenty-one and legally her own mistress she married Pierce Connelly.

The marriage took place from Mrs. Duval's house, on the first of December, 1831, and soon after it the young couple moved south to Natchez in Mississippi, where a living had been found for Pierce by his relations. They were an attractive pair, and must have surprised many in those surroundings where the middle-aged and stuffy are more commonly found. The new rector was young, ambitious and enthusiastic, with unusual powers of attraction; while as for the rector's wife, she might have been described in the same words as Tom Bertram uses to describe Mary Crawford in *Mansfield Park*—"a sweet, pretty, elegant, lively girl."

She did much better, however, than Mary Crawford would have done as a clergyman's wife. She had always been a good churchwoman, and though her duties at that time (two years before the Oxford Movement) could scarcely have been burdensome, she was scrupulous in fulfilling them as well as in caring for her home and concerning herself with the local works of mercy. Pierce soon made himself popular, both by his eloquence in the pulpit and his good influence in the parish, and both he and Cornelia made the rectory a pleasant place, where one could hear good music and join (if one was able) in good conversation. Altogether the Connellys were a great success. Their circle in Natchez was mainly that of the well-to-do planters outside the town and such of its citizens as prospered on the wealth of the plantations. Those were the days of slave-labour, and the whole district was prosperous, with the easy, leisured, cultured prosperity of the South before the Civil War.

It was not, however, such a predominantly Episcopalian society as that which they had left. The States of Louisiana and Mississippi had only recently been taken over from France and Catholicism flourished to an extent which was something quite new in the Connelly experience. In Philadelphia they had had no contact with it whatever—indeed it was not till they came to Natchez that Cornelia had seen even the outside of a convent. But now they were to meet and speak to Catholics, who though not their parishioners were their neighbours. They were not bigoted, nor did they shun all discussion of their religious differences. Cornelia in particular was interested in the strange unknown life that, while she pursued her own cheerful, ordered, prosperous way, was going on within those convent walls.

Four years passed, and the Connellys had a son and daughter,

Mercer and Adeline. Pierce was spoken of as a rising man in his profession, sure of early preferment, and Cornelia was loved for her lightness and goodness of heart. Life seemed to have fulfilled all the happy promises of their wedding day.

But now there appeared in Pierce a growing restlessness. He was successful, he was popular, yet he seemed uneasy. His life as rector of Natchez no longer satisfied him, and after a time he confided to his devoted, anxious wife that he had begun to have doubts as to his position in the Protestant Episcopal Church. Those new contacts with Catholicism had unsettled him. He had heard the call of a higher truth, of Truth itself, from that Catholic and Roman Church of which five years ago he had known little but the name. Now that he knew more, his conviction was growing that it was all that it claimed to be, the infallible interpreter of the mind of God. In which case . . .

It must have been a perfect moment when his Cornelia, whom he had feared might be stricken by this blow at the central order of her life, told him that his doubt and unsettlement had been hers also, that unknown to each other they had been walking the same lanes of thought, and reached the same journey's end.

3

Here I am making certain presumptions. I am presuming that the Connellys did not discuss their changing attitude towards Catholicism until it had crystallised into a definite purpose, and I am presuming that Pierce was the first to put that purpose into words. I have no facts to go upon, only probabilities. I think it probable that during the incubation stage of their doubts, each would have been afraid of upsetting the other. In those days conversions to Rome, especially in clerical circles, were even more rare and more disruptive than they are now. Cornelia especially would have held in check the attraction she felt stealing over her, knowing that her yielding to it would mean the breaking up of her husband's life. In those early stages, before the full truth appeared, she would even have regarded it as a temptation, and it was not till she knew her own joy when he told her his mind that she realised how far she had travelled without him. As for Pierce being the first to speak, I base that assumption on the continuous pattern of their lives, which consistently shows him always taking the first step, to be followed by Cornelia, who then goes far ahead of him.

This was what happened now. After more discussion, some reading and much prayer, their choice was made. They both decided to join the Church of Rome, renouncing the religion in which they had been brought up and which in the providence of God had brought them together. It meant many sacrifices— the sacrifice of their home, of their friends, and, for Pierce, of a good position and a promising future. But one sacrifice was spared them. They were well enough off to have no financial anxieties. Unlike many who were to follow him in later years, Pierce Connelly in surrendering his living did not surrender his livelihood. Indeed by this time he had sufficient private means to be able to plan a visit to Rome, where he decided their reception should take place.

This idea, though it delayed the event for some months, appealed to his sense of fitness, to say nothing of his sense of drama and possibly of his own importance. It would be much better than being received in some small-town church where the priest spoke Latin with an American accent. He pictured a big occasion, a great day, on which he and his Cornelia should be reconciled to their holy mother the Church in the very centre of her life and heart.

But his Cornelia, with a keener sense of the supernatural, could not endure the delay. She longed for the sacraments and hated the thought of having to wait for them till she was in Rome. It did not seem to her to matter where one was received into the Church that is everywhere. The only important consideration was when. As she found her husband determined on this Roman plan, she boldly suggested that she should be received without him while they were waiting for their ship at New Orleans, and it is significant that, adoring her as he did and united as they had been in the adventure until now, he still chose to wait for his big occasion, being only the witness of hers. She was received into the Catholic Church by Bishop Blanc of New Orleans, and made her first communion in the cathedral.

Pierce's great day came later, and very much as he had planned it. The Connellys arrived in Rome with introductions to many important people, and when Pierce was reconciled on the Palm Sunday of 1836, he had a no less illustrious sponsor than the Earl of Shrewsbury. The friendship with the Shrewsbury family thus begun was to play an important part in their lives and to continue through good and evil for many years.

The two young people had always moved in good society, but the society of Philadelphia and Natchez was necessarily very different from the society of cosmopolitan Rome. They found themselves for the first time in the midst of an aristocracy, and the change appears to have gone to Pierce's head. He did not cease to be pious and devout, but his letters to his family at home were so full of talk of "great people" and "valuable acquaintances", that in the end his more democratic brothers revolted and openly called him a worldly-minded snob.

His wife reacted very differently to her new surroundings. The differences between husband and wife were now beginning to show. Hitherto in their five years of marriage they had appeared very much alike in character and disposition—a "happy couple", a "united pair". But Catholicism had turned them into individuals, first revealing, then emphasising, important divergencies of outlook and behaviour.

Cornelia moved easily in the cosmopolitan society in which she found herself for the first time. The admiration which she excited wherever she went was a part of her husband's pride.

He comments smugly, "I am sure that her Christian feelings are far too strong for her ever to be carried away either by love of admiration or love for society." How right he was. Her social success could not give her half the delight that she found in the treasures of Rome—the buildings, the paintings, the music. She decided to take advantage of her opportunities and renewed her studies of music and drawing under the best masters of the city. But neither her own talents nor the beauty with which she was surrounded made the real joy of those months. That joy was the ever-flowing, ever-growing joy of her religion. She had not been in the Church a year, but already she was a creature returned to its natural element—"as a duck to water" . . . only the well-worn simile can express the perfectly unforced naturalness of her plunge into this new environment. At last, though it seemed as if it had been always, she was living the life for which she had been born.

4

Her happiness being of this nature, she was able to take it with her when they left home and returned to Natchez, though it was a return clouded by bad news and straitened circumstances. There had been some losses in the family fortune and for a time it looked as if they would be really poor. Moreover, Natchez was full of their former friends, now turned unfriendly by their change of religion.

Cornelia had much to endure and to contend with during the months that followed. Pierce, always easily depressed, began to feel all the anxieties of a man who has lost the job he was trained for, and does not know how to find another. He declared himself ready to take anything—a clerkship in a bank or a drivership on a plantation, neither of which seemed a practical suggestion. It was a much better idea to become a schoolmaster, which he did on being offered the post of

Professor of English at the College of St. Charles, Grand Côteau, Louisiana.

Both the Connellys must have been greatly relieved to leave Natchez and the shadows of their former life and establish themselves in a new circle which was almost entirely Catholic. They now had three children, for another little son, John Henry, had been born towards the end of their European trip. All the children, of course, were now Catholics, and Cornelia was adding to her delight by teaching them their first steps in religion.

The family's circumstances were henceforth easier—Pierce had his salary to supplement their income, and Cornelia had been given the post of music mistress at the Sacred Heart Convent which adjoined the college. This was for her a very happy situation, for not only did it give scope and value to her great musical gifts, but it brought her into close contact with an order to which she had been specially devoted ever since visiting the Mother-house at the Trinità dei Monti in Rome. There she had made the acquaintance of many of the nuns, and here she became the personal friend of Madame Cutts the superior and profited much from the friendship in her spiritual life.

This was growing apace. Though she had been in the Church only two years she was already treading the higher ways of prayer and sacrifice. Pierce, too, was making progress; indeed the couple were impressive in their piety, in their happiness and in their love of each other. They must have displayed their religion to the world outside in a most attractive light, for all but one of Cornelia's large family became Catholics, and Pierce's brother John was also converted, together with his future wife.

The Connellys lived in a little cottage belonging to the convent, to which they gave the name of Gracemere. Here flourished all the graces of religion and family life. Not content with bringing up her own children in the faith, Cornelia took

E   [57]

into her home a little negro slave-girl, whom she converted and then set free. The old South lives again in this act, as it lives in the sunshine and the shade of the garden at Gracemere, where Cornelia sits watching her children at play, her guitar upon her knee.

"When I first became aware", she wrote at this period, "that the religious state was higher than the secular, I secretly rejoiced that my state in life was fixed and that such a sacrifice would never be asked of me."

She was not one of those ungracious souls who look primly and askance at the gifts of God, as if they were not given us to enjoy. She thankfully rejoiced in her lovely home and happy family. Yet her soul could not forget that her life was not the life of the Man of Sorrows and its deeper knowledge rose suddenly in an act that changed her entire world.

A day came which was to be to her what the day of her conversion had been to St. Catherine of Genoa. Cornelia was never converted, except in the technical, intellectual sense of a change from one religion to another. She had changed her opinions, her allegiance, but her soul was not twice born. All that had happened was the immense improvement of its growth by its transference from an artificial to a natural soil. Nevertheless a day came which was a turning-point in her life. It was a day like any other day of the early Louisiana spring-time, and as on every other day Cornelia sat in her sunny garden, watching her children at play, her guitar upon her knee. Perhaps she sang there in the garden the old songs of the South, "Shining River", and "Shady Grove", her lovely voice rising among the spring voices of the birds, while the flowers in the spring borders matched the gay, streaming ribbons of her guitar.

It was a moment perfect in its beauty, its happiness, its goodness, and suddenly in the midst of it her soul rose up and cried—"Oh, my God, if this happiness be not for thy glory and the good of my soul—take it from me. I make the sacrifice."

[58]

She had done it. She had challenged the divine eagle to swoop on its prey. She had said amen to her own spoliation. It was a heroic act and its reward was on heroic levels. Twenty-four hours later she sat in her garden. The sunshine and the springtime and the flowers were the same, but instead of the guitar upon her knee lay the agonised body of her youngest child, little John, her special treasure, dying in torment after being pushed by a playful dog into a vat of boiling sugar.

5

When a few days later the little boy was buried with all the joyful, tender rites that the Church keeps for those who die "immaculate in the Way", Cornelia could not know that when she herself came to die he would be the only one of her family whom she could confidently expect to meet again in heaven. She had not realised yet the full effect of her offering. She may even have thought that she had already been fully taken at her word. But she had offered all and she had not yet lost all.

Indeed at the moment a new hope had dawned in her life. She was expecting another child, perhaps another son, to comfort her and fill the empty place. On the other hand, she was beginning to feel anxious about her husband. There was something on his mind. She did not think it could still be little John's loss, for he did not seem so much unhappy as preoccupied. There was also a change in his manner towards her, and a withdrawal of his confidence.

She observed these things but she did nothing to change them—she did not coax or plague him to tell her what he obviously wished to conceal. She accepted his withdrawal as she had accepted her other sorrow. It was part of the holocaust she had offered. Yet in the heart of her acceptance was an increasing dread. "Oh, my God," she prayed, "trim thy vine, cut it to the quick, but in thy great mercy root it not up yet."

In those words, "root it not up" lay perhaps a presage of what was coming, for her whole life was shortly to be torn up by the roots. The spring was over, and the long, stifling summer, but though October had come the air was still warm and heavy in the deep South. The morning was as hot as any in an English June when Pierce and Cornelia walked home together from Mass on the feast of St. Edward the Confessor. They had been to Holy Communion and Cornelia's thoughts were still in heaven when her husband spoke. Perhaps we may allow our imagination to build up a conversation of which we have no record except her later declaration that if it had not been for God's grace she would have died of sorrow.

"My love," said Pierce, "you may have noticed lately that there's something on my mind."

"I have indeed," said Cornelia, thankful that at last he seemed likely to confide in her.

"I didn't want to tell you anything till my mind was made up. I would have hid my preoccupation from you if I could, but I know that because you love me you must have seen it in spite of my efforts. I'm going to ask great things of your love for me, Cornelia."

"You can't ask too much."

He took her hand.

"And of your love of God."

What could Pierce have to ask of her love of God? Her mind must have moved among many conjectures, but she was totally unprepared for what was coming.

"I feel," he said slowly—"or rather I'm convinced that God is calling me to be a priest."

The full import of his words can hardly have dawned on her at once. We can see her facing him in a sort of bewilderment.

"Oh, Pierce . . . . but how . . . . ?"

"It can be done," he continued, "if *you* are willing. It is your decision. But it means a great sacrifice from you, my dear. I have gone into the matter and I have found that a married man like myself can be accepted for the priesthood only if his wife before his ordination enters a religious order."

The shock of his words nearly choked her. All she could say was—

"Pierce, the children. . . ."

For a moment he too was silent. Then he said quietly:

"These things take time. It may be some years before I can be ordained, and by then Merty and Ady will be at school. It will merely be a case of providing for their holidays, and I shall be at hand. . . ."

"But there will be . . . . What about . . . .?" Had Pierce forgotten the child that was coming?

He checked—pondered—then said: "If it is God's will that I become a priest, he will provide for *all* our children. There are many things that could happen. My brother and his wife would I am sure be eager to help us, or the child might even be taken charge of by the convent you enter—for a while at least. But all this, as I've said, is far ahead in the future, and we must trust in God. If it is his will——"

"If it is his will," said Cornelia with white lips—"His will be done."

She could say no less, and no more, for she was nearly fainting.

6

The more one thinks of Pierce's announcement, whatever form it actually took, the more one is appalled by the sheer tactlessness (to use no stronger word) of the time he chose to make it. He might at least have waited until Cornelia's child was born. To have compelled her to go through her pregnancy with the knowledge that birth must be followed by separation was a barbarity comparable only to that which, in the bad old days before prison reform, obliged condemned women to see the gallows waiting for them as soon as they had recovered from their lying-in. It is hardly surprising that Elizabeth Fry found these wretched mothers full of a deep resentment. But there was no resentment in Cornelia, though her husband with a few words had turned her deepest joys to sorrows. Her happy home, his tender care, her children's love, were now all so many wounds in her heart. She suffered agony at the thought of the day when she must lose them all and begin a life for which she had never felt any vocation.

It may perhaps be wondered why she submitted so readily, why she had not attempted to argue, or said at least: "This is not the time to talk of such things. They must stand over till our child is born." No doubt Pierce would have listened to her, for he loved her deeply, though he was not always very clever in his way of showing it. But we have to remember that first in Cornelia's heart, before her husband, before her children, came the love of God. Undoubtedly she saw God's will in this decision—following as it did so soon after her offering of herself and all she had. She would not have believed that Pierce could have asked of her such a sacrifice—which after all was a sacrifice for him, too—if he had not been quite convinced that God required it of them both. His call to the priesthood was a great honour for him and for her and for their children. For her too was the special honour of giving her dearest possession to God. He had asked her for this gift, so she gave it gladly with all her wounded heart.

There were, however, some bad moments when her natural, human feelings would have their way, though she was strong enough to hide them from all save her spiritual advisers.

"Is it necessary," she cried to one of these—"is it necessary for Pierce to make this sacrifice and sacrifice me? I love my husband; I love my darling children. Why must I give them up?"

Nothing of course could happen until after the birth of the expected child, and no one but the couple's directors knew what was intended. Cornelia maintained her calm and even her gaiety, showing that integrity and stability of character which was among her greatest gifts. Many a woman, one thinks, would have miscarried her child in such a situation, or at least injured its health and vitality with the poison of hidden distress. But little Frank was born at his full term, a sturdy, healthy baby, untouched by his mother's suffering.

7

A few months after his birth Cornelia went into retreat at the convent, and here and now for the first time she experienced a sense of vocation. Hitherto all her instincts had been opposed to the religious life. She was a wife and a mother and her vocation was to her home and family. When Pierce had spoken of a change it had seemed to her quite impossible that she should ever as it were put her whole nature into reverse.

But she had always believed that the religious life was the higher one, though she had never thought the call would come to her—indeed, she had rejoiced that it could not. Now at last she heard it, and being what she was, she gave her whole heart in response.

This is recorded in the notes she made during the retreat: "Examined vocation. Decided. Simplicity—confidence. Oh, my good Jesus, I do give myself all to thee, to suffer and die on the cross, poor as thou wert poor, abandoned as thou wert abandoned."

Yet even now the future was not decided, and the uncertainty must have acted as an irritant on her sorrows. Such a momentous step as the ordination of a husband and father could not be undertaken without much preparation and time for thought. It was not, of course, the first time that a married man had been ordained, and the procedure for such an event was fixed by custom and canon law. But the Connellys' youth —she was only thirty-three and he five years older—put their separation and the disruption of their family into an altogether different class from that of those elderly or middle-aged couples who, having fledged their children, decide to give up the rest of their lives to religion.

A year had passed since Pierce's announcement, and outwardly their life was the same. Friends and visitors who saw the same happy, cultured exterior could not know that inside the future had eaten it hollow. To change the metaphor, Gracemere was no longer a home but the platform of a railway station where a couple waits, filling with desultory conversation the time that must elapse before the arrival of the train that is to part them for ever.

That train came in some six months later, when little Frank was a year old, taking Pierce away to England and the home of the Shrewsburys while still leaving his ordination a secret and distant adventure. The earl had heard with concern that a man of whom he had always thought most highly had been reduced by financial losses to become a mere usher in a school. He wrote offering to undertake the education at Stonyhurst of Mercer the eldest boy and suggesting that the whole family should move to England, where Pierce would find better opportunities for the exercise of his talents than he enjoyed at Grand Côteau. With the kindest hospitality he invited Cornelia and her children to Alton Towers.

It was agreed that the offer should be accepted only in part. Pierce would go to Europe, taking Mercer with him, but Cornelia would stay behind at Grand Côteau with the two younger children. It would be as it were a dress rehearsal of their final separation, and a test of Pierce's vocation. He would try to find a temporary post, preferably one that would bring him to Rome, and if it all turned out as he hoped and expected he would then ask for ordination.

Gracemere was to be given up and Cornelia and the children were to be lodged at the convent, her part of the dress rehearsal. All the family's furniture and possessions were sold by public auction, and when Pierce and his young son sailed for England they left behind them a wife and mother utterly despoiled.

She now regarded herself as virtually a postulant. She lived with Adeline and Frank in a small cottage in the convent grounds, taught in the school, and joined in the community retreat. Her sister, Mary Peacock, converted by her example, was already a novice, and Cornelia had no thought but of herself becoming a Sacred Heart nun at Grand Côteau as soon as the future should be decided.

But this decision was still like a pilgrim's horizon, continuing to recede. Pierce had arrived in England, had settled Mercer at Stonyhurst, spent a few weeks with the Shrewsburys at Alton Towers, and finally accepted the post of travelling companion to a young Englishman (needless to say "of one of the best families") with whom he was to visit Belgium, Germany, Italy and France.

"What a delightful time," he writes to his brother, "if Nelie were with me! How much rather would I be at home with her and the little ones than anywhere else without them . . . . All the magnificence and greatness I am in the midst of is a poor—very poor—exchange for solitude and holy quiet."

Do we altogether believe him? I am not sure that we do.

8

A letter which Cornelia Connelly might have written to her husband, but did not:

Convent of the Sàcred Heart,
    Grand Côteau,
       Louisiana.

                Feast of St. Aloysius, 1843.

My love,
    It is now almost a year that you have been gone, and little

Frank can hardly remember you, though he prays every
night for his dear Papa. We all, the children and I, follow
you on your travels, spreading out the map of Europe on our
little dining-table and underlining in red ink the places you
have visited, while we read and re-read the descriptions you
give in your letters. What a wonderful tour you must be
having and how you must be enjoying it! I am glad you find
young Mr. Berkeley such an agreeable companion and of
course it must add very much to the pleasures of your trip
to meet so many distinguished people. But, my dear love,
when are you going to Rome? I had thought you would
have been there by now, and as you are so completely in
charge of your route, I am at a loss to understand why you
are not. When you went away you told me that the main
object of your leaving us was to go there as quickly as possible. Yet you write from Fribourg, from Munich, from
Milan, from Ancona, yet never mention Rome. I cannot
help longing for you to go there, so that our future lives may
be settled and the lives of our children. I will not disguise
from you that I find this long period of uncertainty most
trying to my spirits. I am neither in the world nor out of it,
nor know which I shall be a year hence. Nor can I deny
an uneasy feeling that your present life spent in luxurious
travel and fashionable society is not the best possible preparation for a life of prayer and sacrifice. My dear one, I have
given you to God and I want that gift to be as perfect as
human nature will allow. I fear lest it become blemished in
the course of these delays. I do not presume to dictate to
you or even to advise you, but I cannot refrain from asking
you to consider whether it would not be possible to expedite
your journey to the Holy City where alone our case can be
decided. I am sure Mr. Berkeley would not object, having
shown himself so perfectly complying hitherto.

The children and I are well, thank God! Though little
Ady alarmed us all a month ago (when I would not write of

it) by coming out in an eruption of her skin which made us fear the measles. She was of course taken good care of, but as I was teaching in the school I was unable to nurse her or even to visit her in case I should carry the infection to others. I found this a heavy cross, but I realised that as I must learn to live without my children it was good training for me. That being so, I forebore even to inquire after her. So you see, my dearest, I am doing what little I can to fit myself for this great and wonderful thing that is to change our lives.

I am glad you have such good reports of Mercer. I write to him regularly, for I suppose that I shall always be able to do that. He has sent me some nice letters too. But I wish he did not have these day-dreams. His mind seems always to be wandering among castles in the air! I fear that this may interfere with his studies. He has not told me yet where he is in school.

I must go now and prepare my lessons for tomorrow's classes. God bless you, my beloved, and write to me soon—from Rome.

Ever your devoted wife,

CORNELIA CONNELLY.

Actually her diary contains this entry for the feast of St. Aloysius—"Profit by all temptations ! ! ! !"

9

At last Pierce Connelly was in Rome. It is hard to conjecture why he took so long to arrive there, because when he finally did so he immediately set about his petition to the ecclesiastical authorities for leave to separate from his wife as a preliminary to ordination. Their answer possibly surprised him. He was told that nothing whatsoever could be done in her absence.

She must come to Rome and give her consent in person. Till then he had gone his way, prime mover of the enterprise, doubtless imagining that it could go forward and reach its end on his sole impulse. Now for the first time he realised that Cornelia was to have her public say in the matter. It was not enough to inform the authorities that she had freely consented to his wishes from the very first moment of knowing them and was now living a semi-conventual life in anticipation of their fulfilment. She must appear in person and formally express her sanction before anything could be done. The Vatican refused to move without her.

This would mean another delay, which this time would not be Pierce's fault. But once more his behaviour becomes a mystery. He wrote to Cornelia, telling her what had happened and what was required and stating that he himself would come over and fetch her. As bear-leader to the most docile (and well-provided) of bears, he was able, by suggesting the enlargement of a visit to America, to extend his tour and travel free of cost to Philadelphia where she was to meet him. Cornelia, deeply thankful for this call to action, set her affairs in order and left the convent with her children. But when she arrived in Philadelphia she was astonished to find that they were not to go straight to Rome, but stay where they were for a month and then go as guests of the Shrewsburys to Alton Towers. This was not at all what she had bargained for, nor had she expected to find Pierce plunging happily into social life, accepting invitations for them both, and taking all his former pride in the admiration she excited wherever she went.

She had lived a semi-conventual life for over a year and thought she had renounced the world entirely. It was painful to have to make this return and renew the taste of what she hoped she had forgotten. But even Alton Towers did not see the end of it. They left England only for Paris and "half a dozen dinner parties with the Duchesse de D. and the Princesse de B." It was all unexpected and mysterious.

Some might say that Cornelia's own behaviour was as mysterious as her husband's. Why did she put up with all this? She might have challenged him and said: Either we go straight to Rome and arrange for our separation or we return to Grand Côteau and our normal lives. I cannot live indefinitely between two worlds.

The answer lies no doubt in the total offering she had made of herself and her decision to see God's will in her husband's. She was not a mystic. Unlike St. Catherine her Love did not direct her save through the voices of others. Her confessor and her husband were her guides and she would not challenge their decisions—or lack of decision. Besides, she knew herself too well to trust any choice or decision of her own in this matter. Her human longings were all for a return to the family life she had found so happy, and she dared not speak lest self should get control of her tongue. There was nothing to be gained by protest but her own comfort, and that she had learned to do without. She was too holy and wise not to have seen had there been any obvious flaw in her husband's sincerity, and in considering his vocation she could not altogether disapprove of these delays, of this half-return to the world they expected to leave, since both the delays and the return should serve to give him a deeper insight into his own heart. She could not object to them merely because they added to her sufferings the torment of hope, though this torment must have increased almost beyond endurance as the Connellys, always with the faithful and obliging Mr. Berkeley, moved from Paris to Orleans, from Orleans, to Avignon, to Genoa, to Leghorn—making their leisurely way to Rome in the days before the railroads. Often during that slow journey Cornelia must have had to bear the unbearable hope that the course of events would suggest to Pierce that he had no vocation or indeed that the ecclesiastical authorities might decide that it would be inadvisable to ordain him.

10

At last they were in Rome and dining with princes. In the midst of the usual social round they settled in the Via Ripetta and little Adeline was sent as a pupil to the Sacred Heart Convent at the Trinità dei Monti. In visiting her there Cornelia was able to renew her contacts with that other world which she had thought would be her only world by now.

The next delay came from the Church authorities, who made no reply to the couple's petition for separation. This does not seem to have caused any marked distress to Pierce, who at once started making plans for his travels years ahead as the tutor of young Talbot, Shrewsbury's heir. It would, however, be a mistake to attribute his light-heartedness to any relaxation of his desire for the priesthood. Rather, it was due to his conviction that this desire would ultimately be granted. Absolutely sure of himself and of others in their relation to him, he had nothing to consider but how to pass pleasantly and profitably the time of waiting.

Cornelia, on the other hand, found in this ecclesiastical silence a further test of her heroism. It now seemed to her almost likely that the Pope would decline the petition and all she had given up would be restored to her. In her mind must have lived, even if unacknowledged, the thought of Abraham's remitted sacrifice. It was now four years since that St. Edward's Day when to a call very like the call to Abraham she had answered, "Here am I." From that moment her will had never faltered, even in the depths of human grief and loss; and now as the agonies of hope increased there was no change in her. She showed no outward signs of struggle as she went on her quiet, purposeful way. Through complete self-abandonment she had won that rarest gift of complete self-possession. No one could say more fully or more truthfully than she—"Here am I."

She may have been right in supposing that the Papal silence displayed a reluctance to ordain her husband. Pope Gregory XVI had received the Connellys in private audience when they first came to Rome in 1836, and had taken a personal interest in them ever since. He may have hesitated as to the rightness of breaking up so young a family or of ordaining in such exceptional circumstances a man of whose vocation he could not in the nature of things be absolutely certain. Possibly nothing more would have happened if there had not been staying in Rome that winter a very holy American prelate, Bishop Flaget of Bardstown, who had known Pierce and Cornelia for some years and heartily approved of Pierce's aspiration. It is only a surmise that the Bishop intervened on his behalf, but it seems likely that he would have done so and that his better knowledge would induce the Pope to make a favourable decision. Anyhow, delays were ended rather suddenly and on St. Patrick's Day Pierce was able to write to his brother and for the first time make his intentions known.

After giving an account of the matter and explaining the real purpose of his journeys to Europe, with the news that he was to receive Minor Orders almost immediately, he added:

"Nelie at the same time will enter the Convent of the Sacred Heart where little Ady is, not as a novice but only as a postulant, remaining at liberty as long as Frank has need of her. He is to be received with his nurse in a cottage in the garden of the convent just as he was at Grand Côteau. Cornelia will always pass her nights with him, and he has the most beautiful garden you can imagine to play in, large and high, with a sweet view of all Rome."

This happy disposal of those who were to bear the brunt of his sacrifice is characteristic of Pierce, also the paragraph that follows.

"You know the Prince Borghese has taken charge of Frank's education, and he will be put either here in the College of Nobles at Rome, or with Merty at Stonyhurst in England, as soon as he is old enough. So far, you see, things have been ordered very wonderfully. . . . The children are at once placed as well as little princes could desire, with the interest and protection of great and holy people." Even Frank's nurse gets a splash of gilding—"Nelie has the sweetest little person in the world to take care of Frank, well brought up, never at service before, indeed more of a governess than a nurse . . . Lady Shrewsbury's sister heard of her for us."

His brothers John and George must have answered this letter as good Christians, for when he next writes to George he thanks him for "the wise and Christian way in which you judge what we have done". George seems also to have written as a good American, for Pierce continues: "You as well as dear John seem disposed to judge rather harshly of the worldly tone of part of the letters I sent you," and after justifying himself at some length finally clinches the matter by pointing out that Our Lord himself took care that his Mother should be of royal blood.

By this time Pierce had received Minor Orders.

II

On a fine spring day there is no lovelier sight in Rome than the Trinità dei Monti. High above the Spanish Steps the twin towers soar into the breathless dazzle of the sky, while on their flank the convent spreads its great umber façade against dark clouds of ilex in the Borghese Gardens.

On a fine spring day Cornelia Connelly made this beautiful place her prison. She felt it as a prison. For the first time her strong, gay spirit failed. The conflict was over and she had fallen wounded and exhausted on the empty battlefield. "My soul sleeps", she wrote, and she might have added: "My body says, like the starling—'I can't get out.'"

For the first time she experienced the full rigours of convent life—the cold cell, the hard bed, and above all the surrounding, confining walls. The "most beautiful garden you can imagine" and the "sweet view of Rome" were all very well for those who could exchange them at will for the freedom of the streets and the houses of their friends. To Cornelia they were as the exercise-yard of a prison and the view between prison bars. Under the weight of sorrow and reaction her health failed, mentally and physically, and she who had always been so brave, so sane, now longed for death and even thought it was near.

In spite of the presence of her little boy and the kindness of the nuns, many of whom she already knew well, she felt utterly alone. The child was too young to be a companion (when he was old enough she would have to send him away) and the nuns' vocation was so utterly different from her own that it was impossible for them to understand half of what she felt and suffered. "Unless," she writes at this period, "the Lord had been my helper, my soul had almost dwelt in hell."

Pierce had received his Minor Orders in the convent chapel and it was there a year later that she made the vow of perpetual chastity which must precede his elevation to the priesthood. This followed quickly. On the Sunday after she made her vow he received the sub-diaconate and the diaconate a week later. On the third Sunday, July 6th, he was ordained priest.

Cornelia had given her gift to God, and for a moment the clouds parted as she saw her gift accepted and ratified. On the day following his ordination, Pierce said his first Mass in the chapel of the Trinità dei Monti. It was also the day of little Adeline's first communion. Kneeling beside her child at the altar and receiving the sacred host from her husband's hand, Cornelia tasted life, not death, and saw the cross she had carried so long bud like Aaron's rod and become a flowering tree among the brooks of paradise.

It was a moment too big for time, and had soon escaped from it. In its wake the nights and days dragged their slow, hardening length. Cornelia now knew definitely that she was out of place. She found it almost an impossible strain to adapt herself to convent life—at least to the life of this particular convent. The Trinità dei Monti belonged to the same order as Grand Côteau, but this was Italy, not America; if there were no differences of rule there were differences of routine, and of outlook if not of aspiration. She taught in the school, but she had by now sufficient experience as a teacher to have formed her own ideas on the teaching and training of girls. She had an ever-growing conviction that it was not here God meant her to live and work. Yet this Order of the Sacred Heart was the only one she knew. As she was only a postulant she was free to leave it, but where else could she go? Once more uncertainty was added to her trials. She felt that God did not wish her to stay where she was, but his remoter purposes for her were hidden.

Then at last Providence moved, and she was shown her way, no longer through her husband's choices but through the Church authorities who had taken his place. Dr. Wiseman, then head of the Venerable English College in Rome, had just returned from a visit to England where he had been deeply impressed by the Church's opportunities in a country which he felt convinced was now on the brink of a great Catholic revival. He realised the important part that education must play in such a movement, and he also realised that though Catholic boys were already fairly well provided for, very little had been done for the girls. He saw the need for a teaching order on much the same lines as the Order of the Sacred Heart, but with perhaps a more modern outlook and a greater freedom from tradition. It says much for his wisdom and enlightenment that he at once thought of Cornelia Connelly as the best possible leader of such an enterprise.

He had known her since her first days in Rome and thought most highly of her gifts and graces, mental and spiritual. She was thrown away in her present situation and he suggested to the Pope that here was the very woman they needed in England as the pioneer of Catholic education for girls. Pope Gregory, who also knew her well, received the idea with enthusiasm and in a personal interview with Cornelia he sketched for her the Church's plan and the part she was to play in it.

His voice must have seemed to her indeed the voice of God, resolving all her perplexities. Now at last she was to be used, set free from her beautiful garden and sweet view to do a work which she felt capable of performing and which she knew was sorely needed. For the first time she could see her sacrifice as a prelude to a new life for her as well as for Pierce. Her function was not always to be to stand aside, to get out of his way. She at last had a way of her own.

12

In a very few weeks she had left the Trinità dei Monti. She could not go to England till certain preparations had been made and suitable accommodation found for her. But so that she might be at once available when all was ready, it was thought best that she should wait in Paris rather than in Rome. So to Paris she went with her children, staying at the Convent of the Assumption. She must have left the Trinità with mixed feelings. There she had experienced at least one blessed moment and many bitter ones. She had known love and kindness but also loneliness and dereliction.

She went but she left behind her a memorial which will always keep her name in the Order of the Sacred Heart even though it was not to be the order of her adoption. There is a story told by the pilgrims who come to visit the shrine of Mater Admirabilis—of which I believe there is a reproduction in every Sacred Heart convent throughout the world. It concerns a fellow postulant who like Cornelia herself had studied

art and was asked to paint a fresco on the wall of one of the
corridors. But for some reason the painter's skill failed her
and the work was so badly done that the Mother Superior
ordered its obliteration. The next morning, however, when
with a pail of whitewash the order was to be carried out, the
picture had changed. Not only was the painting itself now
beyond reproach, but there was about it a new quality of supernatural beauty which thrilled and awed all who looked upon it.
Such a work must never be destroyed and it was ordered to
remain.

So deeply did it now impress all who saw it, that it soon
became a centre of pilgrimage where many graces have been
obtained and countless prayers answered. It is known that
Cornelia Connelly helped with the painting, though whether it
was her paintbrush or her prayers that changed it so wonderfully I do not know. But as a memorial of her at the Trinità
dei Monti it is singularly appropriate—Mater Admirabilis . . . .
The Mother sits in a sunny green field, her work-basket
beside her, sewing for the Christ who is to come. On her face
is a little secret smile, the smile of a woman who ponders God's
secrets in her heart and waits for the Holy Child.

Cornelia Connelly was thirty-six years old when she
embarked on the great adventure of her life—the founding
of the Society of the Holy Child Jesus. The name had come to
her while she was at prayer, and there is something especially
touching in that placing of Mary's Child in the centre of her
life, instead of her own darling children, now given to God.
For the years that remained to her (and they were many, for
she lived to be seventy years old) she was to have two special
devotions, to the Mother of Sorrows and to the Holy Child.
Between them they tell the story of her life.

She was happy now. She was called to action, to a work
she felt able and eager to do. She was happy about Pierce, too.
After some hesitation as to whether he should join the Jesuits,
he had gone as chaplain to Lord Shrewsbury at Alton Towers.

Cornelia could picture him there, exercising his ministry in surroundings that she herself knew well.

The distribution of Catholicism in England was then very different from what it is now. It was then only just beginning to invade the big industrial towns, and for the most part remained still centred in little groups and communities on the estates of the big Catholic landowners. The Shrewsburys, the Norfolks, the Blundells and many others had acted as protectors to their tenants in penal times, and though those times were over, they still liked to see their estates as centres of Catholic life. Probably all Lord Shrewsbury's employees as well as most of the dwellers in the village were Catholics, and therefore the work of his chaplain would not have differed much from that of a busy parish priest. Cornelia wrote to her brother-in-law from Paris to tell him that Pierce was "deeply engaged in the duties of his ministry, instructing, preaching, hearing confessions, etc., etc." Then she added words that in future years would be painful to read or to remember: "So you see it is not for nothing I have given him to God."

A month or two later Dr. Wiseman called her to England to begin work in his own district. The re-establishment of the Hierarchy was still some years ahead, and the country was divided into missionary districts under a vicar general. Dr. Wiseman as Bishop of the Midland District arranged for Cornelia and her children to be accommodated at the Convent of the Sisters of Mercy in Birmingham.

It was not till she arrived in England that she realised that she herself was to be the foundress of the new congregation. She had always imagined that the work would be organised by someone with more experience than she had of the religious life and that she herself would occupy an auxiliary and subordinate position. But now she found that she, though not yet even a novice, was to do and be everything, and her spirits may well have quailed. The lot of a nun in Protestant England less than twenty years after Catholic Emancipation was not in any circumstances a happy one, and Cornelia's own especial circumstances—a nun with two small children and a mysterious priest husband, an American accent and no money—certainly would not make the situation easier.

However, she set about it all with her wonted drive and courage, and the community already had four members by the time it moved at Dr. Wiseman's direction to Derby. The date of the move must have appeared significant to Cornelia, for it was St. Edward's Day. As she sat with her three companions in the roofless third-class carriage that jogged them mercilessly along one of the earliest railways, she must have thought of that same morning six years ago when in the far-off sunshine of Louisiana she had first seen the terrifying shadow of the life she was leading today.

The little party arrived at Derby (one of them very sick after the journey) to find a vast convent almost without furniture. Kind helpers had prepared for their arrival by cooking a leg of mutton with some carrots and potatoes, but had unfortunately omitted to provide any knives, forks or plates. Nor was there any altar in the convent chapel. Cornelia's first act was to borrow cutlery and crockery, so that she and her companions could eat their dinner, her next to borrow an altar, tabernacle, ciborium and candlesticks, so that they could hear Mass and have the Blessed Sacrament with them in their new home.

Though they were so few in number and the convent did not contain even the necessaries of life, she introduced at once a normal conventual rule and started the society's work of education by teaching in the parish school. It was not, however, till December that Bishop Wiseman gave the religious habit to her and to two other members of the community, so as she put it, they were "all novices together". A year later she was formally professed and installed as Mother Superior of the Society of the Holy Child Jesus.

She was now Mother Connelly, mother of a new family, and a family almost as much dependent on her motherly care as her

[78]

own children had been. For the members of her community were all very young girls, some only in their teens, some recent converts, all quite inexperienced in the ways of the religious life. No doubt they helped satisfy maternal instincts that were otherwise cruelly frustrated. For her own children were no longer with her. Pierce had taken them away.

It is hard to think why he should have done so, for the arrangements for their welfare that had been made at his ordination were working quite satisfactorily. One can only imagine that he was moving in response to the first stirrings of that jealousy of his wife's new position which was later on to become such a disruptive force. He may have compensated himself for the loss of his authority over her by exercising it where it still remained in its full strength. His reasons no doubt were a puzzle even to Cornelia, but his actions were unmistakable. Quite arbitrarily and suddenly he decided that Adeline and Frank should go away to school. Adeline was nearly fourteen and already had some experience of school life, but her mother no doubt had hoped that she would finish her education under her own eye in one of the schools of the society. As for Frank, he was still only a baby, not yet six years old, and it seemed barbarous to send him away. The Church authorities entirely approved of his staying with his mother till he was eight, and to have him snatched away from her like this was enough to break her heart.

There was, however, nothing that she could do about it. Pierce was still the children's legal guardian and had absolute control. She could only face the situation as she had faced every adverse situation in her life hitherto, with courage and the complete acceptance of God's will. She even wrote cheerfully to Mercer about "the nice school at Hampstead where I had put our darling little Frank. . . . Mrs. Nicholson says he has only cried once since I left him."

Mercer was allowed to visit her during the school holidays, but lately he too had become an anxiety and for an even more painful reason. He was turning out badly, showing himself both lazy and deceitful. His schoolwork and his conduct left much to be desired. No doubt his peculiar family circumstances were having the same effect on him as they would have had on most children, and he escaped from them into dreams in which he compensated himself for having a home-life so unlike that of other boys by performing deeds of incredible valour. He attempted the same readjustment in the conscious field by continually begging for money and other things that he thought likely to increase his popularity and prestige. But it was a situation that no Victorian mother, however wise and holy, could be expected to understand. Disappointed and bewildered she asks him: "What do you want with an eyeglass?"

13

But more distressing and alarming than Mercer's behaviour must by now have become the behaviour of Mercer's father. In any attempt to understand Pierce Connelly at this time two facts must be taken into consideration. The first was the death of Pope Gregory towards the end of 1846, the second was the conception and growth of an almost pathological jealousy of Bishop Wiseman.

The late Pope had been a sincere friend and admirer of the Connellys, and Pierce no doubt had hoped great things from his favour. His successor, Pius IX, was not interested, nor had Lord Shrewsbury, on whom Pierce had relied for his advancement, much influence in the new Papal Court. We do not know to what heights Pierce's ambition had soared, but it was probably not far short of a cardinal's hat. Now he saw nothing ahead but monotonous years of work as a country priest. His chaplaincy at Alton had done very well as a stepping-stone to higher things, but as an end in itself he found it stultifying and frustrating.

At the same time his wife seemed to be, in commercial language, on to a good thing, and one uses commercial language all the more readily because Pierce's attitude towards the Church has often suggested the attitude of a keen business man towards a promising enterprise. Apart from his infatuation with high Catholic society, he had always laid great stress on the need for recommending Catholicism to the people at large, and he often wrote of it to his brothers as he might have written of some big business corporation in need of all the succours of publicity and popularity. "Nothing will contribute more to make Catholics popular and do more good than the establishment of Colleges and Convents. . . . Our newspapers and tracts and books too it ought to be the business of every Catholic to encourage and disseminate. . . . If every practical Catholic would deny himself to the amount of one tenth of his income for the sake of works of piety and charity, our Church would double itself in five years from its increased means and its increased respect."

At first he seems to have taken in his wife's new venture the same sort of pride that he used to take in her social success. He writes proudly and happily to his brother about the great work to which she has been called, and does not seem to have been blind to the place of his own ordination in the designs of Providence for the conversion of England. But this commendable attitude soon changed, the change being no doubt due to the second factor in Pierce's deterioration, his jealousy of Dr. Wiseman.

To understand this one must remember that for fifteen years he had dominated his wife to the extent of being absolute master of her fate. She had seen in his wishes the will of God, and in consequence he seems to have done exactly what he liked with her in everything. She had accepted his decisions and also his indecisions, his procrastinations and his sudden acts. But in the end his power had destroyed itself, for its final act had placed her outside his control. Of him, her husband,

Pierce Connelly, she was now completely independent. He had no power over her in her new life or in connection with the society she had founded. It is possible that he had not sufficiently considered this result of his actions. In itself it would have been bad enough. But not only was Cornelia independent of him, she had become dependent on another man.

Very soon after her coming to England Dr. Wiseman begins to appear in a sinister light. In the first place Pierce held him responsible for her not having started her new congregation in America, which he declared had been her own wish. "You ought to know," he wrote to his brother, "it was no doing of Cornelia's coming to England." The bishop had then compelled her to take possession of the convent in Derby "much against her will and even her judgment". Almost immediately after her removal there Pierce set to work to do what he imagined would loosen his rival's hold upon his wife. (It helps towards the understanding of his extraordinary behaviour if we use the language of conjugal jealousy.)

Two of his steps were contradictory. At first he demanded of Dr. Wiseman that she should take her final religious vows without waiting till she had accomplished a year in the novitiate. No doubt he imagined that as a full-fledged religious she would be more independent of her bishop than as a novice. When this move naturally failed he made one in the opposite direction and demanded that she should not take any final vows at all, protesting that if she did so he might be considered responsible for the debts of her community.

Both these attempts at interference failed, but in a third he was entirely and devastatingly successful. Without first consulting either Cornelia or Dr. Wiseman he wrote to a friend in Rome, Dr. Samuele Asperti, and invited him to come to England as chaplain to the new congregation. This was a gratuitous piece of meddling. Cornelia had always been on the best of terms with the Derby priests in whose parish she worked, while the spiritual direction of the community was in the capable hands of the Jesuits. She knew nothing of Dr. Asperti save that he was her husband's friend, and it is at first sight surprising that she should have submitted to this unwarranted intrusion in her affairs. But on reflection one realises that she was no more accustomed than Pierce to the new state of things. She had always let him rule her and could not yet break herself of the habit.

Here one cannot help pausing to compare her with that other saintly wife, Caterina Fiesca Adorna. How would she have reacted if her Giuliano had interfered with her work in the hospital? One can be pretty sure that he would not have been allowed to do so. The medieval wife would have listened to his advice and accepted his co-operation, but with any high-handed acts of interference (had he been disposed to make them) he would have had no success at all. Yet Catherine had not a stronger mind or will than Cornelia. If one thing is proved and certain it is the latter's strength and independence of character. One can only see here a lingering of the Victorian wife who for so long had regarded submission as a religious duty, echoing the poet's: "He for God only, she for God in Him." She had not yet discovered that there was very little of God in the later decisions of Pierce Connelly.

14

It was not till Dr. Asperti had actually arrived and was in residence that she realised all the trouble her obedience had brought on herself and her congregation. The doctor was a fiery Italian, impetuous and bigoted, with characteristically Mediterranean ideas on such subjects as religious communities, Catholic parishes and the conversion of England. He made trouble not only in the society but in the parish, and soon Cornelia's happy, orderly little world was in process of eruption.

To make matters worse, at about this time her friend and protector Dr. Wiseman was removed from the Midlands to the London District. Not only was she left without his counsel at a crisis in her affairs, but he was no longer able to guarantee the society's finances, with the result that she soon found herself seriously in debt. The community now had nearly twenty members, all busily at work. Besides the parish school there was a new school for "young ladies" and a Sunday class for two hundred mill girls. Cornelia had assumed a load of work and responsibility, and it now looked as if it was going to be too much for her. In desperation she appealed to the new Bishop of the Midland District, Dr. Ullathorne.

The Bishop did the best he could. He made the convent a canonical visitation and expressed his unqualified approval of the society and its work. But he considered its temporal difficulties too serious to be overcome under present conditions, and advised Mother Connelly to leave her expensive and unwieldy quarters in Derby and find something smaller and cheaper to run. In fact he advised her to accept an offer which Dr. Wiseman himself had made a short while earlier, when it had occurred to her good friend that her troubles might be a call to move elsewhere. He had therefore written to tell her of "a place prepared, or nearly so, for your reception, where you will be not merely welcomed, but hailed with joy".

The young Sisters of the Community were not pleased at the thought of moving. It seemed like an acknowledgment of failure and the undoing of their work. But Cornelia accepted it as she accepted all that came to her through the voice of her superiors, as the will of God. She said to her nuns: "We are Sisters of the Holy Child Jesus. What must we expect but opposition, persecution, and flight into Egypt."

Egypt in this case was Hastings, or rather the new suburb of St. Leonards which Decimus Burton had designed a mile westward of the town. Here pale Regency façades and colonnades gleamed on the seafront or against the trees of a public garden which he had fashionably embellished with a maze. It was a resort of elegance, shrugging away from the picturesque old fishing and bathing town on the other side of the hill. This hill was a sort of *cordon sanitaire* between fashion and mere popularity. From White Rock where it met the sea, it rose a couple of hundred feet to what had long been known as Spitalman's Down. The name was all that remained of a hospital which Isabella de Cham had built there long ago, and was already in process of changing, as the inhabitants both of Hastings and St. Leonards began to speak of the Catholic Ground.

For the Down was now the property of a Catholic priest, who had enclosed the land and erected several buildings. There was also a chapel, a garden and other grounds, extending to over fourteen acres and completely surrounded by a stone wall. No other houses were in sight and the whole commanded a beautiful, uninterrupted view of the sea. It would be an ideal spot for any convent, but especially for one associated with a school. Hastings and St. Leonards were noted for their healthy climate and the place being already in Catholic hands the transfer could be easily arranged.

Now the reader must meet the Reverend Mr. Jones, the real old-time Catholic priest, survival of pre-emancipation days, with his silver-topped cane and his buckled shoes. At that period secular priests were never addressed as Father (a later custom introduced from Ireland), but he always scrupulously addressed all nuns as Dame. He was a rich man who had laid out his riches for the good of the Church, his ambition being for his establishment to become a centre of religious education. Unfortunately his temper was rather uncertain and former institutions that had settled at All Souls (as the property was called after the dedication of the chapel) had not stayed there long. Dr. Wiseman must have had a real faith in Mother Connelly's wise and peaceable nature when he recommended her to go there.

She went down to St. Leonards to inspect the premises and

had scarcely set foot on the Catholic Ground before her heart was filled with a mysterious sensation of familiarity combined with new experience which she recognised as the memory of a dream. She had already visited this place and it was with a sense of home-coming that she wandered through the buildings and over the grounds with their wide, amazing view of the sea. The last of her fears and hesitations were removed, for she clearly saw God's hand in this. She felt that here indeed was the spot chosen by heaven for her work to go forward in a new strength, and before she went to bed that night she wrote to her community, bidding them thank God for having found them such a lovely and suitable home. Fortunately no dream had told her all that she would suffer there or what would be in her heart as she looked out at that wide, amazing sea.

15

Throughout almost the whole of her stay in Derby Pierce Connelly had been making trouble. His desire to interfere with his wife's congregation had become almost a mania—no doubt because he hoped that by dominating it he could regain some of his lost dominion over herself. When he found that even the appointment of Dr. Asperti was not going to help him, for the chaplain, though a disruptive force, was too conscientious a priest to lend himself to such schemes, he had suddenly left Alton and gone to Italy, crowning the rashness of his act by taking his children with him.

Without a word to their mother he had removed them from their several schools, giving as his reason that the ecclesiastical authorities were plotting to kidnap them. One might almost see here the first symptoms of delusional insanity, and it is certain that Pierce's words and conduct from now onwards show an increasing lack of mental control. Hitherto he had not been in the habit of acting rashly or without realism. He had

[86]

carefully weighed and pondered, indeed procrastinated, the various steps he had taken. But now he rushed wildly into a maze of follies. He suddenly appeared in Rome, assaulting the College of Propaganda with the preposterous demand that the Society of the Holy Child should be exempt from episcopal visitation. His next move was to proclaim himself the society's founder and demand the approval of a rule which he himself had drawn up. Here once again he had gone too far, for Propaganda naturally wrote for confirmation to Bishop Wiseman (then still in the Midland District) enclosing a copy of the imposed rule. The result was an emphatic statement that Mr. Connelly had no authority whatsoever to act in the matter.

Cornelia was in dire distress. She suspected (as indeed he himself confirmed later) that he had taken away her children expressly to have a bargaining hold over her. They were the hostages of her society, and one hardly knows whether to admire most the clear self-knowledge, or the devoted heroism with which she took steps against her own heart. In order to make sure that her love of her children should not betray her love of God she made the following vow: "In union with my crucified Lord and by his most Precious Blood: in adoration, satisfaction, thanksgiving and petition, I, Cornelia, vow to have no future intercourse with my children and their father, beyond what is for the greater glory of God, and is His manifest will made known to me through my director."

She did, however, all she could to calm her husband's frenzy by writing to his and her faithful friend Lord Shrewsbury, beseeching his intervention. After telling him that Pierce's visit to Rome "has been only time and money thrown away", and that she would herself write to Propaganda to decline any changes in the rule of her society, she begs: "Will you, then, my dear Lord, explain all this to him in your own gentle, holy way, and induce him to turn his heart all to his flock for the love of God."

She had given him as a gift to God and she had purchased

that gift with everything in life that she held most dear. It now looked as if her gift might be spoiled, made worthless, leaving her with the payment only. It is easy to imagine what the enemy of her soul would make of this, how he would urge her to cut her losses and keep at least her children. Her vow must have been to her then like a rock in a stormy sea, to which she clung, but against which also she was dashed and bruised so that the whole of her, heart, mind and soul, seemed to be bleeding.

It must be remembered too that this storm broke in the midst of the troubles and anxieties that preceded her move from Derby. If she could ever escape from thoughts of her husband and children it would be into thoughts of the strife caused by Dr. Asperti or of the debts with which she had been burdened by Dr. Wiseman's departure. Only the strongest soul could have survived such a battering.

Then less than a month after her letter to Lord Shrewsbury, her husband came back from Rome to renew his persecution in person. The removal to another part of England of the man his mind had dressed up as his rival and enemy did not cause the improvement that might have been hoped. Indeed, it led to fresh trouble, for when Pierce applied (through his confessor—he scorned to act in person) for facilities for an interview with his wife, the delay caused by Dr. Wiseman's absence was so great that he determined to act without episcopal consent. He suddenly arrived at the convent and demanded to see Cornelia. She, supported by Dr. Asperti, refused. Pierce insisted. She still refused. He refused to leave the convent until he had seen her, but she would not leave her cell. For six hours he raged in the parlour, sending demands and messages by scared lay-sisters. When at last he realised that he could not break down his wife's determination, he went off vowing vengeance on the convent, on Dr. Asperti, and above all on the man he considered the villain of it all, Bishop Wiseman.

It is easy to imagine his reaction to the news that Cornelia was going to follow the bishop into his new district and set up her convent under his protection. Before she herself had actually left Derby (though several of the nuns had already gone) he wrote to Dr. Ullathorne, demanding his intervention. The letter, though it still shows an outer dressing of piety (leaning like so much of Pierce's piety towards smugness), contains some curious phrases for a priest to have written. After an unctuous beginning: "It has pleased Almighty God, more than once, as it appears to me, to call me to hard trials", he goes on to write of "principles which unlike dogmas or matters of discipline are too clear for anyone to doubt about". After that it is not perhaps surprising of him to proclaim: "I am a man, a husband and a father before I am a priest." He then proceeds to announce the real purpose of his letter. "I hear she is about to leave your Lordship's jurisdiction and come again under that of Dr. Wiseman. My object in writing is to beg your Lordship to prevent this if possible." Then comes his threat: "If the laws of justice and honour cannot at once be enforced by the authorities of the Church, I am determined to apply to those of the country."

Poor Cornelia entered her beautiful new convent only to be served with a writ to appear before the Court of Arches to answer her husband's suit for the restitution of conjugal rights.

16

It would be a cynical understatement to call it a bad start. The scandal was nation-wide and the evil which it threatened appeared world-wide. The mere local failure of Cornelia's new school, or even of her society itself, was a minor catastrophe compared with the damage likely to be done to the Catholic cause in England and even abroad. Anti-Catholic feeling had been growing in the country ever since the beginning of the Oxford Movement, and it would now swell on a richer diet than it had known for years. Here was a man

robbed by the Papists of his wife, whom they had shut up
in a convent, refusing to let him even see her. That they had
not done the same with his children was due only to the smart
counter-move by which he had snatched them out of their
clutches. The fact that he himself was a priest may have fogged
the situation a little for some, but for the majority it only set
out the magnitude of the outrage which had driven him to take
such a step against the Church in which he ministered. In legal
circles dry jokes were cracked on this unique event in the history of the English law—a Roman Catholic priest suing a
Roman Catholic nun for restitution of conjugal rights before
the Protestant Court of Arches.

Until the Divorce Act of 1857 matrimonial cases could be
heard only in the ecclesiastical courts (except for those demanding the rare divorce *a vinculo matrimonii* for which an Act of
Parliament was required). So in summoning Cornelia before
the Court of Arches Pierce was taking the only course open to a
husband who wished to get back a runaway wife. The court,
presided over by the Dean of Arches, the chief law officer of
the Archbishop of Canterbury, was an exclusively Anglican
tribunal. It could not be expected to understand the situation,
and its decision was almost a foregone conclusion for Cornelia,
who saw in her husband's action the betrayal not only of herself and her society but of his own priesthood.

There was a rumour that he had publicly apostatised, and
though this could not be confirmed it is obvious that every
consideration both of Catholic loyalty and personal religion
had been swept away by the madness of pride and jealousy.
Cornelia wept for her children who now might fall into Protestant hands. If Pierce had hoped by his action to detach her
from Dr. Wiseman, he had only once again defeated his own
ends. For these terrible events had made her rely more and
more on her kind friend and protector, who stood loyally at
her side from the moment when in answer to her news that she
had received her husband's citation, he wrote, "Fear nothing

. . . you will be fully instructed what to do. No personal appearance will be required of you. I will look after everything for you. I never turn my back on one whom God has given into my care."

As for Pierce, he too must have felt confident of the court's decision in his favour—so confident that he wrote to Dr. Winter, his successor in the chaplaincy at Alton, suggesting that he should escort Cornelia from St. Leonards to Albury Park in Surrey, where friends of his had offered to receive her, and thus spare him the necessity of resorting to compulsion for the enforcement of the Court's decree. "The lawyer's letter in my hands says: 'She may now be compelled by force to return . . . any agreement between you and her, or between either of you and any third person notwithstanding.' They must now therefore know that force can be used and most surely it shall be used."

The case of Connelly *v.* Connelly came before the Court of Arches in May, and as had been generally expected, judgment was given for the plaintiff. Cornelia's counsel at once gave notice of appeal, thus delaying any possible enforcement of the court's decree by its officials. But though no legal compulsion could yet be used, Pierce's earlier threats carried the possibility that he would intervene illegally. His manner both of talking and writing suggested that he was prepared to learn at least one lesson from the ecclesiastical authorities and kidnap his wife. There was a rumour that he had hired a yacht and intended with the help of friends to raid the Convent of the Holy Child and forcibly remove the Mother Superior.

Cornelia's friends urged her to leave the country, but she steadfastly refused, though she thanked them gratefully for their advice and offers of protection. "A flight like this," she wrote to Lady Shrewsbury, "would be an acknowledgment of some cause for flight, which would be contrary to the truth. We have nothing to fear. God and truth are on our side."

[91]

A flight would also mean abandoning her young society, too young to be left without a mother—not only on account of its own tender age (barely three years founded, only six months at St. Leonards), but on account of the age of its members, few of whom were over twenty. It was with that same pity for the youth of her new family that Cornelia decided to keep the news of her tragedy from all save one or two of the oldest. This was of course easier to do in a convent than it would have been in an ordinary household. Nevertheless it required not only constant vigilance but a firm control of her own demeanour, so that nothing could be suspected from any appearances of strain or sorrow. She for whom gaiety had always been a note of life must continue to be gay, to smile as though the enemy of her soul had not snatched her gift out of God's hands and thrown it in the mud. She must busy herself with the small domestic concerns of the community, give practical help to her inexperienced cook, decide how far a pair of shoes had exceeded the requirements of religious poverty. She must sympathise with the small griefs and cares of her postulants and novices as if there were no other griefs or cares.

These young things must not notice that she never went alone either to the parlour or the garden, and of course they did not know that in her cell a disguise hung ready to put on if the worst should happen and she should have to flee. One day it looked as if that moment was near.

"Look, Mother, at that pretty yacht out at sea. I wonder where it comes from and where it's going. It wasn't here yesterday."

Her calm, wise eyes gaze quietly over the edges of the garden to where, below, the Channel spreads like a shining floor round a white ship at anchor. The sudden leap of her heart has already become a prayer as she answers smiling—

"Yes, it's a lovely sight. I often thank God for our view of the sea."

17

For days that must have seemed like weeks that yacht lay at anchor off Hastings. Then one morning Cornelia looked out and it was gone. The Channel lay an innocent, empty stretch of water blinked with sunshine. The yacht had disappeared and nothing had happened. Pierce had made no attempt to carry off his wife. Perhaps his nerve had failed him, or his opportunity; more likely his decreasing funds had disposed him to wait for the almost certain decision of the Privy Council, which would give his schemes the backing of the law.

If it had been a foregone conclusion that the Court of Arches would decide in his favour, the verdict of the Privy Council seemed doubly assured. But now suddenly the power of evil began to fail, as it so often does on the very edge of triumph, thus reflecting the enemy's eternal frustration and final impotence. The case could not have been tried at a worse time. The recent restoration of the hierarchy, combined with Dr. (now Cardinal) Wiseman's somewhat injudicious utterance from the Flaminian Gate, had thrown the country into the grip of the most virulent No-Popery epidemic since the Gordon Riots. The Ecclesiastical Titles Bill (aimed at the new Catholic bishops) was actually before the House of Commons when Mother Connelly's appeal was heard by the Lord of the Privy Council —"the most Protestant Court of what was at the moment the most bigoted country in Europe".

The result was a remarkable instance of the different ways in which God and Satan treat their clients. Incidentally it must also be regarded as a shining example of the integrity of English Law. In spite of the clamour around them the Lords maintained their judicial impartiality and allowed Cornelia's appeal, reversing the decision of the Court of Arches. The matter was not finally closed—there were still certain steps Pierce could have taken towards a new trial. But fortunately by this time he was almost totally without funds and could do no more.

Cornelia was delivered from his persecution, but she was not delivered and never would be from the suffering he had brought into her life. For months, even for years, she had to see him expose himself in frenzied assaults on the Church whose priest her sacrifice had made him. She had to see him rob her children of their faith, and when at last he withdrew with them to another country, leave behind him the smoke of a scandal which it would take years for her society to live down.

The decision of the Privy Council seems to have robbed Pierce of his last few remains of sanity and self-control. His plunge into what an Anglican bishop has described as the Protestant underworld suggests the plunge of the Gadarene swine over their cliff. Down into the depths he hurled himself, with howls of rage against the Church which had now become in his distorted mind the representative and enlargement of his hated rival Cardinal Wiseman.

Only such a supposition accounts for his behaviour and utterances, which are almost those of a madman. They are so wild that one would have expected them to defeat their own ends and cause only incredulity in those who saw and heard him. But those were the bigoted Protestants of mid-Victorian England, already frightened half out of their minds by the restoration of the hierarchy and Cardinal Wiseman's pastoral. Pierce provided these gentry with a veritable armoury of offence. One who until he saw the light had been himself a Catholic priest, fully instructed in the laws of his Church and familiar with all the secrets of the confessional, had declared in all the finality of print that Dr. Wiseman was now teaching the children of England that the burning of heretics "whenever practicable and expedient" was as binding as Friday abstinence. No doubt he himself had given permission to certain of his penitents to poison their relatives, which he proclaimed "according to the Church may occasionally be innocent and lawful", even though he had not had cause to order the shooting of his Sovereign, which was however the sort of thing, he assured his readers, which might happen any day.

His pamphlet *Reasons for Abjuring Allegiance to the See of Rome* went into twenty editions. No doubt it would not have had such a sale in modern times, when the enemies of the Church base their attack on very different grounds. The old-fashioned "hissing Protestant" is almost extinct, though echoes of his voice can still sometimes be heard in remote districts. Only a few years ago a Sussex wood-cutter was told by his aged father when he announced his intention to join the Church of Rome—"Well, well, my boy, if 'ee will do it I can't stop'ee. But mark my words, lad, *dey'll burn'ee, dey'll burn'ee.*"

Pierce Connelly set the Smithfield fires a-smoking in many a nervous Victorian imagination. Then after a time he grew tired of it all and left the country. He took the children with him. By this time the poor things must have grown used to being dragged to and fro between England and Italy. Mercer was nearly grown up, Adeline in her late teens, while Frank was only ten. All three had spent the last few years in an atmosphere with which the home-life of a modern divorced couple would compare favourably. Cornelia was heartbroken at their loss, which involved, she knew, the loss of their religion.

The fact that Pierce was able to apostatise all three may at first seem surprising when we consider how firmly they had been grounded in the Catholic faith and how carefully trained in it during their early years by parents they deeply loved. But we must observe two things. First, that their father was by general report a most persuasive and attractive man. This may hardly appear from his conduct or from such of his correspondence as has been passed on to us, but the evidence is too clear and too consistent to be ignored. "Charming" and even "fascinating" are adjectives which those who knew him personally did not find out of place. He also provided the children with a home which contained at least one resident parent, a luxury they had not enjoyed since the days of Grand Côteau. Life with him must have begun once more to appear normal and respectable—they ceased to bear the stigma of being different from everybody else.

The other consideration is that more than possibly their youthful religion had been tried too high. Children are not unlike Baron Friedrich von Hügel's dog Puck, of whom he used to say that, much as he loved his master, he evidently found it a strain to be always in human company, and sometimes had to run off and be his canine self in the company of other dogs. To what extent the young Connellys were allowed to enjoy the company of "other dogs" is doubtful—it probably was not great. In their home the spiritual atmosphere would have been intense, and Catholic school-life at that period was rigid and demanding, as indeed was all school-life. (A part of Cornelia's achievement with her new society was to soften and modernise Victorian ideas on education.) Pierce in his early Catholic days had been exceedingly stiff in his demands on himself and others. His letters to his brothers are full of exhortations to abjure "pretty things"—displaying a streak of Puritanism as much out of place as his addiction to the "best people". Even Cornelia sometimes appears in her letters to Mercer at Stonyhurst to ask too much of a young boy who already had so many strains upon him.

It was of course a time of stern ideas on conduct and morality, and America before the Civil War was just as "Victorian" as the Queen's own country. Children of the tenderest age have a natural affinity and aptitude for religion, but it is not till they are much older that they begin to have anything in the nature of a moral sense. The grafting of a moral code upon a spiritual attraction is a process requiring great sympathy and delicacy, and one that can easily be mishandled. Above all the child with his supernatural attraction to heaven and God and the saints must not be allowed to think that these things are only means to an end—an end, moreover, necessarily involved with the convenience and credit of his elders. It is a sad reflection that the faith of the young Connellys may not have been lost only through the disruption of their home and the blandishments of their father, but also through a sort of spiritual and moral suffocation in which the very holiest of those who loved them had a share.

Be that as it may, Cornelia's children were lost to her in this world both bodily and spiritually. Mercer and Frank both died outside the Church, and though after her father's death Adeline returned to the practice of her religion, that was not till after Cornelia herself had been dead some years.

18

As for Pierce Connelly, the end of his story is as peculiar as any part of it. If the Gadarene swine had halted their rush "down a steep place into the sea" to browse the scanty pasture of some ledge above the level of the waves, they would have provided a parallel to his last years spent as Minister of the American Church in Florence. One can only guess the considerations that guided him. No doubt they were partly financial, for he had spent nearly all his money on litigation and his chances of finding employment were very much worse than when he had found himself in a similar position fifteen years earlier. Moreover, the last five of those years had been spent in hurling himself against the Rock of Peter, and he was perhaps feeling exhausted and glad to settle down in a position which might by this time have had a certain amount of nostalgic attraction. One may wonder, perhaps, at the American Church authorities receiving him back after his excursion into Popery. But possibly they thought that he had atoned for his lapse by the thoroughness of his anti-Catholic propaganda.

One wonders more at his settling in the midst of a Catholic city, where a sky-line of spires and a clangor of bells would ceaselessly call to his memory past years. In that memory lay buried not only splendours and privileges, not only the love of his wife, but moments of sacred experience and spiritual ecstasy. When he heard, as he must have heard many times of a morning, the three sweet, short strokes of the sacring bell, did he never see Pierce Connelly at the altar, lifting the sacred host? Possibly after banging his head so madly against the Rock he had suffered a sort of spiritual concussion and no longer thought of these things. The same state would account in a different way for his acceptance of what could be considered only a humble position. He was pastor of a church that had no real footing in the city, no permanent congregation, which ministered only to foreigners in transit and was regarded by the citizens as a mere conventicle. From every point of view it seems a strange ending for a man who had once dreamed of a cardinal's hat.

What was really in his heart during those last years of anti-climax, it is only for the Judge of all to know, and we can only guess that it was the prayers and offered sufferings of his wife that kept him thus precariously on his ledge when he might so easily have fallen the whole way into the abyss. But we may be quite sure that she never ceased to pray for him and that her prayers were powerful with God. In one respect Pierce Connelly stands unique in that interesting category of "saints' husbands". It was he who provided his wife with most of the raw material for her holiness. Every step she took on the way to heaven was on his impulsion, either following or resisting him. But for him she would never have founded the society which has spread all over the world and done such an inconceivable amount for Catholic education. Until he confronted her with his desire for the priesthood she had had no thought but of spending and ending her days as his wife and the mother of his children. No doubt Cornelia Connelly would in any event have left behind her a happy and fragrant memory, but it is entirely due to her husband that she has left so very much more. Certainly she had never dreamed of entering a religious order. By the very nature of things that would have been impossible, though there is always that pathetic little note which proclaims her thankfulness that the choice is not and never can be offered her. It is also most unlikely that without Pierce's leadership she would even have become a Catholic. I am not suggesting that she would have resisted the truth, but there is always a stage in a conversion, before conviction has been attained, which belongs to attraction only, and Cornelia with her spirit of self-denial and strong sense of duty would almost certainly have resisted an attraction which threatened a husband's peace.

Then when his leadership had been changed to attack, and instead of being her good angel he became her tempter and soul's enemy, it was through him that she trod the higher, more mysterious paths of suffering. She had already suffered through him in the depths of her tenderest human affections, but now she was also to suffer in the highest peak and summit of her soul. For now she had lost the sustaining thought that what she suffered was the will of God. "I would grind myself to powder," she once had said, "if by that I could accomplish God's will." But this apostasy, this awful dereliction of a consecrated priest, this loss by her children of the gift of faith could not possibly be according to his will. It could only be the work of the devil which for some mysterious reason he had allowed. She knew that God cannot will evil, but that he sometimes allows it, when it is capable of being turned into a greater good. There is always a higher card with which to take the devil's trick, and it was for Cornelia to play that card and win with it, instead of the four souls he had taken from her (and who knows but that she won those too), countless young lives trained in faith and holiness for the greater glory of God.

19

At the time when Mother Connelly started her great work of educating the Catholic girls of England, the education of women was almost at its lowest ebb in this country. Though the position of governess was still practically the only one open to a woman who had to earn her living, very little was done to raise her mental equipment above that of the average schoolboy. Indeed the governess probably knew less about such subjects as arithmetic, history and literature than her younger brothers. "Accomplishments" were still the chief stock-in-trade of the schoolroom. To know more was to be "learned" and to be "learned" was to be unattractive to men and undisposable in the marriage market.

Cornelia Connelly had had a better education than was generally given to girls, and she certainly had a much richer and clearer mind than most of her contemporaries. She also had had some experience of teaching at Grand Côteau and at the Trinità dei Monti, which led her to form certain ideas on what was still known as "female education". These ideas are remarkably enlightened and progressive for her times. Such pioneers as Miss Beale and Miss Buss had scarcely begun their work of reform when she produced her *Book of Studies*, in which she had set down the educational aims of her Society.

These aims include a thorough grounding in English, French, writing, arithmetic, geography, history and grammar. Then, greatly daring, with her older classes, she breaks into the exclusively masculine enclosures of philosophy, astronomy, geology, Latin and Greek, and even architecture and heraldry. At the same time she would not neglect such almost necessary accomplishments in those pre-wireless days as music and singing, and she balanced her curriculum with the usual feminine arts of needlework and embroidery, to which she had added lace-making and other activities useful to the Church such as the making up of vestments.

In none of these things would she tolerate the amateurish standards so prevalent in many girls' schools. Everything must be up to the professional mark, and she engaged specialists from London as instructors. On yet another point she showed her enlightened and adventurous spirit. Those were the days when girls still had to wear back-boards and walk with weights on their heads in the interests of deportment. It occurred to Mother Connelly that a girl could hardly learn better how to move, walk, come into a room, etc., to say nothing of speaking clearly and musically, than by acting a part in a play. The performance of plays therefore became, as it is still, an important part of her curriculum. And this happened at a time when the Reverend Edmund Bertram might still be living at Mansfield Parsonage. Many considered it a dangerous novelty, and some parents were shocked to the pitch of removing their daughters. But Mother Connelly refused to sacrifice her ideals to prejudice, and in time the opposition to her innovations died away, and her boarding-school at St. Leonards became famous throughout the country for providing the very best type of Catholic education.

It was Catholic with a large and a small C. In all knowledge Cornelia aimed at a Christian synthesis. The rule of her society expressly states that it had "chosen education as a means to gain souls to God". All the teaching was given by women leading dedicated lives, and the subjects were chosen with a view to leading the pupils to "the invisible things of God through the medium of the visible". "*Ut dum visibiliter Deum cognoscimus, per hunc in invisibilium amorem rapiamur. . .*" Thus, through the Christmas preface, she united her society with the greatest feast of the Holy Child.

It is interesting to notice here that in the religious training of young people in her schools Cornelia appears to have avoided that rather smothering intensity that she sometimes showed in her dealings with her own children. The type of religious education given by her society shared the enlightenment displayed in other subjects. For instance, in teaching Church history, she insisted that mistakes and scandals should not be left out or glossed over. It was better that the children should hear of these things from teachers who would use them as proofs of the Church's divine origin than, perhaps later on, from those who saw them only as occasions for disillusion and scepticism.

Her schools also, more than other Convent schools, allowed the pupils a great deal of freedom and fun. No doubt her fears for her own brood had led to a state of anxiety in which she had over-stressed the claims of motherhood—requiring, for instance, that poor Mercer should confess his faults to her as well as to his confessor, and showering reproaches where perhaps encouragement, or even a little teasing, would have done more good. The change is all part of the flowering of her nature as it responded more and more closely to the supernatural. The weakness she had shown in her own family—too uncritical an acceptance of the will of a selfish man, too much anxious concern for her children's welfare—have disappeared now that she is the Mother of that so much larger family, the Society of the Holy Child Jesus.

Mother Connelly did not confine her educational work to "young ladies". She started Poor Schools, as they were then called, in St. Leonards, London (where her nuns had to wear the cast-off clothing of the Postulants, in order to escape being pelted in the streets), Preston and Blackpool. Public education was at that time in a shocking state. The school-leaving age was ten, and the subjects taught amounted to little more than reading, writing and arithmetic. Corporations such as the National Society did what they could by establishing "middle schools" for those children whose parents could afford to keep them at school a year or two longer, and Mother Connelly worked on similar lines, adding to the curriculum grammar and geography, as well as such useful though, in those days, unusual subjects as hygiene and domestic economy.

Her work did not go unappreciated. School inspectors praised her highly. One even declared that her school was "one of the most perfect institutions of its kind in Europe". But much dearer to her soul must have been Cardinal Wiseman's words, spoken twenty years after he had brought her to England expressly to salvage and promote Catholic education —"You have realised the desire of my heart."

She had her struggles and many bitter trials and disappointments besides those caused by her husband. Even before the tumult and scandal of the Connelly *v.* Connelly case had died away, she had begun to have trouble with the Reverend Mr. Jones. This was hardly surprising, as no less than six communities had already failed to live with him, but it was a cruel addition to her other cares to think that once more she and her young nuns would have to move house. Taking her usual refuge in prayer, she started a novena for the whole community. They must all have been a little disconcerted by the form taken (presumably) by the answer, for on the last day of the novena Mr. Jones died. He died suddenly and unexpectedly, but he died peaceably, assuring Cornelia that his will would ensure her remaining in her present home, where indeed her society has carried on its work ever since.

For many years it was the mother house, to be succeeded in that capacity by the convent at Mayfield, Sussex, which she had founded as the result of a school picnic among the ruins of what had once been the palace of the Archbishops of Canterbury. When the development and increase of the society necessitated a more central seat of government, Mayfield became the English provincial house and the mother house was transferred to Rome.

At the time of Cornelia's death in 1879, there were convents not only in St. Leonards and Mayfield, but in London, Preston,

Blackpool, Sevenoaks, and at Neuilly in France. There were also three schools in her native city of Philadelphia and one at Sharon Hill in the same State. Since her death four more convents have been established in England (at Harrogate, Oxford, Birmingham and Lancaster), three in Eire, one in Switzerland, one in Rome, six in Africa, and no less than twenty-two in the United States. These convents are all power-stations of Catholic education, energising every sort of school—boarding schools, day schools, grammar schools, parochial schools, preparatory schools, training colleges and university hostels. The Society of the Holy Child Jesus has spread over the world an enlightened, progressive, effective system of Christian education—truly a rich harvest to have sprung from the seed of one woman's broken heart.

20

St. Catherine of Genoa "became a saint because she had to" —because without the support and integration of the supernatural her difficult, introverted nature would have collapsed into hysteria. But no such psychological necessity can have influenced Cornelia Connelly. In any sort of life she would have found a measure of success and happiness. Her charm and her talents would have made her popular in any society, while her strong affections and domestic tastes predestined her to a happy marriage. By giving herself to God, she lost all these things that she would otherwise have enjoyed. Her religion, far from unifying a broken life, disrupted everything except her own being.

I am not thinking here of the religion she was brought up in and practised for the first twenty-six years of her life, but of that more exacting, urgent faith which she and her husband adopted soon after their marriage. If either they had failed to hear or failed to respond to its call, she might have passed tranquilly into old age, watching her children grow up and bring her their children. To the end of her life she would have remained her husband's darling. No doubt he would have given her some anxious moments, but at least she would not have seen him broken on the Rock. Or even if he and she had gone so far as to join the Catholic Church together, they might still have kept themselves in the shallows of Catholicism, where so many paddle and splash, and never risked those deep waters in which she had been cruelly buffeted and he had been drowned. Again, a less holy woman—perhaps only a little less —would have refused to sacrifice herself to Pierce's vocation. If she had refused there would have been no Society of the Holy Child Jesus, but also no broken home or broken hearts.

Certainly the impact of the supernatural on Cornelia's mind and character was more in the way of a test and a purge than a deliverance, and the fact that she survived the ordeal without mental injury bears witness not only to the power of grace but to the psychological integrity of the nature that responded to it.

With so strong and self-reliant a personality it is perhaps surprising to find her consistently moulding her spiritual life on the will of others. In this she could not be more unlike St. Catherine, who for so long went her lone, eccentric way with no guidance save the inward promptings of her Love. Cornelia from the first made a practice of frequent confession and obedience to a director. She also followed her husband's leadership, even at times when perhaps a little opposition would have been good for him. All the more important decisions of her life were his in their first inspiration. Indeed her spiritual life is built on her married life; it begins in her compliance as a wife and crowns itself in the holocaust of her home and family.

When Pierce Connelly's authority was removed by his own act, she turned instead to the authority which that same act had put in its place, and to the end of her life she accepted the guidance either of Dr. Wiseman or (when the new diocese was created) of the Bishop of Southwark. Yet it would be a mistake to regard her as a woman easily led, or so derivative in her ideas that she could not act without advice and example. This is proved by the fact that in every case where authority abused its power she showed herself as firm in resistance as she had hitherto been docile in acceptance. Not only did she reject Pierce's usurped authority at a mighty cost, but at least on one occasion she showed herself equally resolute with Dr. Wiseman when he had, as she thought, taken in a local dispute an attitude unjust and injurious to her community. Her obedience was from strength and not from weakness, and may well have been part of a deliberate plan to subdue and transform her own will which her clear self-knowledge may have shown her as in danger of becoming headstrong. For her the voice of authority, whether her husband's or that of her ecclesiastical superiors, was not its own but the incarnate *logos* of a higher will.

It must be remembered that unlike St. Catherine, she had no inner voice to direct her. The threshold of consciousness in that other's so different nature was, as we have seen, abnormally high. Therefore many mental processes which most of us consciously transact would seem to come from elsewhere, from outside herself and thus appear to be invested with an authority which we can seldom recognise in our conscious thoughts. Had Cornelia had a different mental constitution, with a higher threshold, it is possible that her *Book of Studies* might have been as it were dictated by her unconscious mind and come to her with all the mystery and impressiveness of an inner revelation. Had it done so it would have been neither more nor less supernatural than the reasonings of her normal consciousness, inspired by grace. But Cornelia, as far as we know, had no visions, no locutions, no ecstacies. She followed the normal ways of thought and prayer. Like St. Catherine, she was a teacher, but she expounded no private revelation, only the age-old revelation of universal truth, which it was her task and privilege to adapt to the needs of modern education. Hers is no "difficult" character to be saved by grace from psychological ruin, but one of the sanest, healthiest specimens of mental integrity that ever responded to spiritual inspirations.

Yet these two women, so unlike each other, these two wives, so different in their attitude both to their husbands and to their own souls, have one point of resemblance that wipes out all their divergencies. They have a meeting-place in the gospel of St. Catherine's feast. Cornelia Connelly is not a saint of the Church, but in the gospel of the Mass of "A Holy Woman not a Martyr" her story as well as Catherine's is told. Both Catherine and Cornelia are the merchant who found that treasure hidden in a field, both are the trader who found the pearl of great cost. Both sold all that they had and bought the treasure and the pearl. The only difference lies in the nature of the personal goods that they sold and we could argue as to who paid most. But the point is that both paid all. Indeed for the saints there is no lower price.

THE
MAIDENS

Isabella Rosa de Santa Maria de Flores

I

IT was difficult to enter Lima on that August day some eighty years after the Conquistadors had taken possession of Peru. The streets were jammed with the crowds that struggled towards the Dominican church from every corner of the city. Only a fraction of them could have seen the hearse that was being carried along the principal street, first by members of the Cathedral Chapter, then by the Senators and members of the Royal Council, finally by the heads of the various religious orders.

On the hearse lay the body of a woman, a young girl, slight and small under the folds of her Dominican habit, with her face exposed according to the Spanish custom, to show a beauty that mocked at death under a crown of living flowers. The crowds pressed on the cortège in spite of the Viceroy's Guard along the street, and the soldiers were obliged to drag away those who tried to snatch flowers from the bier or cut fragments from the dead girl's clothing.

Slowly, very slowly, the procession fought its way to the church, where the Archbishop was waiting to receive the body. At last the coffin was placed on a sort of stage in the midst of the Rosary chapel, and immediately the crowd, wedged between it and the walls, began to shout—"A miracle! A miracle!" The statue of the Blessed Virgin, the people declared, had greeted this other virgin who had so often prayed at her feet. Lights poured from the carven whirlings of her robe, and all her baroque movement became alive and gracious as her eyes fixed themselves on the sleeping girl before her. The people burst into tears and the church rang with cries of joy.

Meanwhile the fathers of the convent ranged themselves round the bier, to protect it from the crowd which was becoming beside itself, and to allow the sick to approach and cure their ills by touching the body. Then they began the Office for the Dead; but it was finished only with difficulty, so frantic had the crowd become, pushing and jostling the friars, so that they had to take refuge on the steps of the high altar, and drowning their singing with shouts of joy and gratitude.

"Leave us our Rose—our dear Rose . . . ." and the friars were obliged to put off the burial till the next day.

Reluctantly the crowd dispersed. The chapel was still crowded, but at least one could move in the streets. The traveller from Spain could proceed on his journey after being held a prisoner for more than two hours by these funeral ecstasies. He had left his ship that morning at Callao and was on his way to Cuzco in the mountains, intending to pause only for sight of the capital, with its many fine buildings and innumerable churches, which he had been told were as magnificent as those at home in Spain.

Lima, the new town of the Pizarros, was certainly a beautiful city, lying sheltered in the placid curve of the Rimac Valley, among fields and orchards, well removed from the storms of the Pacific and protected further inland by the whole range of the Andes, whose snowy towers showed him the remoteness of his final destination. He had not time to do more than stop for a meal at the principal inn, but it would be long enough to satisfy not only his hunger but also, which was even more urgent, his curiosity. Who was this mysterious Rose whose name had become a chant on the lips of the crowd? Was she a member of the Viceroy's family? Or a famous courtesan? Or had she at one time saved the city from the plague?—or from some armed attack? What had she done to cause this riot?

The landlord shook his head.

"No, Señor—she is no relation of the Viceroy—though for a time before her death she lived in the Questor's family. Mind you, her people are good people. Her father, Don Gaspardo de Flores, was a distinguished soldier, though now he is old and crippled—I understand that he could not attend his daughter's funeral. Her mother too comes of a good family— de Herrara, of this city. But they are not rich; they lost their money in the wars and the troubles that have been with us ever since the city started. De Flores has a large house and garden, but also a large family, and I understand that he lives very poorly, with only one servant. And this young girl, his daughter, who has just died, she used to work for them, cultivating and selling flowers and making the most ravishing embroideries. My wife says you would think an angel had worked them, so beautiful they are, and I believe they were much sought after by our noble families. I cannot think how the old people will manage without her."

"But then," asked the stranger, "why . . .?"

"Why, Señor? . . ."

"Why this extraordinary outburst—these throngs of people? You would think a queen was being buried."

"Señor," said the innkeeper, "she was greater than a queen. She was a saint."

2

What then was this age and this city wherein a saint was given the honours that in our present civilisation are reserved for film-stars? The crowds that surged round Rose de Flores' bier, snatching at the flowers, snipping bits off her mantle, can be compared only with the bobby-soxers struggling for fragments of Robert Taylor's tie. Certainly saints were no novelty in Lima that the populace should thus lose its head over one of them. Living there at the same time as Rose were at least two who were subsequently canonised—St. Turribius, the Archbishop, and St. Francis Solano—and one *beatus*, the half-caste Dominican lay-brother, Martin Porres.

But though it was a city of saints, Lima was no heavenly city. The streets that had been trodden by the feet of the elect had also run with blood. From the year of its foundation it had been the battle-ground of bloodthirsty desperadoes who had fought not only among themselves but with the powers of the home-country which sought to pacify their disorders.

In comparison with the conquest of Mexico, where the invaders had been opposed by a nation of warriors, the conquest of Peru had been almost peaceful. Several factors had contributed to the ease with which the Spaniards took possession of a country which in its ultimate fastnesses was virtually impregnable. The inhabitants, unlike the Mexicans, were of a peaceable disposition, given more to agriculture than to arms, and even had they been inclined to offer any resistance their defence would have been compromised by the strife that had arisen within their royal house. Two rival Incas, Atahualpa and Huascar, were actually at war when the Spaniards landed. To crown all, the national religion traced back the country's history to a divine couple who had arrived mysteriously from the north, and had taught the hitherto barbarous people the arts of civilisation. Whether the Children of the Sun were a myth, or as is more probable actual visitants from some other country, it is a significant part of the story that they were *white*; and when, having instructed the natives in the use of the plough and the spinning-wheel, and started the royal line of the Incas, they finally disappeared, it was understood that one day they would return, and for centuries the pious Peruvians had watched and waited for the arrival of white men from the sea. For a time at least these white-skinned strangers sailing in from another world were regarded as the descendants of

Manco Capac and Mama Ocollo and the fulfilment of their promise.

The Spaniards were welcomed and might have settled happily in the country but for the unfortunate circumstance that the natives, unprovided and unskilled in the working of base metals, used gold for almost every purpose that iron or copper would be used for in other countries. To the dazzled eyes of the invaders Peru was El Dorado, the golden land, where even the cooking pots were made of gold.

In a passion of greed and excitement they set to work to strip the country, despoiling equally the temple and the kitchen, driving the people to forced labour in the gold-mines and torturing their rulers to find imagined hoards of treasure. The consequences were riots and revolts even in that mild populace, and endless quarrels and assassinations among themselves, so that in the end blood flowed as freely in peace-loving Peru as in warlike Mexico.

Side by side with this strife, spoliation and misery went another sort of conquest. It is difficult for our modern outlook to capture the spirit in which these various expeditions set out from Spain to discover a new world. Side by side with Spanish Imperialism, went the love of adventure, the desire for wealth, and also, strange as it may seem to the modern mind, a genuine desire to convert these undiscovered countries to Christ. From the first, plans were made to plant in them not only the Spanish flag but the cross. Every expedition was accompanied by clergy who were to act not only as chaplains but as missionaries. Ignorance has sadly twisted the story of the evangelisation of the New World. The monks and friars who devoted (and often laid down) their lives to the work of preaching the gospel have been branded with the cruelties of the Conquistadors, to whom they and their methods offered a startling contrast. The fact that the Inquisition was established in Peru in 1570 has been taken to involve the persecution of the Indian population and the forcing of Christianity on those of a different faith. The fact is that by an express provision of the Holy See, the Inquisition had no jurisdiction over the Indians at all, its authority being limited to the Spanish population.

It is remarkable that the country as a whole and without any harsher weapons than preaching and persuasion, very soon yielded itself to Christianity in spite of the cruelties and excesses of its Christian conquerors. This no doubt was mainly due to the enlightened methods of the Dominicans and the Jesuits, who familiarised themselves with various Indian dialects as well as the Quiche language, established a printing press and founded a training college for missionaries as well as innumerable schools, churches, convents and hospitals, thus convincing the people that the white man had other objects besides their robbery and destruction.

Archbishop Turribius, in particular, distinguished himself by his devoted ministry to the Indians. He protected their interests against the Spanish colonists, now two generations settled in the country, instituted many reforms in their government and treatment, and personally visited on foot, no less than twice, the entire territory under his jurisdiction, which comprised at that time nearly the whole of South America. He had started on a third visitation when death came to him suddenly in the spring of 1606.

3

Turribius is the only one of the saints of Lima with whom St. Rose is known to have had any personal association. One would think that she must often have seen the saintly Brother Martin in the Dominican church or out shopping with his basket, and it is certain that she had heard of, though she did not actually hear, the famous sermon of St. Francis Solano, in which he threatened the city with destruction. But there is no record of her having met or spoken to either of these holy men, whereas from her very early days she was in contact with the Archbishop.

Indeed it was he who had given her the name of Rose at her confirmation. She had been christened Isabella after her grandmother, Isabella de Herrara, but so great was her beauty as an infant that her mother invariably called her Rose. And here is our first brush with the hagiographers, who are to confuse our path for the whole of this short life-journey. The simple, pleasing story of a mother who compared her child's fresh loveliness with that of a flower and substituted a floral pet-name for the more pompous mouthful of Isabella, gives way before a "miraculous" event in which a supernatural rose blooms in the infant's cradle. In preferring the natural to the supernatural version of this story I am only following the mind of the Church which teaches that if any event plainly admits of a natural explanation, a supernatural one should not be found for it.

The hagiographers have made the story of Rose de Flores even more difficult to write than it is by nature, and I shall have to cross issues with them on other grounds besides this. There was so much of the marvellous and the inexplicable in her life that it seems unnecessary to add to it, especially as many of the additions have not the simple charm of the one just given. Rose was born covered by a membrane or "caul", an event insufficiently rare, one would think, to require any miraculous explanation, though that is the one offered by most of her biographers. She also yelled lustily when shown by her proud mother to strangers. It requires a hagiographer to transform this all but universal behaviour on the part of infants into a precocious example of humility and the spirit of mortification.

My use of the word hagiographer is no doubt open to criticism. Taken literally, it means no more than a writer about a saint or saints, whereas I am using it to describe someone who writes about a saint in a special manner. Strictly speaking,

Von Hügel is a hagiographer when he writes about St. Catherine of Genoa, but there is a whole abyss between his way of writing and that of those two typical hagiographers Battista Vernazza and Don Marabotto. For my purpose, Von Hügel is a biographer. His aim throughout has been to arrive at the facts about his subject, whether those facts be historical or psychological or spiritual. The aim of the hagiographer on the other hand seems to be to promote a cultus. He approaches his subject from the angle of unqualified admiration, or as Monsignor Alfredo Ottaviani, assessor of the holy office, has more bluntly put it, "with unpardonable levity . . . with more imagination that judgment". Fact (or as some might say, truth) is with him a secondary consideration. He is there to create prodigies, and if there are two versions of an incident, one normal and the other preternormal or miraculous, he will choose the latter. He will also suppress or disguise the weaknesses of his hero, who must be invariably perfect. This leads not only to the omission of anything he may consider contrary to perfection, but the offering to our admiration of that which our judgment tells us is not admirable.

The life of St. Rose bristles with incidents of both kinds—the gratuitously prodigious (using the word in its original sense, before it passed through eighteenth-century slang into a lesser meaning) and the doubtfully admirable. Having in her case no learned, patient Baron Friedrich von Hügel to sift facts and distinguish sources, we must do what we can for ourselves, always keeping in mind the Church's ruling as to the relative values of the natural and the supernatural in explaining phenomena. Indeed the formulated judgments of the Catholic Church provide in St. Rose's case a healthy antidote to the excesses of hagiography. The panel of theologians who examined her during her life records its findings with the most temperate objectivity, while the riots at her funeral and the subsequent exaggeration of her unauthorised cultus led to the decree of Pope Urban XVIII which forbids any public veneration until the ceremony of beatification has been duly performed.

4

A Rose by any other name . . . Rose de Flores started her life as Isabella, but her mother always called her Rose. Her grandmother, on the other hand, insisted on calling her Isabella and considered the use of any other name as a personal affront. The mother, however, persevered, with the result that the unhappy child was badly mauled between them. When she ran to her mother at the call of "Rose!" she would be slapped by her grandmother, but if she obeyed her grandmother's summons to "Isabella!" it was her mother who slapped. We can certainly here agree with the hagiographers that she was an exceptionally obedient child, because whenever and whatever she was called she ran—invariably to be slapped by somebody.

The fixing of her name at her confirmation was due entirely to the inspiration of the Archbishop, for by this time the dowager had won the day and she was always called Isabella. Turribius already had a high reputation for sanctity and his action quelled even Isabella de Herrara, who thenceforward ceased to call her grandchild anything but Rose. Indeed the only opposition was to come at a later date from the girl herself. As she grew older she began to have scruples as to whether it was right for her to be called by a name which had not been given her in baptism but only on account of her personal beauty. She did not like to take this problem to her confessor, but in the end it was solved, as so many of her problems were to be, in the Rosary chapel of the Dominican church. Here was a statue of the Blessed Virgin which she specially loved, and as she knelt in prayer before it she heard these words in her heart: "My divine child prefers the name of

Rose, but he would like to add to it the name of his Mother."
From that day she called herself and persuaded others to call
her Rose of St. Mary.

But that was some years later, and in such a short life no
years should be passed over. So once more we return to her
baptism. This was privately administered as, though her birth
had been unwontedly easy for her mother who had had already
ten similar experiences, the child herself seemed likely to
die. She had not only the beauty but the fragility of a flower,
and her health was not improved by her mother's methods of
rearing her. When she was nine months old, Maria de Flores
found herself unable to suckle her any longer, but out of pride
and obstinacy refused to engage a foster-mother, with the
result that her daughter nearly died of starvation. The hagiographers leap exultantly upon this incident, pointing out that
the saintly infant endured the pangs of hunger without complaint. No doubt the poor little thing was too weak to cry.
Indeed, all things considered, her survival both now and at a
later date is a marvel as great as any that the hagiographers have
recorded.

All her life she was sickly and delicate, prone to mysterious
ailments, and from her earliest years she was subjected to the
most clumsy and mistaken treatment, yet she survived to
inflict on herself penances that might have been expected to
kill the stoutest and toughest. Rose is yet another instance of
that extraordinary power of soul over body which we have
already observed in St. Catherine of Genoa, and which indeed
in some form or another is characteristic of all types of
sanctity.

Her first penances were not of her own seeking, but were
inflicted on her by the medical practice of her day. "When a
man hath sinned," says the Preacher, "let him fall into the
hands of the physician." This reads strangely to us now, but
it must have seemed apt enough to Rose's generation, when
often the most painful part of a disease would be its cure.

A thumb caught under the lid of a heavy coffer, an irritating skin rash, an aural abscess, a nasal polypus, are all in themselves heavy tests of endurance; but the fact that Rose endured with unflinching heroism not only these ills but their remedies, speaks highly for her courage and self-control. The de Flores' surgeon, Juan Perez de Zumeta, was a great believer in corrosives, which he used as a preliminary to the knife, but the child's worst sufferings were caused by her own mother who insisted on treating a painful rash on her face and head with an application of mercury that nearly removed the scalp.

On this occasion Rose revealed the sources of her courage, for her mother when she discovered the damage she had done relieved some of her anger with herself by blaming her victim: "Why didn't you tell me it was hurting you? Why didn't you cry?"

Rose pointed to a picture of Our Lord wearing the crown of thorns.

"It didn't hurt me as much as that hurt him."

From her earliest childhood she had been attracted by this picture, and when other children were at play, she would steal away and sit before it, pouring out her treasures of prayer and pity. At the inquiry made later in her life by the ecclesiastical authorities into her methods of prayer she stated that from the very first she had practised the prayer of union—she had known no other. She had learned to pray before she had learned to speak—at least with any ease and precision. Her prayer was a wordless flow from the heart, and its first object was the suffering Christ who, probably through some crude daub of a travelling artist (for in those days it was impossible to reproduce works of art), had captured her childish imagination.

It was his suffering which enabled her to bear her own, and so lost did she become in the contemplation of it that when she had nothing to bear, being rid for a time of her ailments, she would feel as if something were amiss and lacking in her life and would take steps to restore it. She could not possibly ask any member of her family for help in such a matter, so she turned to the servant of the household, a simple Peruvian girl called Marianna, whose mind was probably of the same age as her own. Between them they got hold of a heavy beam, which Rose would carry on her shoulders as if it were the cross. Alone with Marianna she would perform the penances that her childish mind dictated, all with a view to making herself more like the object of her love.

5

Unlike most delicate children, Rose developed early. She learned at an early age to walk and talk and also to read. Accounts of her education are conflicting. According to one, she was educated at the Dominican convent, but the difficulty here is that there was no Dominican convent for women in Lima until after her death. It is more likely that she was taught by her mother in such moments of leisure as the poor, flustered woman could command in the midst of her household toils. This fits in with the accepted ideas on female education at this period, but there is a difficulty, if it is really true that Rose knew Latin—knew it well enough not only to read her office but to compose verses that have come down to us as her work. I am inclined to solve it by considering them the work of her biographers.

The reason she learned to read so early was not, however, the skill and patience of her teacher, be that teacher Maria de Flores or somebody better qualified. Like so many children she learned to read mainly through her desire to master a special book. This in her case was the Life of St. Catherine of Siena, whose story had taken hold of her imagination, possibly because the home conditions of the saint were so very like her own. Like herself, Catherine was the youngest of a large family—indeed of a family more than twice the size of Rose's, for she had twenty-three brothers and sisters. Like herself, Catherine had felt an early attraction to prayer and penance, practising both in the face of family mockery and parental opposition. In later life the resemblances became even more striking, but this no doubt is due to the fact that Rose deliberately modelled her behaviour on that of her heroine.

There seems little doubt that it was in imitation of St. Catherine that she made the vow that invariably causes the hagiographers to lift their hands in respectful wonder while reducing the scoffers to ribaldry. The pious infant's vow of perpetual virginity is a phenomenon that has possibly edified the faithful less than it has amused the profane. Rose made hers at the age of five, and one naturally asks—what could a child of five have known about virginity? The question is of our own time, but the answer comes from hers and is probably: More than you think. In any case, the vow may have amounted to no more than a promise not to marry, or more positively to enter a religious order. Of its binding nature one may well be in doubt. Few confessors, I imagine, would consider binding a vow made before the age of reason, and many girls may have looked back on such a vow from the safe shores of marriage with a smile or a sigh.

Above all it is necessary to keep our Rose within the setting of her own time and country. If we move her into ours we shall probably be guilty of more blunders and misunderstandings than ever sprang from the roots of an imprudent admiration. She lived for the whole of her short life in a Spanish colony at the meeting of the sixteenth and seventeenth centuries. It was a time when in England young minds were being fed on tales from the classics and European history—such as form the subjects of Shakespeare's plays. In Catholic Spain—more temperamentally opposed to the Renaissance than any other country—the romantic imagination was still supplied from tales of chivalry and the lives of the saints. It is unlikely that Rose ever read the former, but she certainly studied the latter and modelled her life upon them. It was as natural for her to do so as for a modern girl to model her appearance on that of an admired film-star, and who shall say that the result was any worse?

We must certainly leave our times behind us and enter hers if we are to understand a childish episode which her biographers have enlarged out of nature. Though a quiet, delicate child, more fond of solitude than of company and of reading than of play, she was so sweet and accommodating that other children loved to come and play with her. One day a party of little girls brought their dolls into her parents' garden, but instead of joining them with her own doll like any normal little girl, Rose ran away from them, leaving them to play by themselves. The reason she gave was that dolls reminded her of idols; therefore she refused ever to play with them or even to possess one.

We surely are not bound to see this incident as a shining example of "precocious maturity in a mind above the puerilities of childhood". It translates quite easily into natural childish behaviour if we consider her upbringing and surroundings. She lived in a country still partly pagan, and no doubt had heard some terrifying stories of the old Indian gods from the Christianised Marianna. She would probably also, though the Peruvians were not strictly speaking idolators, have seen effigies of Mama Ocollo and Manco Capac, which, made according to the traditions of Indian art, would have seemed to her hideous and frightening, apart from her acceptance of the belief that "out of the mouth of idols the devil sometimes speaks". And it is quite true that these images and her friends' dolls would have been very much alike, for we must rid ourselves of our naturalistic pretty-pretty conception of a doll if we are to imagine the dolls of Lima in the fifteen-eighties. They were probably crudely painted unjointed wooden objects, presenting no difficulty to the maternal imagination of the average little girl, but also providing matter for the imagination of a little girl of a very different type, a little girl who feared and hated evil, so was afraid of idols, and therefore, because these dolls reminded her of idols, was afraid of dolls.

But in spite of her behaviour on this and doubtless other occasions Rose continued to be sought after by her little friends. She was an entirely lovable child, always ready to help, always willing to give up her own way in matters that did not involve her ideas of good and evil, so she could be allowed a few eccentricities. As she grew up her favour increased and began to cause her anxiety. She feared that it might be at least partly due to her personal beauty, which her mother's friends did not scruple to praise to her face, and she began at an early age to take strong measures against that which some might have thought a subject for thanksgiving, the gracious gift of a God condescending to bestow on a creature the reflection of one of his own attributes.

We shall find it easier to understand some very strange conduct if we can continue to see Rose as a child, one who throughout her life never lost the clear black-and-white vision of youth or learned to sophisticate the simple logic of innocence. Certainly her almost vindictive hatred of her own charms started in a thoroughly childish manner. She was playing in the garden with one of her brothers—Ferdinando was her favourite, the one with whom she "paired" in that large family—and the game was becoming, as games with boys often do, a little rough. Even Rose's gentle spirit was roused to anger when Ferdinando pulled off her veil (the inevitable headgear of a Spanish woman in the colonies, though little worn elsewhere) and rubbed earth and sand into her hair. When he saw that she was furious, he mocked her. "What's all the fuss about?" he cried as he danced round her—"Why should you mind having dirt in your hair? You mean to be good and holy, yet you carry on your head what is highly offensive to God. Don't you know that a woman's hair is a net to drag men down into hell? That there are souls who owe their damnation to nothing but a woman's beautiful hair? Isn't your hair an instrument of perdition? So why shouldn't I rub dirt in it?"

Rose was thunder-struck. Her blood ran cold. She had never thought of this before, that she should carry on her head what might be a weapon in the devil's armoury had never occurred to her till this moment. But now that it had, she could endure the thought no longer. She must act at once. She went quickly and quietly into the house, and taking a pair of shears from her mother's work-basket cut off all her beautiful hair.

6

It was perhaps lucky for her that the great veil which even a little girl had to wear concealed the damage from her mother until the hair had begun to grow again, for Maria de Flores took a very different view from her daughter's on the subject of personal beauty.

And here we must pause to consider the woman who played such a leading part in our saint's life. Of her father, Gaspardo de Flores, we know little except that he was one of Lima's "new poor", a man of ancient family, who had lost his substance and his health in the Peruvian wars. No doubt it was his indifferent health that made him such a cipher in his own family, for it was his wife who ruled the household, brought up eleven children on a small income, and tried in vain to bring her youngest daughter's unruly sanctity into line with her own ideas of worldly advantage and decorum.

We have already written of saints' husbands and studied the parts that two not very holy men played in the lives of two very holy women. But now we are to meet a saint's mother and watch her behaviour under the impact of her daughter's particularly disconcerting type of holiness. Maria de Flores does not appear at first glance to have been a very good mother. She certainly was a hot-tempered, excitable woman, who relieved her feelings not only with words but with blows. We hear of her not only slapping and cuffing her delicate child, but beating and kicking her. She is fond of her, she is proud of her, but again and again she injures her not only by violent but by careless treatment. We have already seen how she nearly scalped her with an application of mercury, and there is another story of her wrapping uncured furs round her daughter's hands when these were swollen with rheumatism during an unhappy visit to the marshy country outside Lima. The furs, securely bound over the hands, caused a devastation second only to that caused by the girl herself when she plunged those same hands into quicklime because someone had praised their beauty.

This brings us to the other side of the question. We may blame the Señora de Flores but we cannot help pitying her, nor can we entirely withhold our sympathy. Her daughter Rose must have been in almost every respect a sore trial to her. She was sweet, she was submissive on all the points that her mother would have told you did not matter, but she was as iron on the subject dearest to that mother's heart—the making of a prosperous marriage.

Rose was the beauty of the family. The exact form that beauty took we do not know, for we have no contemporary portrait of her and very little detailed description. We are told that she had huge dark eyes with very long lashes, but that would hardly have distinguished her in a Spanish-Indian city such as Lima. We can only conjecture from her name that her beauty had a fresh and flower-like quality. The Spaniards have always admired fairness, and probably she was lighter-skinned than most Spanish girls, with rose-petal colouring in her cheeks. Certainly her beauty is emphasised by her biographers to the point of legend, and it must have been considerable, since it was enough to cause her to be sought in marriage by more than one young man of wealth and position in spite of the absence of a dowry.

It is easy to see how dear this project would be to her mother's heart. A rich marriage would set the family up for good and the only obstacle to it came from Rose herself. Maria de Flores was not likely to have been deterred by a vow of virginity made at the age of five, but Rose's adolescent and adult opposition to the plan was something really formidable. It endured, without flinching, ill-treatment from both her parents, and there was always the uneasy thought that if driven to desperation she might so disfigure herself as to become completely unmarriageable.

The canonisation of a saint does not mean that the Church approves of every one of his or her actions, and the ends of sanctity are defeated by uncritical admiration which sees all behaviour on the same level of perfection. One resents the facile assumption that by refusing to go out visiting with her mother Rose was acting in a more edifying manner than if she had cheerfully faced the stiffness and boredom of Spanish-Colonial society. Moreover, the shifts by which she contrived to make her mother leave her at home are scarcely in themselves admirable, and to explain them by enlarging on her love of quiet and solitude is only to attribute a selfish motive. Why is it that pious writers never seem to realise that a love of quiet and solitude can be just as selfish as a love of noise and company?

In order to sympathise with Rose in this matter we must remember the end and object of it all. Her mother's social schemes, her dressing up of her reluctant daughter in silk and velvet, her adornment of her lovely head with flowers, were all part of a major campaign for getting her married, and the best tactics lay in resistance even in the smallest skirmishes. The battle swayed to and fro. Sometimes Maria de Flores won and took out her daughter dressed in silk, crowned with flowers and looking even more beautiful than she need have done because of her refusal to wear cosmetics. At other times Rose was the winner, with eyelids puffy and inflamed after an application of pepper or with a bruised and swollen foot on which she had cunningly dropped a stone. In the end it was Rose who won. The mother grew weary, the pepper-in-eye treatment really frightened her; moreover in time her daughter's refusal to marry became well known among her friends, so there was no longer any use in offering her as merchandise.

Like a prudent general, Rose consolidated her victory. Not content with merely stopping her mother dressing her up, she persuaded her to let her wear the shapeless, dun-coloured cloak that was the uniform of the pious women of Lima in contrast to the gay, many-coloured attire of their more frivolous sisters. The existence of a definite style of dress for the ultra-devout, distinguishing them not only from the fashionable world but from the religious orders, seems an improvement on the modern custom of the ultra-devout seeking an unworldly attire in the fashions of the day before yesterday. The wearing of her cloak was a public proclamation that Rose, though not belonging to any religious order, was not in the marriage-market and must not be expected to take any part in the ordinary social life of the city.

But though she was no longer required to go visiting with her mother, she still found that she had to confront the enemy, who had adopted methods of infiltration. One of the differences between the frivolous circles of old-time Lima and present-day London is that while our frivolous society mainly ignores religion, the gay ladies of Lima were much occupied with it as an entertainment. Many of the social occasions that Rose had shunned were pilgrimages to popular shrines, and now the rumour that the Señorita de Flores had dedicated her virginity to God drew to her mother's house curious sight-seers whose relation to the holiness of their objects was about the same as the relation of a football crowd to the actual players of the game.

Rose shrank from these people, but found it more difficult to escape them in her own home than in theirs.

Her deliverance came with the help of her faithful friend and brother Ferdinando. She persuaded him to help her build herself a little cell in the depths of her father's garden. They chose a spot as far as possible from the house, in a thicket of plane-trees and wild sugar-canes. Here, like two children playing "house", they wove together branches with creepers, making a green lattice for the walls, and a green thatch for the roof. Inside Rose built a little altar with a large cross made out of two boards and stuck over with flowers and feathers. That cross was the brightest, gayest thing in the whole garden, adorned as it was, not only with all the colours of tropical flowers, but with the iridescent feathers of humming birds, parrots, minahs, flamingoes, all the glowing aviary of Peru. Before it in her dun cloak knelt Rose like a little brown dove.

7

No one was more fully aware than Rose herself of what her family had lost through her refusal to marry, and no one could have been more generously determined that as far as possible their loss should be made good. They should have no cause to regret her continued presence among them. She had always been useful in the home, helping her mother and the servant to cook and keep house, and lately she had taken upon herself the nursing of Isabella de Herrara, now bedridden. These activities saved money, since they spared her parents the necessity of employing others, but they did not make it. Rose was determined in future to make money and do what she could to revive the de Flores fortunes which were drooping apace.

It is not quite certain of whom the household consisted at this particular moment. As Rose was the youngest, her sisters were probably all married, though not we may believe advantageously. Of her brothers Ferdinando was still living at home and apparently earning nothing. There were also two invalids or semi-invalids to support. Nevertheless Rose's decision was a bold one, for in those days it was almost unknown for a woman of gentle birth to earn her living, and the fact that she worked to support her family must have appeared quite as unusual and astonishing to her friends as her anchorite's cell in the garden.

It was that garden which became the scene of her labours. The de Flores' house faced the street, opposite the church of the Holy Spirit, but at the back of it was a large rambling garden or paddock, which for lack of money to pay a gardener was now almost a wilderness. Rose took upon herself to make this wilderness blossom as her name. She made flower-beds and grew flowers for sale.

Lima was a city of flowers. The soil and climate encouraged the growth not only of tropical varieties but of many that flourish in temperate zones; and, which was perhaps unusual in a place where flowers grow almost too easily, the ladies of Lima could not have too many of them. They liked to have flowers in their hair as well as in their houses, and Rose soon found her wares in great demand, especially as she was by all reports an expert gardener. She not only grew flowers but she grafted them and improved their species. Of course the hagiographers would credit her with miraculous out-of-season bloomings and miraculous out-of-nature blossoms, but we need not look further than the climate and soil of Lima, in which orchids grow side by side with wallflowers, and roses bloom all the year round, and the undoubted fact that Rose had a green thumb.

She was also, besides a gardener, an expert needlewoman, and not content with making flowers grow in her garden she made them grow on silk and damask and velvet. Her embroidery was we are told of almost supernatural beauty and commanded as ready a sale as her flowers, and doubtless higher prices. Indeed the de Flores family were probably better off for her labours than they would have been for her marriage, unless her husband had been exceptionally accommodating. It was their realisation of this which made them oppose a suggestion which was made at this time that their daughter should join a religious order.

It may seem strange that she had not already done so or thought of doing so. Apart from any question of personal holiness, the convent was then the only alternative to marriage, and we may put down the fact that she chose instead to lead a semi-conventual life in her own home to her persisting devotion to St. Catherine of Siena. This saint had occupied a cell in her parents' house, and Rose would apparently have been content to do the same but for certain developments for which her friend and confessor St. Turribius was mainly responsible.

She was of course leading a life very little different from that of a nun who has made the vows of poverty, chastity and obedience. Her poverty was independent of any vow and her vow of chastity was already fourteen years old. Obedience was more uncertain, because in some respects she was bound to remain her own mistress, but she sought to observe it in obedience to her confessor and to her mother. The former was sensible and practical enough, the latter involved her in more than she would have had to endure from any novice-mistress or mother superior. This was partly due to her own methods which left all initiative to her mother, even in such a matter as a drink of water. Rose would never ask for a drink—her mother must offer it or she would go thirsty. Maria de Flores was a busy woman and a worried woman, therefore probably a forgetful woman. Rose often went parched for days. But here again one cannot feel for her without also feeling for her mother. It must have been as great a trial to have this responsibility forced upon her on the top of all the other cares as it was for Rose to endure her failures to meet it.

No doubt Archbishop Turribius realised these and other objections to the religious life at home. There was also the question of Rose's penances, which we shall consider later. He possibly thought that they needed regulation and supervision. Though he knew of her parents' very natural objection to her removal, he used his influence to persuade them to let her join a convent of Poor Clares which his aunt was setting up in Lima. Turribius must have had great persuasive powers. Not only had he in the past induced a redoubtable dowager to renounce the use of her own name in her grandchild, but he was now able to convince a not particularly devout couple that they must do without their breadwinner. A certain amount of opposition seems to have come from Rose herself. She did not fail to realise that she could lead her special sort of life more satisfactorily in a convent than at home, but, still faithful to St. Catherine, she would have preferred a Dominican to a Franciscan house, and she had a presentiment (afterwards fulfilled) that one would be opened in Lima before very long. She also seems to have had some real scruples about leaving her family to shift for themselves. She probably knew better than Turribius how completely they depended on her.

Certainly it was in a divided frame of mind that she at last set out for her destination, escorted by her devoted Ferdinando. They went on foot, and on the way, her heart still full of her heroine, she asked if she might pause to say a prayer in her favourite haunt, the Rosary chapel of the Dominican church. Here a marvellous event took place. Though the mechanism of it is obviously psychological, that need not exclude a supernatural inspiration. Rose found herself unable to rise from her knees before the statue of the Blessed Virgin. In vain did Ferdinando urge her to hurry, reminding her that where she was going she would have plenty of time for prayer; in vain did he even try to drag her away. She was as if nailed to the ground, until she suddenly realised that this was God's way of showing her she was not to be a Poor Clare. Then she found

[133]

that she was able to get up and go home to her parents, and take up her old way of life in spite of all its drawbacks, because God had shown her plainly that that was the way he wished her to live.

8

Her decision to join the Dominican third order came shortly afterwards. There might be no Dominican convent for women in Lima, but there was a flourishing branch of the secular third order, and our only surprise is that Rose had not joined it before this. St. Catherine of Siena had been a tertiary, and on her feast day the tertiaries of Lima carried her statue, adorned with silks and flowers, round the city. It was while Rose was embroidering a robe for this statue, that the call to join the Preaching Friars came to her characteristically through the persistent flutterings of a large black-and-white butterfly, which flew round and round her, and backwards and forwards in front of her eyes, as if determined that she should admire its display of the Dominican colours.

The Third Order of St. Dominic, unlike so many tertiary bodies, is organically a part of the society to which it is attached. Indeed it was usual then for tertiaries to wear the Dominican habit (a privilege now generally reserved for their burial), and Rose forthwith exchanged her dove-like garb for the black-and-white vesture of a magpie.

The Black Friars were established to fight heresy, and for that reason have not enjoyed outside the Church the popularity of their Franciscan brethren. Certainly their connection with the Spanish Inquisition makes a dark episode in their history, but it must not be thought to express either the mind of their founder or the spirit of their order. St. Dominic had intended that heresy should be fought with the weapons of study and of argument, and the preachers were, as their name implies,

primarily evangelists. It was not as inquisitors but as missionaries that they accompanied the Spanish invaders of the New
World. We have seen that in Peru the Inquisition, though
established, had no concern with the pagans of the country.
It did not even, as in Portuguese India, concern itself with those
who relapsed after baptism. The Preaching Friars were a powerful missionary force, and so little did their methods resemble
those of the Conquistadors that we have the strange and
pathetic spectacle of the Inca Atahualpa, basely betrayed by
Pizarro and cruelly ill-treated, asking for baptism at the hands
of the saintly Father Vincent Valverde.

The order stands, in general terms, for the approach to God
through the mind, and has produced such intellectual giants
as Albertus Magnus and Thomas Aquinas. It is perhaps a little
difficult to see Rose in that company. She is not an intellectual
saint, her mysticism has not the mental grounding which
distinguishes that of St. Catherine of Genoa, and she also lacks
that other Catherine's virile intelligence and sturdy common
sense. If one were to hazard a guess as to her most suitable
setting it would be among the Carmelites. But heaven chose
that she should join the Black Friars, ultimately to shine with
her heroine in the Dominican firmament, twin stars of the
Old World and the New.

This regularising, as it were, of her religious status made a
certain difference in her daily life. She used it to persuade her
mother to allow her to have a cell built in the garden, in succession to the childish wigwam which she and Ferdinando put
up together. This tiny dwelling, five feet by four, was she
assured her confessor quite large enough for her and her
Bridegroom to keep house in together. It was furnished with a
stool and a table only, for Rose still slept in the house. She had
given the key to her mother and would neither leave it at night
nor return to it in the morning without her escort.

Her refusal to walk even across the garden without Maria
de Flores, which must have added considerably to that poor

lady's normal harassments, was no doubt a part of her interpretation of the vow of obedience. But it also expressed her
reverence for that decorum which Spanish custom had exalted
almost into a moral virtue. Rose carried it to the extreme of
refusing even to go to Mass unchaperoned, though the Church
of the Holy Spirit was only just across the road. But she told
an officious lady who marvelled that anyone of her piety should
not attend Mass every day, that she did in fact hear Mass daily
in several churches, visiting them in the spirit when her mother
was unable to escort her bodily.

There were also no doubt practical reasons for not leaving
the house unaccompanied. Rose was already famous in the city
for her holiness and no less famous for her beauty, and it would
be only natural for certain of the more light-minded citizens
to want to see just how much the one was able to safeguard the
other. There is indeed a story of a terrified Rose being pursued
across the garden by a handsome young man. The hagiographers insist that he was Satan in gallant disguise, but I
prefer Rose's own version of the evil-one as a huge black dog,
smelling abominably of sulphur.

Her days and nights were now mapped out with religious
exactitude, but in a proportion she would never have been
allowed to keep in any religious house. She gave no less than
twelve hours in the twenty-four to prayer, for ten she worked
to support her family, and for two she slept. How she managed
to live so long with only two hours' sleep at night (except
when ordered by her confessor to make them four) is one of the
many mysteries of her physical life. She had been a delicate
child and all her life she was a delicate girl, prone to illnesses
both known and unknown to the medical science of her day.
Yet not only did she deny herself some two-thirds of the sleep
considered essential to health, but she was able to live for long
periods without food or drink, keeping an absolute fast for as
long as ten days. We have seen that St. Catherine of Genoa was
able to go without eating for the whole of Lent, but in her case

the fast was not absolute. She would swallow a draught of vinegar and salt which probably counteracted the acid-forming tendencies of her body, and she was moreover powerfully sustained by her daily communion. Rose was able to receive Holy Communion only at her mother's convenience, and throughout her fasts would deny herself not only food but water. Her normal diet, when not fasting, seems insufficient to sustain life. She would never eat meat, fish or eggs, and to join in the ordinary meals of her family made her vomit (as happened to Caterina Adorna when to avoid singularity she ate during her fasts), but she throve on a soup made of bitter herbs, sheep's gall and ashes. "*Ce curieux potage*," as her anonymous French biographer temperately calls this concoction, was brewed by herself, and as soon as the natural and inevitable battle with Maria de Flores was won, constituted her main diet when in health, though in sickness she would occasionally take a little chocolate, considered in those days less as a food than as a medicine.

Most certainly Rose, like St. Catherine of Genoa, had a soul firmly seated in the saddle of Brother Ass; but unlike St. Catherine she beat and belaboured that poor animal with a fury that ceased only with his life. St. Catherine did penance for four years for the sins she had committed before her conversion, but at the end of that period she relaxed and adopted another mode of life—for we cannot consider as expiatory her great fasts in Lent and Advent, which were rather an inspired movement of her body in sympathy with her Love. Rose had no "unconverted" period to atone for. From her babyhood she had been a child of God. It is most unlikely that she had ever committed a mortal sin—her baptismal innocence was like dew upon her. Yet her penances never ceased, piling up in savagery until only to read of them is painful and even shocking.

She had by now at twenty years old moved far from the child who used to trudge about with a log upon her shoulders.

These childish penances seem first to have been undertaken out of love and pity for Our Lord in his Passion, but later on the motive power changes and looks more like hatred—hatred of sin and self. Rose's treatment of her own body is positively vindictive. She assaulted every part of it. On her head she wore, carefully hidden beneath her veil, a crown of nails and spikes; next to her skin was a hair shirt—not the token garment that is little more than a scapular, but a full-size shirt reaching to her knees and with sleeves that came to her wrists. Round her waist she wore a steel chain, pulled so tightly that it bit into her flesh. We have seen how she plunged her beautiful hands into quicklime, though these could not be punished as much as the rest for fear that they should become unfit for work; but having one day realised that from her catalogue of bodily chastisement she had left out the soles of her feet, she repaired the omission by walking to and fro on the red-hot top of the kitchen stove.

Her bed, which might have been expected to provide some refreshment and repose, even if for no more than two hours— *Exsultabunt sancti in gloria: Laetabuntur in cubilibus suis*—was a terrible construction of stones, shards, nails and thorns. She also scourged herself regularly—with steel chains until stopped by her confessor. When she died there is said to have been found among her papers the following "design for a spiritual trousseau for the infant Jesus":

"In the year 1616, with the help of my Saviour and of his holy Mother, I prepare a garment for my very dear Jesus, who is soon to be born naked and shivering in the stable of Bethlehem. To weave his little shirt I made use of fifty litanies, nine rosaries and five days of fasting in memory of his Incarnation. I shall make his napkins of nine stations before the Blessed Sacrament, nine divisions of the rosarian Psalter, and nine days of fasting to honour the nine months he spent in his Mother's womb. I will make the swaddling bands in which he is to be wrapped with five days of abstinence, five rosaries and five stations in honour of his Nativity. I will make him a coverlet with the devotion of the Five Crowns of Our Lord, five absolute fasts and as many stations in memory of his circumcision. As for the trimming of his dress and the canopy that is to protect his crib, I shall make them of thirty-three communions, thirty-three attendances at Mass, thirty-three hours of mental prayer, thirty-three Paters, Aves and Credos, with as many Glorias and Salve Reginas, thirty-three rosaries, thirty-three days of fasting and three thousand lashes of the scourge, in veneration for the thirty-three years he spent on earth. Finally, I shall place as food in his cradle my tears, my sighs, my affections, and above all my heart and my soul, so that I shall henceforth possess nothing that does not entirely belong to him."

9

This document, both terrible and touching, gives us a portrait of Rose in her ferocity and in her innocence. We must not lose sight of her innocence. We must not allow the black cloak to hide the white robe beneath, or we shall find ourselves turning away from her, as a saint we cannot bear to look at. She is without question a very "difficult" saint and one almost impossible to commend to an age in which suffering has become something of an indecency, a thing to be put an end to at all costs, even of life itself. That a young and beautiful girl should so afflict her body seems to us not only less admirable than it seemed to her contemporaries but positively repulsive. We have studied psychology and find ourselves confronted here with the abnormal. Let us face it. It has never been claimed that all the saints were normal people, in fact some of them were distinctly otherwise. The point we must keep in mind is that even the abnormal can be sanctified.

It is impossible to understand Rose without her penances

and we had better begin our attempt by clearing the air. The fog here is partly due to the general but mistaken idea that the saints are all for our imitation, whereas some of them are for admiration only—using the word in its strictly Latin sense of wonder. St. Rose is most emphatically not for imitation. I do not suppose that there now exists in Christendom a director who would allow his penitent to practise even half of her penances. Her own spiritual advisers seem indeed to have done what they could to abate their violence, but though she would always obey she would also plead, and her pleading was apparently irresistible. She had too a method of finding a way out of their prohibitions. When forbidden to scourge herself with chains, she remembered that she had not been forbidden to tie those chains round her waist, and when Father Juan de Villalobus took away her crown and refused to give it back unless she let him file down the nails, she restored those nails to all their former powers of penetration by hammering her head with her fists.

Rose had no less than eleven directors in her short life, which does not mean that they wearied of her obstinacy or that she wantonly changed them. Clerical circles in Lima were far from static, for Peru was still in a sense a missionary district and an outlying part of the Spanish empire. Journeys to and from the motherland sometimes took several months, and several more would be required for journeys into the interior such as that on which her most important confessor St. Turribius lost his life. Certainly none of those who had the privilege of directing the soul of this ferocious child failed to attribute its violence to its purity. They saw both the black and the white. With a clearer vision than we can easily command in these days that are cloudy with false conventions and philosophies they saw the black and the white as irreconcilables which must always be at war. It was Rose's innocence which showed her the infinite nature of sin. Had she been less of an innocent creature, she would probably, like most of us, have seen it only in its finite aspects. It is only if we see sin as finite that we can call her penances exaggerated. If we see it as she saw it, as an infinite transgression against the Infinite God, there is no possible exaggeration of punishment short of an infinity which can be attained only in hell.

The sin of Pizarro against the Inca Atahualpa revolts us in its finite aspects as a crime against humanity, but there are sins which in their finite aspects are hardly revolting at all. Yet those sins, if they are sins in any degree, are sins against God and therefore infinite. This truth of which Rose was fully aware accounts for her horror of what most of us would call trifling sins. She can never have appeared to her confessor as St. Catherine of Genoa appeared to Don Marabotto, as an ingenuous boy bashfully owning to some small delinquency. She was a fanatic about sin, afraid of it as some people are afraid of disease, and in her fear detecting the symptoms in her own body—for had not Ferdinando warned her that beauty like hers is the noose that catches men and drags them down to hell? When in the last few years of her life she received and nursed the diseased women of the town, no doubt she saw in them the triumph of evil in girls like herself, girls who perhaps still were beautiful and once were innocent.

But, unlike St. Catherine of Genoa, her penances were not for her own sins and she probably knew nothing of the sins of the Conquistadors. She saw sin apart from human attachments, in its diabolical essence, as an immanence from another world, and she met it with weapons that belong to that world rather than to this. Certainly all of her directors believed that her desire for penance was supernatural and were diffident in their efforts to control it, fearing no doubt lest they should be found to fight against God—the God who, after all, has said: "He who loves his life shall lose it, he who is an enemy to his own life in this world shall keep it, so as to live eternally."

10

We have done our best to understand how it was that Isabella Rosa de Santa Maria de Flores became the enemy of her own life, so perhaps we may now ask her to take off her black cloak and show us the more attractive white robe beneath it. Though the Dominican black stands for penance, a cloak is a misleading symbol in Rose's case, since it is worn externally and her penances were performed so secretly that none knew of them save her confessors and occasionally, when she needed a confederate, the faithful servant Marianna. Indeed, she was so anxious to conceal them that when in course of time they came to affect her looks, making her face drawn and haggard, she prayed to have the healthful curves and colours of her beauty restored, preferring to fly the flag of Satan on her cheeks than risk his entering, through the treacheries of pride and human respect, the inner fortress of her soul.

Her penances were certainly rumoured but they were never certainly known, though we are told that once the intervention of her guardian angel was required to hide her discipline. The attraction which made the ladies of Lima flock to her cell was, as far as we can judge, a mingling of her saintly reputation with a most winning personal charm. Perhaps too they hoped to be admitted to a share of those supernatural favours which constituted what we might call the white side of her life. It was the gossip of the city that Our Lord and his Mother visited her daily—mysterious voices had been heard talking in her cell; and more than once a child (the little daughter of Isabella de Mexia and the child of a servant in another house) had actually, with the privileged eyes of childhood, seen the Infant Christ in her company "wearing a dress of purple and azure blue".

Certainly her Dominican robe of innocence is not only white but glistening in the light of visits from another world.

When she told her confessor that her little cell was quite big enough for her and her Bridegroom to keep house in, she had meant her words to be taken literally. Like her heroine, St. Catherine of Siena, she had gone through the mystical experience known as the spiritual marriage. In a vision, Our Lord, disguised as "a sculptor in marble or precious stones", had told her that if she would henceforth live for him alone, he would take care of her family; and shortly afterwards, in her favourite haunt of the Rosary chapel, she had heard the voice of the Holy Child speaking from his Mother's arms: "Rose of my heart, be my bride." She had answered: "Lord, if you desire that which I should not dare to hope for, I will be yours and remain eternally faithful to you." Thus by means of visual and auditory symbols a spiritual event of the first magnitude was accomplished in Rose's soul. Though it had some of the effects of conversion it bore no other resemblance to it, being in the nature of consummation rather than of transformation. From henceforth her union with her Bridegroom was complete.

But her heart was still the heart of a child, and she remembered that a wedding requires a ring. How should she obtain a ring? She could not afford to buy one, but who had ever heard of a bride without a ring? As once before, when the child-nun needed a cell, she turned for help to her kind brother Ferdinando. She had grown in the last years very close to this brother, whom she was instructing in the ways of interior prayer. Would he make her a ring? We are told that he hesitated a moment, and then as if suddenly inspired, seized a piece of paper and drew on it a ring with a stone inscribed with the Holy Name. Rose asked for an inscription inside, and to her intense delight he wrote the very words she had heard in the Rosary chapel, but which he had never heard, the words of the Holy Child himself—"Rose of my heart, be my bride." We have no idea how Ferdinando was able to make this ring for her. Doubtless he had his ways and means, for nothing miraculous has been suggested (apart from its sudden transference

from the altar on which she had placed it on Maundy Thursday
to her finger on Easter Sunday), and she put it on to wear till
the day of her death.

Her confessor at that time was Father Juan de Lorenzana,
O.P., a man of great sanctity combined with worldly wisdom.
He was frequently consulted by the Viceroy. He knew of the
rumours going through the city and thought it wise to make a
thorough investigation of his penitent's supernatural experiences. There is a curiously modern note about his procedure,
for he appointed a commission of theologians to inquire into
the matter, choosing as his principal collaborator a doctor of
medicine, Juan de Castillo. Other members of the commission
were two Dominican fathers, Louis de Bilbao and Juan Pérez,
and the learned Jesuit Diégo Martinez. All five interviewed
Rose in her cell, chaperoned by Maria de Flores and by Maria
de Usateguy, wife of the Questor Gonzalez de la Massa, who
had become a close friend of the de Flores family.

It would indeed have required a miracle to squeeze without
suffocation eight persons into Rose's five-by-four cell. Doubtless the meeting overflowed into the garden, where it must
have made a bright pool of colour in the shade of the plane-
trees. The black of the Jesuit and the magpie vesture of the
Dominicans would have acted as foils to the scarlet of the doctor
of medicine, while the two duennas stood on either side of
Rose's black-and-white in the sombre yet glowing colours
of Spanish ladies dressed for an occasion—Maria de Flores
doubtless looking a little shabby, Maria de la Massa more
richly attired than her friend but still after a fashion that had
long gone by in the mother country.

The proceedings opened with a number of questions from
the doctor of medicine. These, however, were not medical but
theological, designed to discover Rose's method of prayer and
how she had come to learn it. She confessed that she had read
few if any books on theology, and had only her own words in
which to describe her experiences. But it was obvious that she

had practised since early childhood the very highest form of prayer, which is the mystical prayer of union. She had not learned it from books—it had come to her naturally from the very first. In it she was transported into wordless, imageless union with God, her senses being in complete abeyance (up till her twelfth year she had suffered occasionally from distractions, but never since then), though she was capable all the time of continuing satisfactorily any work she was engaged in, and many of her embroideries had been worked while she was in this state of prayer. She did not, however, neglect vocal prayer, for apart from saying the Little Office of her Dominican obligation, she spent every day three hours of her allotted twelve in thanksgiving.

Dr. Castillo examined her on the subject of her penances, and here she gave only muted replies, assuring him (as indeed in her simplicity she believed) that she did nothing very extraordinary and nothing without the approval of her director.

On the subject of her visions she was more detailed and illuminating. She told him that she frequently saw Our Lord, both as a child and as a man, and also his Mother, and that she talked to them familiarly every day. She described how she saw her Saviour "clearly but in a fugitive manner. He comes towards me and then disappears." Nor did she ever see more of him than his head and shoulders. When he appeared as a child, she saw him completely and for much longer, though generally as a tiny figure only an inch or two high. He would run about between the lines of a book she was reading. At other times he would be as large as a child of eight. Once he had challenged her to a game of cards, the stake being a peculiarly severe headache she was suffering from at the time. She won and the headache immediately disappeared, but he demanded his revenge and this time he was the winner. "Lord," she asked, "what do you claim as your winnings?" He replied: "Your patience," and the headache returned with redoubled force, so that she did not sleep at all that night. But the next morning she had never felt so full of health and vitality.

This artless tale was actually told to her mother on another occasion, but it is representative of many of what might be called her lesser spiritual experiences. She seems to have had quite an exceptional faculty of visualising her thoughts and imaginations, but when as the result of their examination the theologians told her that her visions were imaginary they did not mean what we should mean by the word.

Strictly speaking, imagination is "the faculty of representing to oneself sensible objects independently of an actual impression of those subjects on our senses". Common use has shrunk the meaning to a representation of objects which have no real existence at all. Theologically, of course, it by no means follows that an object which makes no impression on our senses does not exist in reality, and the last thing which this commission would have wished to convey was that Rose's visions were in any sense illusions. What their findings made clear is their belief that these supernatural experiences had been clothed in images projected from her own mind, and that the external visions seen and words heard were hers and must in no sense be taken as literal representations of what lay behind them—which has been the teaching of the Church throughout the ages.

Psychologists have suggested that the externalisation of images, which normally happens only in our dreams, would be equally frequent and normal in our waking hours if it was not inhibited by some other faculty. This inhibiting faculty may be reduced in power by illness or fatigue, and Rose as we know was frequently ill, and constantly working and fasting. Her spiritual life, therefore, very easily became externalised and the value of its impressions does not lie in their externalisation but rather in the hidden depths of the supernatural experience of which they were the symbols.

This her examiners made clear. When, however, she told them in answer to another question that she saw God "as it were in a light which could be compared to nothing in nature, a light without form, without limit, without measure, a light that is pure and changeless, penetrating everything and always the same in all places", they decided that in this case the vision was intellectual, that is perceived by the mind and soul.

They questioned her further on various dogmas of the Church—the Mystery of the Holy Trinity, the Hypostatic Union, the Real Presence in the Eucharist, predestination, grace, and the joys of the blessed in heaven—also on such mystical subjects as the Illuminative Way and the Dark Night of the Soul. To all these questions Rose gave gentle, modest answers which showed nevertheless that grasp of divine truth which lay within her simplicity.

The findings of the commission were unanimous. They declared (1) that she had arrived at the Prayer of Union by a direct route, and not by the usual approach through the Purgative Way, (2) that she had endured the terrors of the Dark Night with heroic courage and perfect submission to the Will of God, (3) that undoubtedly the Holy Ghost had spoken to them through her mouth. It is noteworthy that they made no further comment on her visions or her penances, regarding the former no doubt as a bye-product or outward projection of her intense life of interior prayer, while the latter were the private concern of her director.

From that time Dr. Castillo frequently visited her, declaring that every time he did so he came away refreshed and fortified. This indeed was the experience of all her confessors, who drew strength from her as they dispensed sacramental grace. Once when the sacristan of the Dominican church told Father de Lorenzana that "Little Rose" was waiting to make her confession, he replied: "This Rose whom you now call 'little' will soon have her greatness known throughout the world."

One result of the commission which deserves recording is its effect on Maria de Flores. She came at last to appreciate her daughter now that others had declared her exceptional nature. Until then Rose had been more of a nuisance than a credit, but now that all those learned theologians had spoken of her so highly, her mother might believe that there was something admirable in her after all. Which shows that she was very like almost any other mother of a difficult daughter.

II

The proper setting for a rose is a garden, and our especial Rose passed most of her life in hers, making it the centre of her work and prayer. In the interests both of safety and decorum her brief nights must be spent in the house, but the first grey of dawn sees her threading her way through the bushes and flowers, and her matins are far ahead of the first bird-song.

The hagiographers have strange tales to tell, and as they are also rather enchanting tales and have about them the freshness of early morning, we shall not be too critical of the evidence. Moreover, even if the details of these reports would not have satisfied Laplace, the general atmosphere they create is, we are sure, the right one. For it is only to be expected that this innocent creature should share the delights of man's first innocence and be on terms of love and friendship with the whole of God's creation.

We are told that God placed Adam in a garden, and a garden is the type of a friendly, co-operative natural order, subject to man and serving him. When Adam sinned he was exiled from the garden, and went out into the wasteland, where nature is unfriendly or at best neutral. She holds aloof, and our efforts towards communion with her suggest the wooing of a frigid bride. She does not want us or need us. If she yields her secrets it is only to our importunity—there is no response on her side. Set against this general indifference, we sometimes meet pathetic instances of individual devotion, of animal turning to human as to a lost mediator, while on the human side a guilt-complex expresses itself in pathological cruelty or pathological doting. The final enmity of nature, outraged and vengeful, is typified by hell fire.

But paradise remains, and those who while still on earth yet live in paradise, have a foretaste of its delight. Stories of friendship between man and nature are common in the lives of the saints. Those who become the enemies of their own lives sometimes become the friends of all other forms of life. The friendship between St. Francis of Assisi and the birds, to say nothing of the wolf of Gubbio, is nearly as well known outside the Church as within it. While in Rose's own city of Lima, her holy contemporary Martin Porres was soon to embroil himself with his superiors by admitting sick animals to the Dominican hospital.

Her own especial friendship with nature is distinguished by a wider reach than such friendships usually attain, even in the lives of the saints; for it included creatures that the most fervent animal-lovers generally choose to ignore, such as gnats, wasps, and mosquitoes, while extending itself beyond the animal kingdom into the realm of plants and flowers.

Flowers indeed were her livelihood, whether she grew them in flower-beds or embroidered them on silk, and we might wonder why she has never been made the patron saint of gardeners, so successful was she in their cultivation. We are told that flowers would grow for her when they would grow for no one else. She is credited with a whole miraculous bed of gillyflowers, sprung up where not even a bud was to be seen the night before. A fellow tertiary, Sister Caterina de Santa Maria, used sometimes to walk with her from her house to her cell in the garden, and she has given her account of a whole garden waking to greet its gardener as she passed through it in the dawn. "The trees bowed over her as she walked, the leaves rustled and made sweet music as they scattered their pearls of dew, the flowers swayed their stems and hastened to uncurl their petals, from which floated delicious scents. The birds began their song as they fluttered around her, perching freely on her arms and shoulders while the insects came in swarms and greeted her with their humming."

Sister Caterina's reaction to the insects was not unlike what would have been our own; on being stung by a lively mosquito she squashed it flat against the wall. "What are you doing, Sister?" cried Rose in dismay—"You are killing my guests." "That," said Catherine coldly, "is not the name I should give them." "And why not?" asked the mistress of the house. "Why should we refuse these poor creatures a drop of our blood, when Our Saviour so often refreshes us with his [the word-play here suggests the marvel unknown in her time of blood transfusion]. However, I don't want my guests to hurt you, so if you promise not to kill any more of them I will promise that they shall sting you no more than they sting me."

Which they never did. Rose's sufferings did not include the common ordeal of being stung by insects. "When I settled here," she said to her confessor, who had some difficulty in approaching her through swarms of gnats and mosquitoes, "I realised that it was necessary to live on good terms with my neighbours. So I made a treaty with them, to which they have been faithful. They don't hurt me and I don't hurt them. They often take shelter under my roof, and in return they accompany with their humming the praises I sing to God."

And indeed, says her biographer, it really was so. "Now, my friends," said Rose of a morning, opening her door, "let us sing together the praises of God Almighty." Whereupon the insects would divide themselves into two choirs, to accompany her recitation of the office till she dismissed them with: "Go, little sisters, and find your next meal among the flowers."

This transfer from an animal to a vegetable diet may account for the fact that not only Rose but her visitors suffered so little from mosquito bites. Her mother, her confessor, Sister Catherine, and Gonzalez de la Massa and his wife were all immune.

[150]

Another tertiary, Francesca de Montoya, had however to pay a quittance of "three stings in honour of the Blessed Trinity".

12

There were others who shared Rose's garden sanctuary besides her friends in the various orders of creation. As the rumour of her holiness grew, the poor and sick of the city began to stream out to her for comfort. Her Spanish rigidity of decorum did not oppose a ministry to the diseased women of the town, whose souls she tended equally with their bodies. Her parents' house was large, so she was able to accommodate her patients in her own home, an arrangement to which her mother strangely enough made no objection. She had already shown her nursing skill in her ministrations to Isabella de Herrara, who had spent her last days under her care. She also undoubtedly had the gift of healing. Nursing and prayer were her medicines and with them she worked some remarkable cures.

One in particular wakes echoes in our day. A certain religious had become what must have been one of the first victims of the tobacco habit. He had acquired it to such an extent that his health was affected and in vain his physician and his monastic superiors sought to break him of it. "For a trumpery satisfaction this monk risked death and perhaps eternal loss." His friends begged Rose to help him, but for a time humility made her hesitate. How could she succeed when so many with greater skill and authority than herself had failed? But charity prevailed, and with it the inspirations of common sense. For years everyone had been reasoning and pleading with this poor man. There were no words left for her to speak *to* him; so instead she would speak *of* him. For five days she prayed without ceasing and "suddenly the sufferer conceived such a horror of tobacco that the smell alone became unbearable to him".

Most of Rose's patients, however, were of her own sex and kind, that is women and girls of good family reduced to poverty. She helped them by every means in her power, and having nothing of her own to give away she lavishly disposed of the goods of others. This curious form of generosity is common in the lives of the saints, and one would like to suppose it the invention of those biographers "with more imagination than judgment" whom the Holy Office deplores. According to one account, Rose would read her victims little lectures on how pleased they ought to be at this diversion of their possessions to others more in need of them. But I prefer the excuse she made to her mother when the latter very naturally protested at the bestowal of one of her only two cloaks on the Señorita Francesca de Montoya, who had none and therefore by all the laws of Spanish colonial custom was unable to go to church. "Do not fret, my dear mother. I did this only because I know that two new cloaks are shortly to be given you." As indeed they were. An unknown benefactor sent Maria de Flores forty silver pieces for the express purpose of buying herself a cloak, and hardly had she begun to wear it when her friend, Maria de Sala, presented her with a beautiful piece of silk to make another.

As time passed Rose's desire to comfort souls and bodies reached an intensity that could not be satisfied with the few she was able to nurse in her parents' house. She became a regular visitor at the hospitals, where her nursing and her cures were as successful and numerous as they had been at home. In this sweeping of the mystical impulse into practical work for humanity, this emptying of the love of God into the love of man, she resembles none more than St. Catherine of Genoa, and there is an incident in one of the hospital wards which brings them close to each other in a likeness which also presents a significant contrast.

We have seen how St. Catherine caught the plague because, carried away by the love of God, she kissed the mouth of a dying woman, or rather the Name that mouth was trying to utter. Rose, moved by another sort of frenzy, drank a bowl of blood which had been drawn some hours before from a sick woman and was beginning to putrify. "What!" she cried to herself, "you have a horror of the blood of your sister in Christ, and you are yourself but a miserable creature? Drink up!" In both saints the gesture is one of love towards the neighbour, but whereas in the case of the Italian matron it is prompted by the love of God, causing an utter self-forgetfulness, the Spanish maiden's impulse is the desire to punish her own shrinking flesh. Both do a deed which is terrible, but in Catherine's case also lovely, whereas our reaction to Rose's is conditioned by those very shrinkings she attacked so fiercely in herself. There is the further consideration that it could not have been of the smallest comfort to the poor creature who had inspired it, while Catherine's kiss must indeed have been a lovely memory to take out of the world.

13

It would have been fitting and would perhaps have pleased us better if our Rose had died in the garden where she had lived for so many years. But, as so often happens to her namesake, it was her fate to be plucked and carried away to die in a house.

For a long time now the de la Massa family had been the friends of the de Flores. Gonzalvo de la Massa was the questor or chief tax-gatherer of Lima, and a wealthy man in high position, whereas Gaspardo de Flores had sunk into poverty and obscurity. But wealth had no social significance in that city, where birth, that is pure Spanish blood, and military prowess were the touchstones; and de Flores, as an old soldier and pure-bred Spaniard, would have considered himself the equal of any nobleman in Peru.

Early in 1614 the de la Massas made the surprising suggestion

L

that Rose should come and live with them. It is surprising because hard to account for by any reasoning we should consider cogent now. It certainly was not a case of relieving her parents of an expense, because she must have cost them almost nothing. Moreover, the family was largely dependent on her labours, and when their consent was finally given for her removal it was made a condition that those labours should continue. We may also feel surprised that the de la Massas should invite into their household a young woman whose ways were so remote from theirs or indeed from the ways of ordinary mankind. But here, of course, we judge from the distance of our own time and society. A saint in the home—and all Lima now believed Rose to be a saint—would have been considered an honour worth paying for in a certain amount of inconvenience. Her love of solitude, her hours of prayer, her fasts, her flagellations would all have shed lustre on those who had invited her to share their life.

But I suspect the real motive for the adoption (for adoption was what it amounted to, though Rose was in her thirtieth year) was their affection for their friends' daughter combined with a true appreciation of her holiness and a desire to please God by giving it scope and protection. No doubt they knew that things were often made hard for her in her parents' house, for in spite of Maria de Flores' improvement since the visit of the theologians, she still suffered from a sharp tongue, a rash judgment and an explosive temper.

Rose too had reached an age when her frequent sicknesses and ferocious penances had at last begun to affect her health. This is hardly surprising; indeed the only surprise is that it had not happened till now. A year of Rose's life would probably have killed any ordinary human being, but it was not till she reached the age of thirty that her friends began to feel any real anxiety about her health.

Certainly she led under their roof a life that was very much easier than the life she had led at home. She protested to her director that she was now without opportunities for sacrifice. Her bed of brickbats and potshards had been thrown by her mother into the river, and though she had permission to construct one like it for Lent, her confessor forbade its use at other seasons. Maria de la Massa gave her as a bedroom the room already occupied by her own little girls, which sheds a curious light upon her as a mother but also illuminates Rose's sweetness and adaptability, for apparently the arrangement was accepted with the greatest goodwill on both sides.

Waking after her self-allotted two hours, Rose would creep out of bed and spend the rest of the night on a wooden stool, to pray while the darkness lingered, then to take up her sewing with the first light. The Señora de la Massa allowed her to observe her fasts, when she saw that they and her peculiar diet improved her health rather than otherwise. She also allowed her to build in an attic under the roof a cell to which she retired every Thursday night, remaining there undisturbed till Saturday morning.

Rose sadly missed her garden cell, where she had spent so many happy hours, conversing familiarly with her Bridegroom and his Mother, and reciting her office with the birds and insects. For she now lived a life which, except for her retirement from Thursday to Saturday, was almost bereft of solitude. But she had grown in spiritual stature since the days when she believed that solitude was a good in itself, to be clung to and fought for at no matter what cost to herself and others. She accepted the new arrangement as the will of God, since it was the will of her parents and of her director, and fulfilled its conditions faithfully and without complaint. Her vow of obedience was now divided equally between her mother and Maria de la Massa, who in her turn became the dispenser of that unasked-for cup of water.

A twenty-two-hour day allows plenty of time for work as well as for prayer, and Rose spent much of her time in household tasks, though these could hardly have been as necessary in the wealthy, well-staffed household of the de la Massas as they had been in her old home, and must we fear have demoralised the servants, who doubtless came to look upon her as one always available to do the more unpleasant work. She also, of course, continued to work at her embroideries for the good of her family. We are not told whether she still grew flowers for the market, but as she constantly visited her parents' home it is probable she did so. She also continued her nursing in the hospitals. In fact, except that it became a little more normal, her life with the de la Massas differed but little from her life with the de Flores.

It was at the questor's house that she reached the climax of her fame. Long rumoured for her holiness and charity, she came at last to be regarded as the preserver of the city of Lima. This city, like most in the Spanish colonies, was a city of contrasts, of black and white, light and darkness. On one side we find a sturdy growth of piety, fruiting in no less than three saints and one *beatus*, on the other inconceivable licence, debauchery, bloodshed and violence. There was also within its walls a large Indian population, always trembling on the verge of paganism. We have seen that heroic and self-sacrificing missionaries had accompanied the Conquistadors without imitating their methods. But though most of the native population of Peru was by this time nominally Christian, there were still in that vast country tracts of forest and mountain that had not been evangelised, and as the inhabitants of these invaded or drifted into the Christian parts, old habits of thought and worship only too readily came back. The Peruvian Indian was a docile, easily-influenced creature, and those characteristics which had aided the work of the missionaries were also favourable to its destruction.

At about this time the village of Anco-Anco, between Lima and Potosi, was wiped out by an earthquake. Earthquakes are not uncommon in Peru, but public opinion decided that this particular disaster had been due to the sins of the inhabitants, who had all relapsed into paganism and had all perished, except it was said for one young woman who in her extremity had invoked the Blessed Virgin Mary instead of Manco Capac.

One could hardly expect the clergy and religious of Lima to forgo such an opportunity to put the fear of God into their congregations. It was a clear case for the text: "Except ye repent, ye shall all likewise perish." But apparently they had little success until a Franciscan friar, Francis of Solano (afterwards canonised) came marching into Lima from Tucumen, like Jonah marching into Nineveh or George Fox into Lichfield—crying, "Woe! woe! to the bloody city ! . . ." In the market-place he preached a sermon which achieved in an hour what the local clergy had failed to achieve in seven weeks—he thoroughly frightened the citizens. Indeed he frightened them beyond his own intentions, for his warning had been given in general terms: "Now is the axe laid to the root of the tree and every tree which does not give good fruit is cut down and cast into the fire." His terrified hearers took his words to mean that Lima would be destroyed that very night, like Anco-Anco, by fire and earthquake. Many fled into the country, others rushed into the churches; others still ran to the questor's house to beg little Rose de Flores to intervene with heaven on their behalf and save them.

It is not likely that Rose shared the general panic, but the child who had been afraid of dolls because she was afraid of idols must have found a voice in her prayers as she thought of Anco-Anco and its idolatries. We are told that she scourged herself that night as never before, and in the morning the city of Lima was still there. The dreaded catastrophe had not happened. Not a stone of the Pizarro palaces was out of place, while the great yellow frontage of the cathedral blazed in nothing fiercer than sunshine.

It was a miracle, of course. No citizen would believe that he had not been the day before doomed to destruction. That the doom had been averted could be due only to prayer, pre-eminently to the prayer of the city's flower of sanctity, little Rose de Flores. From that day she was to be more loved and reverenced than any other within its walls. The holiness of a Turribius or a Francis or a Martin must bow to hers as the patriarchs' sheaves bowed to little Joseph's. There were no scenes of mob excitement, such as attended her funeral, nor was she even followed in the streets by curious gazers as she made her way to the church or to the hospital, the only places where she appeared in public. Her modesty was respected because in all those stews of violence and promiscuity it yet was understood, existing as an ideal long after its image had been lost. But the city's life seemed to centre more and more closely upon hers, as pulses beat to the measure of an invisible heart.

Only for a short time longer was she to go to and fro in its grateful streets. Early in 1617 she announced that she would die that year. She had known and proclaimed since childhood that she would die on the feast of St. Bartholomew.

Rose had the gift of foretelling the future. There is too much evidence for this to be in doubt. Five years earlier she had told her mother that she would end her days as a nun in Lima's Dominican convent—which did not then exist. She had been throwing rose petals into the air as an act of homage to their Creator when her brother Ferdinando joined her with the bet that he could throw them higher than she. So he could, but in spite of that, his sister won the game, because her petals as she threw them stayed in the air where they formed a cross in the midst of a crown. Rose who "scried" rose petals as others have "scried" tea-leaves, interpreted this to mean a convent in which many souls would leave the earth to make a crown for the Bridegroom whose crucified life they shared.

From that day she talked constantly of this convent, declaring that it would be built in Lima and named after St. Catherine of Siena. Another time in a dream she saw the adventure expressed in lilies. When Father Louis de Bilbao, who was then her confessor, spoke his doubts that another convent should ever be built in a city already chock-a-block with them, she quietly informed him that at the laying of the foundation stone he would say the Mass. As for her mother, when she told her daughter bluntly not to make a fool of herself with her day-dreaming, she was informed that she herself would be the first to take the veil. Whereupon the poor woman burst into a perfect frenzy of rage, asking how on earth she "who was busier than God" could possibly leave all her chores and cares to become a nun, and anyhow who was to pay her dowry?

It was paid in fact by Lucia de la Draga, a young woman whom while still a wife and mother Rose had recognised as the first prioress of her convent. In 1622, five years after her death, the Convent of St. Catherine of Siena was built in Lima. Father Louis de Bilbao said the Mass at the laying of the foundation stone, and the widowed Lucia de la Draga was made prioress under the name of Sister Lucia of the Trinity. It was she who remitted the dowry of Maria de Flores, when the latter—now also a widow, though at a very different age— asked to be allowed to take the veil. For many years our saint's mother lived in the convent of her daughter's day-dream— still, no doubt, occasionally restless or even bad-tempered, but growing steadily more happy and at ease with her surroundings till death at last brought her to the peace her life had never known.

Poor frantic, flustered, frenzied Maria de Flores! It seems just possible that her restlessness and bad temper were the result of a missed vocation and that her ill-treatment of Rose was due to a secret jealousy. The emergence of a religious vocation in the children of parents who have missed it is a phenomenon we shall observe more closely in the life of St. Thérèse of Lisieux. It is by no means uncommon in the secular as well as in the religious life. Dr. James Bridie has used the idea for his play, *A Sleeping Clergyman*, and it is for psychologists to decide whether a past renunciation or a present though hidden desire is the more potent influence on the child who finally redeems the failure of those before him.

14

All through her life Rose's penances had been laced with the greater merit of suffering she had not chosen for herself. She seems to have experienced almost every sort of illness—asthma, pleurisy, headache, stomach-ache, palpitations, a sore and swollen throat and a most painful arthritis in her hands and feet. She was seldom without one or more of these complaints, and shortly before she died it was revealed that in her last illness she would suffer from them all.

That was her own interpretation of her famous vision of the two rainbows, on which she was minutely questioned by her friend the doctor Juan de Castillo.

"I found myself," she told him, "surrounded by a dazzling light, in the midst of which was a many-coloured rainbow. Beyond that was another, just as beautiful, which bore in its centre a cross dripping with blood. Behind them both and filling all the space they occupied was the Divine Humanity, which formed as it were the background to the picture."

Until then in her visions she had seen only Our Lord's head and shoulders, apparently at some distance. But now he was close to her and visible from head to feet. A fire radiated from him which seemed to consume her soul, filling it with such bliss that she thought she had left this world and was already in heaven. Then she saw those celestial scales which appear in most representations of her, on which the Saviour "as if he had wished himself to take charge of such a delicate operation," weighed her sufferings against her graces. When they were exactly balanced she heard him say, "Suffering and grace are equals, and grace is given in proportion to pain. The cross is the true and only way to heaven."

She had already put these words into the mouth of St. Catherine of Siena, when in the course of some earlier illness a sympathetic friend had asked her why she did not beg her heroine for a little respite. "What would be the use? I know beforehand what she'd say. She'd ask me if I expected to go to heaven by any other way than the way of the Cross."

Dr. Castillo questioned her with theological minuteness on the details of her vision. What were the colours of the two rainbows? Under what similitude did grace appear on the scales? When Our Lord spoke was his voice audible in her ears or only in her heart? Her answers to these questions are all in the vague, struggling terms of one trying to transpose a supernatural spiritual experience into the limitations of the natural and physical. The colours of the rainbows were so many, so varied, so different from earthly colours that she could not describe them. Grace had "no physical shape or beauty. Without being God himself it was like God," while the divine voice had been "like a ray of light in my soul, leaving there the impression he wished to give me".

The impression that she herself gathered from this vision was of her own imminent death in conditions of great agony. She warned Maria de la Massa that she would die in her house: "And there is one thing I beg of you. When I am all dried up with fever and beseech you for a cup of cold water, please do not refuse me." This pathetic plea was so unlike Rose that her friend was astonished as well as deeply moved. She readily gave the promise, which she afterwards broke. When the time came and Rose, burning with fever, made her request, she dared not fly in the face of medical orders and was forced unwillingly to deny it. Rose understood that she must accept her share of the pains of Calvary, and all she did was to murmur with her parched lips: "*Sitio*—I thirst."

Her illness, which came upon her suddenly one night, completely baffled the physicians. Most of her biographers regard this as a proof of its supernatural origin, but if we consider the state of medical knowledge at that time—when the circulation of the blood had not yet been discovered and the body was still an affair of "humours"—it seems unnecessary to turn to the miraculous for its frustrations. The wonder is that the doctors were able to do as much as they did in the way of diagnosis and alleviation. The various accounts, with their long list of symptoms, suggest, as in St. Catherine's case, a breakdown of the entire system through poisoning from the kidneys, and the marvel is that it had not happened years earlier.

From the first there was no hope of her recovery. To have hoped would have been to fly in the face of religion as well as medicine, for the saint herself had announced that this was her last illness, giving the exact date of its end, and making all the dispositions of a dying person. She made a general confession of her whole life's sins, received the viaticum and extreme unction, renewed her religious vows and asked to have her scapular spread upon the bed. She then asked for all the de la Massa household to be brought into her room, the servants as well as the children, and with touching humility begged their pardon for all the inconveniences caused them by her unusual way of life. Then she thanked them for their care of her—"For two days more you'll have this heavy burden, and I'll ask God that you do not lose the fruits of your long patience."

Everybody cried, but Rose herself was joyful. She was going to her Bridegroom, and going to him directly, without making any dark detours in purgatory. Of that she was certain. Hearing two women talking at her bedside and one of them proclaiming that God was merciful in allowing souls to come to him that way, "and as for me, I desire nothing better," she broke into the conversation: "As for me, I carry my hopes higher. Jesus Christ is my Bridegroom, and such a favour, though it would exceed my merits, would not exceed his power."

One might think that if any human being could claim to have had her purgatory here on earth it would be Rose.

Nevertheless, she had made what was at that time a very startling utterance. Contemporary ideas on the after-life were tough. Divine Truth, though itself eternal, takes on the reflections of the various ages through which it travels on its passage through time, and Rose's age had an eschatology which our own has softened almost to pap. Certainly the idea of hell was no stumbling-block to the faithful. Everyone was afraid of hell, even the good and the devout. The Renaissance had not brought scepticism to the lands of the Spanish Main, and it was in a very far country that a poet could sing:

> "I have a sin of fear that when I've spun
> My last thread I shall perish on the shore. . ."

The fear of extinction is probably the mortal fear of a generation that has learned to doubt. In the ages of faith, which in Lima were extended well beyond their European end in the sixteenth century, it was the idea of hell which absorbed all the unresolved fears of the psyche, fears cast not by Calvinism but from those shadows whence Calvinism had sprung, blind fears which had lost the lights of hope and reason. To such terrified souls purgatory would be not a threat but an escape and the hope of avoiding it a challenge amounting almost to blasphemy.

But Rose trusted in her Bridegroom, and as death drew near her happiness grew greater. Like St. Catherine of Genoa, she had in the midst of her pain and fever reliefs of ecstasy, and on her return from one of these she said to her confessor: "Oh, Father, if my time wasn't so short I should have such beautiful things to tell you." Her physical sufferings decreased as her body weakened, till at the end she was left lying only in great exhaustion. Both her parents were at her bedside, though her father, who himself was seriously ill, had had to be carried into her room. She asked for their blessing and also begged that of her adopted parents, the two de la Massas. She was so clear in her mind, that Father de Lorenzana thought she would last some hours longer and wished to defer his final blessing till the next day. But Rose assured him with a smile that the next day she would be very far off.

It was nearly midnight on the eve of St. Bartholomew, and she knew that she would not outlive the striking of the hour. She begged the watchers to lift her off her bed and lay her on the floor, so that like her Bridegroom she should die on wood. When they refused, she turned for the last time to her faithful Ferdinando, who had so often helped her to fulfil the strange demands of her sanctity, and asked him to take away her pillow. He did so, and her head found the cross on the wooden frame of the bed. In her hand was a blessed candle, and she signed herself with it as the clocks began to chime. From the belfries of Lima's innumerable churches midnight went out in twelve strokes over the city, and when the last had sounded she repeated three times the holiest Name, adding the prayer "Be with me," and was gone.

15

"Almighty God, giver of all good gifts, Who didst will that blessed Rose, a flower of purity and patience, nourished betimes with the dew of thy grace, should blossom in the far Indies, grant that we thy servants may hasten to follow where the fragrance of her passage beckons us, and so deserve, we likewise, to become a perfume offered to the Father by Christ."

Thus the collect for her feast takes us back into the garden where her soul grew and sweetened the streets of a city. Rose's canonisation was not delayed like that of St. Catherine of Genoa, but followed swiftly on her death, almost as a necessity. The scenes that attended her funeral, when popular devotion reached such a pitch of delirious obstruction that her body had finally to be buried by stealth, prolonged themselves into a public cultus which was with difficulty halted by the decree of Pope Urban VIII. Her post-mortem miracles, including two raisings from the dead, were noised through the city of Lima which had also been swept by a religious revival that spread from it throughout Peru, indeed throughout the whole of the "far Indies". It would seem as if she had by her penances made satisfaction for the sins of the Conquistadors and redeemed her country's unhappy past. Certainly new tides of penitence, purity and charity washed over those bloodstained cities and idolatrous villages. Once more the confessionals were thronged, though this time it was not in fear of a threatened catastrophe, but out of love for a gracious, humble, childlike presence which still seemed to dwell among them.

The Dominican order was not slow to act and her "cause" was set in motion very soon after she died. According to the decree *Caelestis Hierusalem cives* fifty years must elapse between death and canonisation, but almost as soon as this period was over the final ceremony was performed, and Isabella Rosa de Santa Maria de Flores became St. Rose of Lima and patron of the New World.

"Hail, St. Rose! Hail, joy of Lima, precious pearl of the Pacific, pure gold of Peru, precious balsam of the Andes and inestimable treasure of America!" In these terms, which we imagine would sound better in another language, our little Rose is invoked from Baffin Land to Cape Horn.

O Rose, fecisti viriliter—Rose, thou hast done manfully. The antiphon to the Magnificat of the second vespers of her feast brings out the fiercer aspects of her character, as opposed to the fragrance manifested in the Collect. Ferocity and fragrance . . . these express the two sides of her difficult sanctity. Together they form that cross which she set up in her childhood's first cell, the cross that was gaudy with feathers and flowers. At first it must have looked almost like a child's toy, or the ornament of a young girl's dressing-table; only a closer inspection would reveal the hard, rough wood under all the colour and perfume.

During her lifetime Rose's penances were known only to

a few. It was not till the minute examination of her character and conduct required by the canonisation process that they were revealed to those outside the little circle of her intimates. No doubt it is mainly those penances which make her such a difficult saint for our own day. We are tempted to look at them from the psychological rather than the theological angle and to see them as sadistic and abnormal. I have already suggested that their ugliness is due to the simplicity of her nature which would not allow her to reason against her own impulses or to make terms with sin. We must further take into account the age in which she lived and the race from which she sprang. It was an age of unbridled cruelty, legal vindictiveness and domestic violence. This was so in all countries (it would be an error to except our own, where Topcliffe had just gone into comfortable retirement), but in addition Rose belonged to a nation which has always carried a strain of cruelty, and even today can find excitement rather than sickness in the sight and the smell of blood. In her cruelty to herself Rose offered up and sanctified the cruelty of her age and nation. Her cruelty sanctified because its impulse was the hatred of sin and its victim was none other than herself. To all that was not herself, whether human, animal, bird or insect, she extended a measureless love.

But even apart from her penances Rose is not an easy saint. One obstacle to any present-day devotion comparable to that which she enjoyed in the past is the absence from her life of almost any form of action or achievement. It is true that she was a mystic, but the lives of most mystics have borne fruit in some definite act or message. St. Teresa not only wrote her treatises but reformed the Carmelite order, St. John of the Cross left his poems and a map of the spiritual life, St. Margaret Mary brought into prominence a doctrine which till then had been only in the background of the Church's theology and based on it a popular devotion. Rose's own heroine, St. Catherine of Siena, had varied her life of contemplation with some remarkable excursions into the ecclesiastical politics of her day, while even St. Catherine of Genoa, that lonely soul, left behind her a body of doctrine in addition to having worked for years as matron of a hospital—a circumstance more likely to impress the modern mind than Rose's private ministrations to harlots and distressed gentlewomen.

If only when she worked in her parents' garden she had created a new variety of her own name, or if even a shred of her embroidery remained in some Peruvian reliquary. . . . We have nothing of her but some notes which she may have written and some Latin poems which she almost certainly did not write. Her visions too lack any wide significance. They are entirely personal and miniature. I own that I find them more convincing than many larger canvases. The tiny child running about between the lines of Louis de Grenada's *Interior Prayer*, the distant oval of Our Lord's head and shoulders, carry for me the same conviction as that voice "like a horse-fly in a bottle" among all the lights and spiritual elegances of Fatima. But though they must have brought the joys of heaven into the purgatory she had sought on earth, they have no special message for our own day, any more than they had for hers. They were her private property, her personal reward.

She seems to be essentially a saint more easily seen from heaven than from earth. Indeed there is something of the heavenly visitant about her—her beauty, her innocence and her horror of sin. Imagine if it were possible for such a being to come among us, would not its reactions be very much like hers?—a horrified recoil from the mess we have made of so much beauty and a movement of love and pity towards all the sufferers from that mess, whether partakers of our own humanity or of the natural order we have betrayed. I am not suggesting that her soul had different origins from any other, but as it most wonderfully and beautifully preserved its innocence, it was indeed among us as a heavenly stranger.

"The fragrance of her passage. . ." In days of old it was

thought that the sweet scent of flowers was a disinfectant, a protection against disease; so we can see our Rose as a nosegay carried through the wards of a hospital, followed by the turning faces of the sick. Even though our vision of her day may have become blurred by facile assumptions and too ready drifts with changing fashions, we still may "follow where the fragrance of her passage beckons us" and find through her some of the sweets and sunshine of the garden we have lost.

Thérèse Martin

I

"*On voit bien que nos cloîtres sont balayés par une enfant de quinze ans.*"

The Mother Superior's cold, inspecting eye travelled over the wall to where a spider's web had escaped the novice's broom. Then she walked on towards the chapel.

It was cold. There was a chill in the air from the snow that had fallen yesterday. The child had been so pleased. She loved the snow, she said, but had scarcely dared hope that a fall of it would decorate the day of her clothing, for the temperature had been unseasonably high. She regarded the fall as a special grace, a delicate compliment from her betrothed. Well, it might seem like that to her, but it was a compliment her elders could well have done without. Mère Marie de Gonzague shivered. Of course when you were as young as that you did not feel the cold, but the day would come when little Thérèse Martin would not be so glad to see the snow.

Little Thérèse Martin . . . . she had known her from childhood, though that did not mean for very long. What funny little letters she used to write—signing herself "Thérèse de Jesu", as if she pictured herself treading in the footsteps of the greatest of all Carmelites. She had always longed to enter Carmel, or rather she had longed for it ever since her favourite sister Pauline had entered the order. She had not missed Marie, the eldest, so much. Now there were three Martin girls in the Carmel at Lisieux, and if the old man were to die (and he had had two strokes) there would be four, for she knew that

Céline wished to enter and was withheld only by the claims of home. Four sisters in one Carmel—was not that too many? It would surely be difficult to spiritualise so much family affection. . . . The Reverend Mother rebuked herself. Who was she to talk of difficulty when it came to the things of God? The God who could send snow out of a warm air . . . . again she folded her lips. The child was so young—young even for her age and that was too young for Carmel. But she had been frantic to enter at fifteen. She had appealed to the bishop —she had appealed to the Pope; or rather she had made a personal assault upon him . . . Reverend Mother shuddered. Would she ever forget the story she had heard so many times of what had happened on that pilgrimage? It seemed wrong that such presumptuous daring should be rewarded. But it had been rewarded. Little Thérèse Martin was safe in Carmel, and clothed as a novice though still only a child— a child whom no one apparently had taught how to use a broom.

Mère Marie de Gonzague was now in chapel and on her knees. She begged God on her knees to forgive her and change in her this spirit of criticism and antagonism, to help her to resist the temptation to dislike this girl who was now one of her own daughters. Oh, my God, help me to be patient, help me to be just, help me to love little Thérèse Martin.

2

To turn from Isabella Rosa de Santa Maria de Flores to Thérèse Martin is nearly as big a change as that from Peru to northern France. These two seem as unlike each other as a couple of maiden saints could possibly be. Since we have now approached the toy-cupboard of the Infant Jesus we may perhaps without irreverence hear them singing to each other across the continents and the centuries—

"I'll tak' the high road and you'll tak' the low road
And I'll be in heaven before ye."

St. Rose was a saint in the grand manner, a mystic, an ascetic, a visionary, a prophet, a worker of miracles. St. Thérèse professed to have had no extraordinary experiences and certainly worked no wonders in her lifetime. Rose was the enemy of her own life in ferocious penances, yet her soul so fortified her body that it survived its maltreatment for thirty-one years. Thérèse practised no austerities beyond those required by the order to which she belonged, yet died unresisting of a Normandy winter's cold. Rose was a recluse and a solitary, who nevertheless reigned as uncrowned queen of a city; while Thérèse lived either with her family or with her fellow Carmelites and was known to few outside those circles. Rose left behind her no special message, no body of doctrine, no revelation—her sanctity rests on "the fragrance of her passage" through this world. Thérèse passed through it almost unnoticed, but bequeathed it a legacy that has made the fortune of countless humble souls. Finally, Rose is not a saint for imitation. She stands for impetration only, a victim for the sins of others, a sign in the spiritual heavens, a strange, starry light. But Thérèse has proclaimed herself a model that all can imitate and leads the way to heaven by a road on which even the smallest child can follow her.

The country we have just entered suggests another simile and we may compare Rose to some wine of rare vintage, the *grand vin* bottled at the château for a special occasion, while Thérèse is the *petit vin* drunk at the family table. The first is for connoisseurs only; no one would dream of using it merely to quench his thirst. Nor is it a wine of which one can drink more than a small quantity—it would probably disagree with a delicate stomach. St. Rose is such a wine, she is not for the ordinary drinker, but St. Thérèse declared herself expressly as the friend of the ordinary man, the man who is not a connoisseur, who does not understand the subtleties of holiness, who would be afraid to search very deeply into the things of God. Yet such a man has his thirst, and little Thérèse Martin offers him a small wine *pour le soif.*

When we leave interior things and study the externals of these lives, the differences are not so great, indeed there are certain resemblances. It is true that Rose was a well-born though impoverished lady, whereas Thérèse was only a *petite bourgeoise* whose family had always been comfortably off. Nevertheless the two girls have some remarkable points in common. One is their childlike approach to the things of God. With Thérèse this is deliberate, a part of her doctrine, which is indeed an elaboration of the text beginning: "Except ye become as little children. . . ." With Rose the outlook seems unconscious, expressing itself in the clarity of a child's vision and the uncompromising directness of a child's innocence. Both were lovers of the Holy Child. Thérèse bore his name in Carmel, while St. Rose more sensationally received his daily visits and wore his nuptial ring. Both young women, too, loved flowers—Rose using them realistically as a means of livelihood, Thérèse using them symbolically to describe herself and her work. Rose is one saint's name while the other calls herself the Little Flower and promises a shower of roses. But here once more a contrast is at work. Rose's life suggests little of her namesake save the fragrance, and if we were to choose a floral symbol for her we should take one of those huge, rare, waxy, orchidaceous lilies that lighten the darkness of some tropical forest; while Thérèse is the "*petite fleur blanche*" which her father picked one afternoon in his garden—a little white rock-plant growing on a wall, a small affair to wear in the button-hole.

A last most significant resemblance in the exterior lives of these two is the isolation in which they lived from their own times. With Rose the isolation was natural. Born in a Spanish colony, the child of parents themselves born in exile, at a time when communications were both difficult and dangerous, she had only the most tenuous contacts with that Old World far away across the ocean. In Europe the Reformation had been followed by the Counter-Reformation, yet in Rose's life there is no trace of either. She did penance for the sins and idolatries of Peru, but apparently never thought of offering herself as victim for the heresiarchs of Europe and their dupes. Her world was entirely the New World of the Americas, as remote from the changing fashions of Europe in religion as in dress, a world in which idolatry and not heresy was the enemy, a world which ignored not only the Reformation but the Renaissance and carried its religion still along the straight line of the ages of faith.

Thérèse's isolation was not natural but artificial. She belonged to that social group which the French have called "*les emigrés de l'interieure*", a group largely provincial and middle-class which for half a century had held itself aloof from the main social, political and artistic life of the country, inhabiting its own little private world of domesticity and religion.

Its withdrawal had followed almost immediately on its emergence, which was later than that of the English middle class, and it justified itself against those already in the field by methods very different from those of its British counterpart. The middle classes in England have always had an important share in the political and cultural life of their country. Their defences have been social rather than moral, the ramparts of a class-consciousness which in most countries is to be found only in the aristocracy and the proletariat. The group from which our saint comes is really a group within a group, a sub-section of the *bourgeoisie*, and its withdrawal from the rest is on moral rather than on social grounds. It disapproved of contemporary morals, of contemporary politics and literature and art, so it cut itself off from them—in the case of politics almost completely, while in the cultural field it clung to conventional, out-moded forms which it had purged of all that it considered morally undesirable. It was an escapism which impoverished both camps. The main body of political and artistic life lost some valuable ideals and restraints, while the fugitives themselves suffered all the losses incidental to their seclusion.

Our saint was born into an inconceivably narrow society. We know from her own statement that she was not allowed to read a newspaper (her violation of this rule on a certain occasion had some important results) and she certainly never went to a theatre or to a dance, while even a game of cards was regarded with suspicion. She had literary and artistic gifts which though not of a very high order would in her British counterpart almost certainly have involved some contacts with the literature and art of her day. Thérèse was a contemporary of Renoir, Cézanne, Van Gogh, Verlaine, yet there is no evidence, external or internal, that she had ever heard of them. It is true that she entered a Carmelite convent at the age of fifteen, but drawing, painting and writing were all part of her occupations there without apparently involving standards much higher than those of a Christmas card.

It would seem, then, that Thérèse was not only a little flower, but a little flower growing in a very little garden, a prim, neat, safe small-town garden, where a tiny square of grass is mown and nothing is attempted that the neighbours might disapprove of. This is the soil from which she sprang and spread over the world.

3

The reason no doubt is the same as that of all flourishing growth—a fertile soil, a favourable climate. Thérèse is the only one of my four subjects who comes from a really pious home. The homes of the three others were religious in the sense that religion was taught and practised in them all. Caterina Fiesca, Cornelia Connelly and Rosa de Flores were all brought up in good moral surroundings and the orthodoxy of their day, but we have no evidence of any extremes of piety in their families, whereas of the Martins it might be said that they were a household of saints only one of whom was canonised.

Both Thérèse's father and mother were exceptionally holy, and both had at one time desired a religious vocation. Here indeed we have "a sleeping clergyman". Louis Martin had tried in vain to enter the monastery of Great St. Bernard, while Zèlie Guérin had been refused by the Sisters of St. Vincent de Paul. They met and married and all their five daughters became nuns.

Thérèse's sanctity begins with an old soldier living at Alençon. We know little about Monsieur le Capitaine Martin except that "it was impossible without emotion to hear him recite the Paternoster". Unlike that other old soldier who fathered St. Rose, he was not poor, nor was he particularly well-born. He came of good, sound *bourgeois* stock and his children adopted superior trades rather than professions. His favourite son, Louis, became a jeweller in Alençon—that is after he had recovered from the disappointment of his rejection by the Prior of Great St. Bernard. It was really not so much a rejection as a postponement. He had not finished his studies so he was told to go back and do so before he applied again. But those few months must have shown him a different way of serving God, for he had made no further attempt to leave the world when fifteen years later his marriage took place.

The reasons for Zèlie Guérin's rejection by the Sisters of Mercy are not recorded, but the occasion seems to have convinced her that her true vocation lay in marriage and motherhood. Her great hope now was for a son who would become a missionary priest. . . . This hope must have received as heavy a blow as the first when on their wedding night her husband told her he wished them to live as brother and sister.

The story of the "white" marriage in which the wife is the

reluctant partner and the husband the wooer who finally establishes normal relations used to be a fairly popular subject in fiction; but in this case the reluctance was the bridegroom's and it was the tact and patience of the bride which in the end persuaded him that her ideal was the more supernatural of the two, as well as obviously the more natural. Many years were spent in trying to give this missionary to God. Four daughters were born before, after many tears and prayers, there came a son. He lived five months. More tears, more prayers, and another son who lived only a few months longer. After that we are told that the parents ceased to pray for a missionary. Then their last child was born—the child who is now the Patron of all the Missions.

She was christened Marie Françoise Thérèse, and as in the case of St. Rose her name became an early subject of controversy. Zèlie Martin's elder sister was a Visitation nun at Le Mans, and Thérèse's middle name was doubtless intended to please her. But Sister Marie-Dosithée was not content and wished the child to be habitually called Françoise, whereas the parents preferred to call her Thérèse. It was the battle between Isabella de Herrara and Maria de Flores fought again on more decorous lines, and when the baby became ill soon after her christening the Françoise party gained a temporary advantage. "You must invoke St. Francis de Sales," wrote Sister Marie-Dosithée, "and promise him that if my little niece recovers she shall be called by his name." One cannot repress a shudder at the thought of the kindly, courteous, debonair St. Francis (a saint who is "meek" in the true sense of that much misused word) being used for this sort of pious blackmail. As might have been expected, he would have nothing to do with it, and when the mother, broken with anxiety, decided to make the promise, but only if and when all hope was lost, her child immediately recovered.

Zèlie Martin was a woman with a job. She had her own lace-making business in Alençon, which she continued even after her husband had retired and given up his jeweller's shop. He was ten years older than she, but she was the first to die, after an operation for cancer, when Thérèse was only four years old. The little girl's memory goes back far, very far, and in her autobiography she has much to say about her mother and obviously remembers her death with sorrow. But in a family where the eldest daughter is nearly old enough to be the mother of the youngest, such a loss is not likely to have the domestic or psychological effects that might follow it in a different sort of home. Zèlie's place was taken by the eldest daughter Marie, or rather it was shared between her and the daughter next in age, Pauline.

To Thérèse her sister Pauline had always been an almost heroic figure. She day-dreamed about her as some children day-dream about the heroes and heroines of their imagination. Whenever her mother asked: "What are you thinking about?" the answer invariably was: "Pauline." And Pauline was to be not only her heroine but virtually her mother for almost all her life, first in the home where for many years she kept house for her father and took charge of the younger children, and finally in Carmel itself where as Mère Agnes de Jesu she is the "mère chérie" to whom the classic *Histoire d'une Âme* is addressed. "It is to you, my darling Mother, you who are twice my Mother. . . ."

The Martins were an exceptionally devoted family and Thérèse loved all her sisters, even though she loved Pauline the best. Next to Pauline in her affections came Céline, who was nearest to her in age, near enough to be played with and quarrelled with; the confession to her mother: "*J'ai battu Céline*," has the genuine nursery tone. Thérèse was obviously the dominant sister in spite of being the younger, but the accounts show her as an amiable tyrant, only once descending to rapacity. That was when, on being asked with her sister to choose some dolls' clothes from a basket and having seen Céline modestly help herself to a scrap of trimming, she calmly announced: "I'll take the lot." She could not, however, be happy without Céline, and later on even her life in Carmel was incomplete till this nearest if not dearest sister (who alone of all the Martin girls seems to have cast a glance towards the world) joined her there.

4

But more than any of her sisters or than the mother she had lost Thérèse loved her father. We have already had two glimpses of him, but they are not very illuminating, for they shed their light only on one side of his character, a side which did not develop, since it embodied a world-fleeing impulse that God did not wish to gratify. We have glanced at the would-be monk and the would-be continent husband, and seen how he renounced both these ideals for one which only a fanatic would consider lower since it so plainly represents heaven's choice against his own.

Louis Joseph Stanislas Martin is the fourth member of that shadow quartet which has been assembling behind our quartet in heaven. We have already two saints' husbands and a saint's mother. Now we complete the number with a saint's father. Freud has traced the idea of God to a primitive father-complex. The Old Man of the prehistoric tribe has in the course of the ages become the Father in Heaven. And though I am given to understand that the theory is not much sounder anthropologically than it is theologically, we must all recognise the germ of truth that lies in it. A child's idea of God must inevitably be conditioned by its idea of its own father. It has no other content to put into the word when first it learns to pray. "Our Father" cannot be so very different from "My father", and he becomes either a symbol of love, care and kindness, or of severity, harshness and caprice.

For Thérèse Martin fatherhood was a state made up

altogether of goodness and love. Monsieur Martin was not only the friend, counsellor and companion of his children but the friend of all his little world. His mind might be narrow but his heart was big with charity, and his personal holiness makes him only a little less of a saint than his daughter.

In nineteenth-century France, where even the rudimentary social services that existed in our own country were unknown, every good man was still his brother's keeper. Monsieur Martin held himself responsible for his neighbour's welfare, and was always ready to help the unfortunate, whether they deserved it or not. There is a story of his hauling a drunken man out of the gutter where he was lying and helping him home with one arm while with the other he carried his tools. Another story lights up a gracious custom one hopes has not quite died out. When Léonie Martin (the middle sister and the only one not to enter Carmel) made her First Communion, her family took it upon themselves to "dress" a poor child who was making hers at the same time. The custom, at least in their case, went further and involved the child's presence throughout the day in the home of her benefactors and her equal share of the First Communion celebrations, including a dinner with a *"pièce montée"*. This reminds us of an episode in Maxence van der Meersch's novel *La Pauvre Fille*, in which a family living horribly in an unspeakable Paris slum is sustained not only by the gifts of the charitable but by the manner of their giving. One of the losses that must be set against the gains of a modern system by which the state takes upon itself offices until recently performed by individuals, is the loss of all that is contained in the word charity.

It is a word that has lost caste with us. It has joined that ever-lengthening list of words, all most significantly denoting virtues, that have been twisted out of their original meaning, sometimes into their very opposites. Thus candour, which once stood close to its derivation in sweetness, is now only for the unpleasantly outspoken; meek, which once meant the same

[179]

as gracious, has now almost reached the meaning of its own rhyme in weakness; while nice has broken out of a fastidious discrimination into a vague, general sound of approval. Last and saddest of all, charity has become the symbol of a degrading dole by a superior person, instead of representing the highest form of love—love of man in and for the love of God, as against the intellectual loves of the "phil" prefix and the longing loves of Eros. Who in our present meaning of the word would live on charity, and who in its true significance would live on anything else?

It was charity which impelled Caterina Adorna to kiss the mouth of the plague-stricken woman, and it was charity which impelled Louis Martin to lift the drunken man out of the gutter and arm him home. Charity too was the impulse of his love for his daughters, for only charity, having loved them so much, could give them all to God—feeling only pride and delight when one by one they left him to enter Carmel or the Order of the Visitation. Without charity parental love can be the most possessive of all the instincts, just as it can be one of the most foolish, the most vain and the most blind. Monsieur Martin's love for his daughters was none of these things. He loved them, yet he made no claims on them; in his gentle way he ruled his family, but it was a rule of love. Can we wonder that in Thérèse's idea of God love had completely cast out fear?

Instead of fear was a contrition which, motivated by love, became that perfect act which outstrips penance in the soul's return to grace. Thérèse herself tells of how one day as a very small child she was "fooling about" on a swing when her father asked her for a kiss and she refused to give it to him. Her sister Marie at once told her that she was a naughty little girl, an idea which does not seem to have occurred to her till then. But immediately she realised how she must have hurt her father's feelings by what she had done, she was overcome with sorrow, and as she ran to ask his forgiveness and give him the kiss she had denied, "the whole house echoed with my screams of penitence".

"Oh, my God, I am heartily sorry and humbly beg pardon for all my sins. . . ." So begins the familiar Act of Contrition, and St. Rose, scrupulous and fearful in the shadow of her parents' capricious ill-treatment, continues with the next phrase: "Because they have deserved thy dreadful punishments," while St. Catherine embarks on her four years of penance and reparation, "Because they have crucified My Lord and Saviour Jesus Christ." But it is Thérèse who has learned from her father's love to complete and perfect the act with its final phrase: "But most of all because they have offended thine infinite goodness and mercy." As she runs through a house echoing with her "screams of penitence", and throws herself into her father's arms to ask his forgiveness and make reparation with a kiss, she spontaneously performs that act which throughout her life will be the pattern of all her returns to God.

5

"One day God showed me an old tree laden with five lovely fruits about to ripen, and ordered me to transplant it into my garden. I obeyed and the fruits ripened one by one; the Child Jesus, as is told in a legend of the flight into Egypt, passed five times and made a sign; the old tree bent itself lovingly and each time, without complaint, let one of its fruits fall into the hands of the Child-God. What a wonderful sight, this new Abraham! What greatness of soul! We are only pigmies when compared with that man."

Thus Monsieur Guérin wrote of his brother-in-law's coming to Lisieux, which happened soon after the death of his wife. He wished to be near the Guérins and to have their help in the bringing up of his family. He was not a poor man, and was able to afford himself a pleasant villa on the outskirts of the town.

Les Buissonets has always been one of the most personal attractions of a pilgrimage to Lisieux. The very short time that elapsed between the family's leaving it and Thérèse's canonisation has allowed it to be kept very much as it was in her day. Indeed, in this respect it can be compared only with the otherwise so-different Haworth Parsonage. Furniture, pictures, toys remain, and the trim little façade smiles on the pilgrim as it smiled on Thérèse. The place might well have been left to speak for itself, but alas! has not been allowed to do so. The statuary group in the homely little garden is a truly dreadful example of what might be called the meringue complex in French ecclesiastical art. Thérèse and her father might be fashioned out of white sugar, except that unfortunately they do not melt in the sun; nor do they appear to have suffered from the bombardment which in the last stages of the second world war destroyed most of the picturesque and interesting old town. Their situation makes them even more distressing than the huge white basilica (also spared) which hits the eye from a neighbouring hill-top, but will no doubt in time weather down to something no more unpleasant than the Sacré Coeur on the hill-top of Montmartre.

Thérèse from the first was delighted with the garden, wherein she became remarkably like St. Rose. No more than Rose did she like playing with dolls—"*Je ne savais pas jouer à la poupée*"—but amused herself by making tisanes and similar decoctions out of seed-vessels and the bark of trees. Unlike Rose, however, she did not swallow these herself as a penance, but gave them to her devoted father, who only pretended to drink them. She also grew flowers, probably not so expertly as the older saint, but enough to adorn the little altars that she built in corners and decorated, much as Rose decorated the cross in her home-made cell. Thérèse was as full of piety as Rose, but her piety expressed itself in play rather than penance. When the family had gone to evening service, which she was too young to attend, she would light up her toy altar with wax-vestas or saved candle-ends and recite the *Memorare* with the servant Victoire (the game was to see if you could finish the prayer before the vestas burned out)—a daylight variant of Rose making and carrying her wooden cross with the help of the servant Marianna.

Thérèse's life may be said to have moved in a groove of piety. Religion conditioned all that she did, her work, her play, her affections, her ambitions. The Martins had no existence apart from it. The day started with prayer and, for the elders, with Mass. In the afternoon Thérèse would go with her father for a walk which always included a visit to the Blessed Sacrament in one of the town's churches. In the evening a game of draughts would be followed by a reading from *L'Année Liturgique* and some book which Thérèse is anxious to assure us was interesting as well as instructive. Then all the family went upstairs to pray with the child before she was put to bed. No doubt they had their recreations—Monsieur Martin we know was a keen fisherman, and there would be visits to the Guérins and other members of their small circle, and sometimes expeditions into the country. But in the main they led a cloistral life in preparation for the cloister.

One by one the elder girls left their father and their home: first Pauline, then Marie, both entering the Carmel at Lisieux; then Léonie to join the Order of the Visitation at Caen, after a trial of the Poor Clares which failed on account of her health; then Thérèse herself for Carmel, leaving only Céline to take care of the old man who knew that at his death she would become his last gift to God.

His health had begun to fail some little time before Thérèse's admission to Carmel. He had had a paralytic stroke the year before, and though he made a good recovery there was a second attack shortly before her clothing. Whether the struggle to part with this dearest child—his little queen, he called her—had been too heroic for his declining strength we do not know. All we do know, because Thérèse herself repeats his words, is that one day on a visit to Alençon he had in the Church of Notre Dame (the church where he was married) received such graces that he cried out: "My God, it is too much. I am too happy. It isn't possible to go to heaven in this way. I want to suffer for you. . . .": a challenge not unlike that made by Cornelia Connelly in the garden at Gracemere.

He was well enough to lead his little queen in her bridal dress of white velvet and swansdown up the aisle of the Carmelite chapel on the day of her clothing, but subsequent attacks paralysed him completely and veiled at last the brightness of his clear and ardent mind. For three years he was in a mental home, though he died at the home of his brother-in-law who finally took charge of him. On his last visit to Carmel, helpless and almost speechless, when his daughters bade him *"Au revoir"*, he pointed upwards and after a struggle to find words and then to utter them, murmured: *"Au ciel."* Of his five daughters only Céline was with him when he died.

6

By writing her own autobiography, Thérèse Martin has robbed the hagiographers of their prey. *Histoire d'une Âme* is written with a most deceiving artlessness. From the style one might think that any future biographer would at least have the pleasure of assessing characters and incidents at their true value, and of giving as it were an adult shape to the whole. But in fact Thérèse has left very little of this to be done. Not only has she acute powers of observation and a clear, discriminating memory, but she is quick to interpret past events in the light of future development, and she is extraordinarily keensighted in regard to her own failings. "I saw that my great longing to make my final vows was mixed with a great self-love. . . ." cuts away the ground from under the critic's feet.

Thérèse, trained from earliest childhood in the examination of conscience, knows about herself all and more than anyone else is ever likely to know. And what is more she is not afraid to say it.

The best approach to her life is to see it as the expression of her doctrine, for Thérèse, like St. Catherine of Genoa, is a saint whose greatness lies not only in her life but in her teaching. Yet it would be hard to imagine anything more remote from the *Vita et Dottrina* than *Histoire d'une Âme*. Not only is the latter a first-hand almost unedited account, whereas the former is the compilation of good people who were not always accurate or discriminating, but the whole width of the kingdom of heaven seems to lie between the mysteries of those Hidden Worlds and the simplicities of that Little Way. St. Catherine was a mystic and an intellectual, and her life was the vehicle rather than the expression of her teaching, whereas with Thérèse her life *is* her doctrine; for that doctrine does not involve a theological or a philosophical system, but a practical design for living. She calls it a "little" way to signify its ordinariness, its simplicity, and its possibility for all.

The word "*petit*" in French is not quite the same as "little" in our language, and this has led to a certain amount of misunderstanding. Miss Sackville-West in her sympathetic and illuminating study of the two Teresas in *The Eagle and the Dove* is obviously misled by her second subject's use of diminutives and goes so far as to accuse her of "*niaiserie*". Certainly if the word had no wider meaning in France than it has in England the accusation would be justified. But in that country it stands for a good deal more than size—otherwise should we have a newspaper called *Le Petit Parisien*, to say nothing of *Le Petit Paroissien* in church and *Le Petit Precepteur* in school? A French working man will address his companion as "*mon p'tit*", for which the best translation would be "old man" or "old chap". Indeed it has much the same function as the English "old" in denoting familiarity and easy, informal relations.

And this I think is what Thérèse wishes to convey in most cases where she uses the word "*petit*". For her it means something ordinary, something for the rank and file, for the plain man. After all the dictionary gives "*les petits*" for the English "common people". I am not suggesting that Thérèse's "little" is never the same as ours, but it certainly is not always so; it is rather her own special reference to the ordinary ways of holiness as distinct from the extraordinary ways of such saints as St. Rose and her own namesake in Carmel, St. Teresa of Avila.

"You know, Mother," she writes in the ninth chapter of her autobiography, "I have always wanted to be a saint; but alas! I have always realised when I have compared myself with the saints that there exists between them and me the same difference that we see in nature between a mountain of which the summit is lost in the clouds and a grain of sand which is trodden by the feet of passers-by."

Without measuring the depths and the heights quite as she does, we can appreciate the difference between her and the "great" saints—the visionaries, the ecstatics, the miracle-workers, the self-macerators, the martyrs. Here indeed there is a contrast of great and small. But "instead of being discouraged, I said to myself: 'God would not inspire desires that cannot be realised; so I can in spite of my lowness, aspire to sanctity'." It is notable that many saints besides Thérèse have deliberately set out to be what they are. Neither humility nor modesty can hold them back from such a vast ambition. "It is for the glory of God that we should be saints. God wills what is for His glory; therefore God wills us to be saints. God wills me to be a saint. I will be a saint. *Therefore I shall be a saint*." So writes Cornelia Connelly, and if the truth were known most people who love God at all have at one time had the hope and the desire to be a saint, and the tragedy of many lives has been the loss of just this hope and just this desire. In a number of cases the loss is due to discouragement by what should have been its strongest inspiration. We read the lives of the saints and are discouraged. We could never rise to anything like this.

It is for such souls as these that Thérèse points out a simpler way to heaven, a way for ordinary, commonplace folk, who have no special gifts nor in their own opinion anything of what it takes to be a saint. There are aristocrats in the kingdom of God but there are also the common people—"*les petits*", in fact. For these she has found a little way to heaven and provided a map in the story of her life.

7

That map might be compared with a map of her own Normandy countryside—a homely, friendly landscape, with no unusual features, no high peaks, no large towns, no dense forests or dark gorges. Beyond Lima tower the Andes and the Alps are not far from Genoa, but outside Lisieux are only gently rolling hills and little valleys sheltering farms among their orchards, a pattern of fields and "*bocages*" no bigger than our Sussex shaws. It is not so much a contrast of great and small as of the impressive with the commonplace, the exotic with the homely. So in the map of Thérèse's life we shall not look out for any remarkable features, for great depths or heights or for anything startling or strange. But everything is there, suffering, love, endeavour, renunciation, everything that is required to make a saint.

When we come to look at her sufferings we do not find the rare and terrible anguish which fell to the lot of Cornelia Connelly, nor the equally rare and terrible penances self-inflicted by St. Rose. The earthly sorrows of Thérèse are the kind we all have to bear, chiefly the loss of loved ones, while her spiritual sorrows are the lot of all who aspire to any degree of holiness—misunderstanding, discouragement, aridity and "temptations against faith".

Yet she suffered acutely. We cannot measure pain by its causes. Toothache can be and often is more painful than a mortal disease, and the loss of a parent or a sister may hurt more than the break-up of a marriage or the blows of a leaded scourge. Thérèse was only four when her mother died, but the depth of her sorrow can be measured by its effect on her character. From being a merry, carefree, rather obstreperous little girl she became a quiet, shy one: "Immediately after Mamma's death, as you know, Mother, my happy nature changed entirely. I who used to be so lively and open-hearted became timid and gentle, sensitive in the extreme; a single look was often enough to make me dissolve in tears, it was best for no one to notice me; I could not enjoy the company of strangers and was never merry except in my family circle." This period of her life was the unhappiest, for she had not yet found the spiritual strength that was to sustain her under later, heavier sorrows. She calls it the second period and it lasted until she was fourteen, prolonged no doubt by a further bereavement on the departure of her adored sister Pauline for Carmel.

She had not expected this to happen so soon. She had always known that one day Pauline would become a nun, but no doubt she had not thought she would leave home before her eldest sister Marie who had the same ambition. She had moreover misunderstood some words that Pauline had uttered on the subject of their going away together "into a far wilderness". She was shocked and grief-stricken when she found that she had never intended to wait till Thérèse was old enough to go with her.

The separation took place and it was as if the little girl had lost her mother all over again. She fretted to such an extent that she became ill, and so ill that she very nearly died. We need not regard this illness as another instance of the "mystery sickness" beloved of the hagiographers. There is, however, little doubt that pining and grief had predisposed her to it by reducing her bodily resistance. "My life seemed to me full of suffering and repeated separations. . . . I knew nothing then of the joys of sacrifice. I was weak, so weak, that I regard it as a great grace that I was able to endure without dying a trial well above my strength."

This may seem exaggerated language. Pauline was not dead. She had only as it were gone a few yards down the street, to a convent where she could still be visited by her small sister, who moreover was already forming in her mind the project of joining her there. But as we have said before, pain cannot be measured by its causes, and those parlour interviews did little or nothing to fill the gap in the little girl's life. They were necessarily short, limited to a few minutes at the end of the "*parloirs de famille*", and as Thérèse owns that she spent most of this time in tears, they cannot have been very enjoyable to either party.

Thérèse was very ill indeed. By sheer will-power she forced a sufficient recovery to attend the clothing of her beloved sister, but next day she had a serious relapse. She became delirious—"My bed seemed to be surrounded by horrible precipices; certain nails fixed in the walls of the room took in my eyes the terrifying shapes of great, black carbonised fingers. . . ." She attributes this to "*le demon*", but those, and they are many, who have lived through similar experiences and seen innocent pictures and calendars become horrid shapes of hell, will recognise as it were the "ordinary" workings of that demon, through a body poisoned with fever and exhaustion.

All her life Thérèse was to remember that illness with terror and its cure with thankfulness and delight.

8

We have now come to one of the few events in her life which might be called preternatural. She had by her bedside

a small replica of the statue of Our Lady carved by the eighteenth-century sculptor Bouchardon for the Church of St.
Giles in Paris. It had belonged to her mother and the whole
family was still much attached to it. When the little girl became
ill her father asked for a novena to Our Lady of Victories.
The bedside statue bears no resemblance to that in the famous
Paris church, but the two are linked together both at the beginning and the end of the story.

On the Sunday of the novena Thérèse was so ill that for the
first time she failed to recognise her sister Marie, who had
taken her mother's place ever since Pauline entered Carmel.
She lay in bed calling piteously: "Marie! Marie!" but when
her sister entered the room, "though I perfectly well saw her
come in", she was a stranger. Marie knelt down weeping
before the statue and prayed "with the fervour of a mother
who demands, who *will have* the life of her child". Léonie and
Céline who were there too knelt down and joined in her prayer.
"Marie! Marie!" The sick child and her sisters were all calling
the same name.

Then suddenly and wonderfully Thérèse was herself again.
She recognised her eldest sister, she smiled, she talked, she
cried with joy. All three girls noticed the change in her, as they
had noticed the look on her face that preceded it. Marie in
particular was convinced that not only had her prayer been
heard but that some miraculous favour had been shown her
little sister to account for that almost luminous look of ecstasy.

Perhaps unwisely she determined to find out. Thérèse did
not want to tell her, but she was too young to be able to keep
a secret from anyone she loved, and bit by bit in response to
Marie's coaxings her story was told. The Blessed Virgin had
smiled at her. Thérèse had seen the statue move, come towards
her and smile. At that ravishing smile all her griefs and sufferings had faded away and she had been filled with a joy that
might have been the joy of heaven.

Poor Thérèse! She had not wanted to tell her secret, and now all her vague fears and reluctances were to be justified. Marie had asked her permission to tell the nuns on her next visit to Carmel, and it was they who with what can only be described as pious pawings rubbed the bloom off that exquisite experience so that "for four years the memory of that ineffable favour became for me a real grief of soul".

When on her recovery she went to visit Pauline, now Sister Agnes of Jesus, she found a crowd of nuns assembled with their Reverend Mother to question her on the miracle. They probed and pried. Some asked her if the Blessed Virgin was carrying the Holy Child, others if she was accompanied by angels, and so on. "All these questions confused me and hurt me; I could make only one answer: 'The Blessed Virgin looked very beautiful. I saw her move towards me and smile at me.'"

The poor child, seeing her rainbow experience thus translated into the plaster imagery of the ecclesiastical emporium, failed to recognise it and thought that she had been lying. "If only I had kept my secret I should have kept my happiness." She felt painfully humbled and conceived a real horror of herself, "Oh God, you alone know what I suffered."

Here in my edition of *Histoire d'une Âme* comes the footnote: "This distress could be nothing but the effect of a mysterious permission of God." Permission—yes, as always. Mysterious—no. It would have been mysterious if any nature as sensitive and high-toned as Thérèse's could have endured all this spiritual vulgarity without shrinking. She was too young to fight it, so she succumbed. For four years she was robbed of what should have been the happiest moment of her life. Her deliverance came when she was nearly fifteen years old, in that very church of Nôtre Dame des Victoires where the novena for her recovery had been said. Pausing there at the outset of her pilgrimage to Rome in 1887, she found graces that reminded her of those that had followed her First Communion, and "it was there that my Mother the Virgin Mary *told me clearly that it really had been she herself who had smiled at me and cured me"*. At once all her joy in the memory was restored. The colours flashed once more on the butterfly's wings and the rainbow spanned the sky.

Was Thérèse's cure miraculous in the strict sense of a divine intervention in the ordinary ways of nature? Her illness was far from being one for which there was no hope of recovery. As there is no record of her receiving Extreme Unction she obviously was not considered in danger of death. It was only the swiftness, the suddenness of the cure which made it remarkable. This swiftness is a characteristic of all preternatural cures, where often there is nothing surprising in the recovery of the patient but in the suddenness with which it takes place. As for the other circumstances of her recovery, they are allied to the illness, when nails in the wall appeared as ghastly carbonised fingers. The change was in herself—horror and hell changed to beauty and heaven by her soul's contact with supernatural power. I see Our Lady's smile as Thérèse's own personal translation of an experience that in itself was incommunicable, and all her later unhappiness as the result of her attempt to communicate it.

Her only other preternatural experience is of a different kind and consists of one of those apprehensions of the future which are not uncommon. It is of earlier date than the adventure of the Smiling Virgin; Thérèse was only six years old when looking out of the window she saw her father (then far away on a visit to Alençon) walking in the garden. He walked as an old man, with bent and shaking legs, and over his head hung a veil or cloth that completely hid his face. It is easy to interpret the vision in the light of what happened later, of the physical and mental disintegration that preceded his death. At the time Thérèse was bewildered and distressed. In vain kindly grown-ups told her that she had seen the maid walking with her apron over her head. She knew exactly what she had seen and could not forget it.

Afterwards she regarded the episode as a divine revelation of the "precious cross" that was to come, but added the pertinent question: "Why did God give this light to a child who if she had understood it would have died of sorrow?" She was not aware that her experience, though unusual, was not unique nor necessarily supernatural. Many of us, not specially gifted spiritually or even psychically, have known what it is to "dream true". The difference here lies in the fact that the child was wide awake, and also, more significantly, in the many years that were to elapse before the dream's fulfilment. Most cases of prevision extend only a few hours in time, even a lag of days is unusual and here we have years. Her report, of course, is written some time after both events, but he would be indeed a sceptic who could doubt Thérèse's word.

9

These two contacts with the preternatural are her life's only contribution to any sort of pious sensationalism, and are on a very small scale when compared with the exploits of others in the same field. It might be said that they are out of place in a life that professes to display nothing out of the ordinary; to which the rejoinder is that most people, if they are honest with themselves, will acknowledge that they have experienced something of this nature—an answer to prayer which verges on the miraculous or some contact, not obviously religious, with a world existing outside space and time. Our model in such cases must be Thérèse's restraint and delicacy. To neither of her experiences did she give any exaggerated importance. The change that came over her and transformed her life is not to be attributed to the cure of her illness but to something totally different.

Indeed after her recovery she was very much as she had been before, a quiet, shy, ultra-sensitive girl, devoted to her family but slow to make friends outside it. She was now fourteen and had been at school some years, but had no close friends among her schoolfellows. Moreover, she had lately become a victim to scruples. These added to the sensitive melancholy of her life, and when in her turn Marie left Les Buissonets for Carmel, her state of mind was critical. Céline was too young to give her the help and comfort she had found in her eldest sister, so in her distress she turned to those members of her family who had known only a few months of earth but must now have reached wisdom's full stature in paradise. She begged the help of the two "missionaries" who with Hélène and Melanie were in heaven. The answer came at once and her scruples troubled her no more. But she was still a prey to that emotional inflammation which if unchecked might have infected her soul with a sickness very much more dangerous than that from which her body had just recovered.

A family love which includes not only the living but the dead is unusual even among the saints. Next to her love of God it was and remained all her life Thérèse's strongest passion. But at one time it had its dangers. The youngest of so many adoring sisters, the petted darling of a doting father, she had no inducement to grow up into a woman, and was still, though nearly fifteen, obstinately remaining a child.

Her "conversion" is nothing else than the conquest of that debilitating state of prolonged childhood into which she had fallen. In other words, by God's grace she made herself grow up. Unlike St. Catherine's conversion, the battle was fought in entire consciousness and the victory won by a deliberate effort of the will. The occasion was so trivial as almost to appear ridiculous. After the midnight Mass of Christmas it was the custom of the Martin family to watch Thérèse examine with joy and excitement the treasures in the "magic shoes" that like any other little French girl she had left on the hearth. Her father's pleasure in her pleasure had lately become the best part of it and she looked forward to his gaiety even more than to the pretty trifles he would give her. This Christmas of 1886, as she ran upstairs to take off her outdoor clothes, she heard him say: "All this is too childish for a big girl like Thérèse, and I hope this will be the last year of it."

These words, she tells us, pierced her heart, and watching for the inevitable tears, Céline urged her not to go down immediately: "You would cry too much." But something had changed in Thérèse; she did not cry. With a violent effort she not only held back her tears but managed to check the wild beating of her heart. She ran downstairs and went through with all her old joyfulness the little ceremony now robbed of all its joy. Her father laughed, Thérèse laughed, and what was more for the rest of her life she hardly ever cried again.

"A small miracle was necessary to make me grow up." Certainly the Christmas Grace, as she calls it, seems a very small specimen in the way of conversions, but the change it wrought in her was a big one. Extreme sensitiveness need not necessarily be a sin but it can be a most degrading imperfection, and Thérèse confesses that hers had made her "positively unbearable". From this event she dates the third period of her life, the one most filled with graces. "In one moment the work that I had been trying in vain to do for years was done. Jesus did it, contenting himself with my goodwill. 'Lord, I have fished all night and have caught nothing.' Even more merciful to me than he was to his disciples, Jesus himself took the net and cast it, and drew it out full of fish; he made me a fisher of souls."

She caught her own first fish very soon afterwards. Having discovered God's power with her she was next to discover her power with God. We know that Thérèse was not allowed to read the newspapers, a prohibition which we find mildly surprising when we realise that Monsieur Martin's daily paper was *La Croix*, but the common talk of Lisieux had told her about the multi-murderer Pranzini, now in prison awaiting execution. Prominent in all the gossip that she heard was his impenitence. He obstinately refused to make his peace with God, and Thérèse was filled with the fear that his soul would be lost. It is worth noticing that she saw this soul not so much as that of a fellow creature in peril as the precious treasure of her Saviour of which he was about to be robbed. As far as Pranzini was concerned, Christ would have died in vain, and the thought appalled her.

She determined to obtain the murderer's salvation. No milder statement covers her prayer, and she felt convinced that it would be heard. Nevertheless she asked for a sign. "Oh God, I am quite sure that you will forgive poor Pranzini; I would believe it even if he did not confess himself or show any sign of contrition, so much do I trust your infinite mercy. But he is my first sinner, and because of that I ask only *a sign* of repentance for my own consolation."

On the day after the execution she juggled delicately with her conscience and opened the forbidden *La Croix*. Pranzini had indeed gone to his death without confession or absolution, but at the very last moment, when the executioners were dragging him towards the *bascule*, he turned round, seized the crucifix which the priest was holding up, and kissed three times the sacred wounds. The sign had been given.

10

"My first sinner" . . . There is a touching innocence about those words with which Thérèse inaugurates a mission that is still in action nearly sixty years after her death. From the moment when she knew that her prayers had saved a murderer whose soul would otherwise almost certainly have been lost, the longing to save souls fused with her earlier, vaguer longing to enter Carmel. When later on, at her religious profession, she was solemnly asked her reasons for leaving the world, she replied, "I have come to save souls and above all to pray for priests."

Those who know little of the religious life often imagine a convent as a place where timid men and women take refuge from the trials of the world. I will not say that such a world-fleeing emotion is never the basis of a vocation, but it is not likely to produce the best type of religious, who enters a convent to work, either actively in some Christian enterprise such as nursing or education, or spiritually with tools of penance and prayer. No matter what may sometimes have happened in the past, there is nothing in modern conventual life to encourage the fearful or the lazy. The Carmelite order is one of the oldest and the most austere. The convents for women are strictly enclosed and the ordinary routine is a discipline of the utmost severity.

Thérèse longed to enter Carmel, and to enter as soon as possible. She was now fourteen and a half, and her life ever since the Christmas Grace had taken on fresh tones of spiritual quality. She was like a fledgling bird that is losing its down and sees every day a gay new adult feather. Soon it will spread its wings and fly, and Thérèse longed to fly, even from her darling father.

In a scene that has been so perfectly described by herself that no one would presume to describe it again she won his consent to enter Carmel as soon as she was fifteen, if the necessary permission could be obtained. This included the permission of her uncle, Monsieur Guérin, and when Thérèse had attached the little white flower her father gave her to a picture of Our Lady of Victories, she set about obtaining it, and did so at last, after a bad start in a downright refusal. She then addressed herself to the even more intractable Church authorities.

Their answer can be guessed. What she asked was quite impossible. Sixteen is the lowest age at which a girl can be accepted by a religious order, and in the case of a very severe order like the Carmelites, the age required is twenty-one.

In vain Monsieur Martin took her for a personal interview with the Bishop of Bayeux. The bishop was very kind and fatherly, but he would make no promises. Before anything could happen there would have to be an interview with the Superior of the Carmelites, the mere thought of which brought to her eyes and cheeks the tears that had now become so rare. Monsieur Martin had planned to take his two younger daughters on a pilgrimage to Rome, and the bishop considered this would be a very good test of her vocation. It was her father who then told him that she would not hesitate to attack the Pope himself on the subject if she had not already obtained the permission she was asking.

So had they hatched this scheme together, or was a mere joke of Monsieur Martin's responsible for his daughter's personal assault on His Holiness Pope Leo XIII? This is perhaps the most startling episode in her life. We can hardly compare her with a débutante in the British Court accompanying her curtsy with a personal appeal to the Queen, for there is an admixture of homeliness in the magnificence of the Vatican which has no parallel in this country. But it was certainly a proceeding very much out of order, and we are surprised that Thérèse was able to get so far as an argument with His Holiness before being forcibly removed by the attendants.

The pilgrims approached the audience throne singly, and each knelt down to kiss the Pope's foot and hand before passing on into an adjoining room. The priest conductor of the pilgrimage, the Abbé Révérony, had given orders that no one was to speak a word, but this did not make Thérèse falter by more than a look at Céline, who murmured: "Speak." She spoke.

"Holy Father, I have a favour to ask of you. . . ."

The eagle head with its piercing eyes bent swiftly to her as she repeated—

"Holy Father, in honour of your jubilee, allow me to enter Carmel at fifteen."

At this the indignant vicar general of Bayeux interjected:

"Holy Father, this child wants to be a Carmelite, the question is being examined at this moment by her superiors."

"Well, my child," said the Pope, "do what your superiors decide."

But Thérèse now had her clasped hands on his knees.

"Oh, Holy Father, if you say yes, everyone will agree."

Still gazing at her fixedly he slowly pronounced these words: "*Allons. . . allons . . . . vous entrerez si le bon Dieu le veut.*"

Thérèse, who seems completely to have forgotten her surroundings, would have continued the argument. But things had now gone too far and the spectators intervened. Two members of the Noble Guard took her by the arms to lift her up, but required the help of the Abbé Révérony before they could release her grip of the papal knees. Just as she was being taken away, the Pope gently put his hand over her lips, which he may have seen parting for further speech, then lifted it in blessing.

Poor little Thérèse. No doubt she had embarrassed a number of exalted personages, while she herself was humbled and disappointed by what I hope I shall not be called irreverent for describing as an ecclesiastical example of "passing the buck"— the final recipient being *le bon Dieu*. It was in these last words of His Holiness that the only comfort lay for her ardent spirituality. She still trusted in God.

II

She was not disappointed—not in that last issue, though there were lesser disappointments which show how much she was still a child. Without the smallest regard for probabilities, she had set her heart on being admitted to Carmel on the first anniversary of the Christmas Grace, even at the very hour. She would not be fifteen till January the second, but the anniversary meant everything to her, and she was bitterly disappointed when the necessary permission (which in her simplicity she had never doubted, in spite of all discouragements) failed to arrive. It came on New Year's Day, which one would have thought soon enough, but brought with it a further disappointment, for Mère Marie de Gonzague, the Mother Superior, refused to admit her till after Lent.

"I could not restrain my tears at such a long delay." One is tempted to ask: "Why in such a hurry?" She could surely have waited three months beyond her fifteenth birthday to start a life which might have lasted another sixty years. Had she a presentiment that the years would not be more than ten? In her eagerness we may see a twofold inspiration. One part is the surviving child in her, for to a child three months can seem eternity; the other and the strongest is her consuming desire to give herself entirely to God. The sooner she gives herself the more she gives, and she suffers all the thwarted generosity of a lover who longs to give all but is compelled to hold something back—three months of eating and drinking, of sleeping and waking, of walking and talking, of reading and resting and praying and playing, three months of daily experience, three months of life, three months of Thérèse.

It was also no doubt discouraging to have this last prohibition come from the convent itself, from the Mother Superior on whose goodwill and good understanding her religious future, under God, depended. She might have expected that Reverend Mother whom she had known from a child would be delighted to receive her and would welcome her most kindly. A great deal has been written about Mère Marie de Gonzague which suggests that she did not really like Thérèse Martin. Thérèse herself tells us that she treated her very severely. "I could never meet her without being blamed for something," and it was before the entire community that she made the remark:

"*On voit bien que nos cloîtres sont balayés par une enfant de quinze ans.*" Possibly she did not want to receive Thérèse, and did so only under pressure from her superiors; probably she thought her too young and not improbably she considered two daughters from one family enough for any convent. When Thérèse entered there would be three Martin girls and later possibly four. It looked as if the cloister might well become a family affair.

Perhaps we ourselves may wonder how much family affection had to do with Thérèse's eagerness and haste. From very early childhood she had known that Pauline would one day become a nun and had planned to go with her when she left home for Carmel. When she found that Pauline would not wait for her, the shock and disappointment were enough to make her ill, and Marie's departure a few years later brought almost as debilitating a sorrow. Was it not likely that such a warm-hearted, sensitive, highly-strung girl as Thérèse should be unable to face life without the comfort and protection of her sisters and should take the shortest way to be with them again?

We could of course argue that she left behind her as much as she went to join—Céline, the sister next her in age and her closest companion, and above all her adored and adoring father. No sister, however kind or wise, could take his place, and from him the separation (which with Céline might be ended by her own admission) must be life-long and complete. But it is almost certain that her early longings for Carmel contained a large admixture of her love for Pauline and Marie. After all, was there ever such a thing as an absolutely pure motive? "Who shall be found willing to serve God for naught?" I can think of only one thus willing and he was the victim of a monstrous error—James Weller when he said amen to his own damnation. One of the wonders of free grace is the use that it can make of motives and instincts that are in themselves only just worthy. In Thérèse's case it had to work upon that which

o   [201]

in itself was good; and as fine materials lend themselves to finer achievements than what is shoddy or defective, we have in her life the rare sight of a truly supernatural family affection.

Her love for her sisters in Carmel need have caused Mother Marie no apprehension, for it passed without apparent pain or struggle into the paradisal world which St. John of the Cross describes when he writes to Donna Juana de Pedraga: "All that is wanting now is that I should forget you. But consider how that is forgotten which is ever present in the soul." Thérèse's letters to her loved ones outside Carmel and the notes that passed between her and the loved ones within all express an affection "as pure as it was particular . . . . fully accepted and willed and acknowledged to its immediate object".* They are brimming with family love transformed into heavenly love, a transformation which does not prevent terms of endearment, nicknames or family jokes. The type of convent where these freedoms are forbidden seems unsure of itself in the supernatural field. With Thérèse they are celestial coinage, small change, but new-minted, clean and shining. Never is there the slightest evidence of the Martins becoming an *enclave* within the cloister, even after their number has been augmented by the admission of their cousin Marie Guérin. During the last years of Thérèse's life it could have been said that the whole family was in heaven, some one side of death and some the other but all equally supernaturalised citizens of the kingdom of God.

12

With her entry into Carmel Thérèse ends *L'Histoire Printanière d'une Petite Fleur Blanche* which makes up the larger part of *Histoire d'une Âme*, the part written expressly for her sister Pauline. At that time Pauline, otherwise Mère Agnes de Jesu,

* Von Hügel, *The Mystical Element of Religion.*

was Prioress of Carmel and had as it were commissioned the work. But two more chapters were added later at the behest of Mère Marie de Gonzague during her next term of office. Mère Chérie becomes Mère Vénérée, and the tone of the writing is altogether more restrained and remote.

But Mère Marie was no longer the dragon guarding the treasure of Thérèse's first weeks in Carmel. The girl's humility and perseverence had ended in removing her superior's distrust. There is little doubt but that much of Mère Marie's severity was deliberately intended to discourage a faltering vocation. If Thérèse had entered Carmel on the spur of her longing to be with her sisters or of a romantic infatuation for convent life, the sooner she was taught to realise her mistake the better. A child of fifteen is, humanly speaking, too young to know her own mind, and in charity to her as well as the community, enlightenment should come before she has made any irrevocable decision. So Mère Marie de Gonzague scolded—"On the rare occasions I was with her for an hour I was scolded almost all the time"—and postponed her profession eight months (which was certainly not a sin against prudence), and though she suffered much, in the end Thérèse completely understood her and even thanked her.

Apart from the scolding of Mère Marie, she found no difficulty in adapting herself to convent life. She was entirely without romantic illusions and must besides have been well informed by her sisters. Anyway, "I found the religious life just what I had imagined, no sacrifice surprised me." Yet it would be difficult to picture a greater change from her comfortable life at Les Buissonets. It is true that she had spent the last three months in training, but such mortifications as she practised were entirely of the spirit. "Far from being like those beautiful souls who from their childhood practise all sorts of macerations, I made mine consist only of breaking my will, of refusing to answer back, of doing little services without letting them be noticed, and a thousand other things of this kind. By the practice of these nothings I prepared myself."

She was wise indeed; yet one would have thought that some sort of physical training was necessary for a life in which the body had to take its full share of penance. In Carmel a rigorous fast was observed during the most trying months of the year, the discipline was in regular use, the beds were so hard that one would hardly imagine that sleep could be found on them, and the corridors and cells were entirely unheated. Yet Thérèse accepted it all without flinching and almost without comment —all except the cold.

This she considered one of the greatest trials of her religious life, especially since she could not feel that it was willed by God, but was due to an exaggerated rigorism in the interpretation of the Carmelite rule—in her own words: "permitted by him, but not willed by him." We have suggested that Cornelia Connelly found the bitterest of her sufferings in the thought that as they originated in her husband's sin, they could not be according to God's will, and here we have a situation not unlike hers, though typically reduced in scale. Thérèse could not believe that a rule originally made in Spain where heating might rightly be considered a luxury, or at least not a necessity, should be rigorously enforced in the north of France through winters of rain and snow. "Not to take into account differences in climate and diversities of constitutions, was to tempt God and sin against prudence." St. Teresa allowed heating only in the common room, where Thérèse, having spent the day "*transie de froid*", would warm herself for a few minutes before making her long way to her cell through open cloisters and down a freezing corridor, to arrive at last in an icy room where the only warmth was provided by two thin coverlets.

One may well be amazed at the conservatism which refused to adapt to such conditions a rule obviously intended to be no more than austere. The explanation belongs, perhaps, less to the spirit of the cloister than to the spirit which for several hundred years has kept so much unchanged in our public schools. Knowing what she thought about it all, we may wonder that Thérèse did not complain till she was on her deathbed—she could have obtained certain reliefs from the novice mistress—but she wished to accept this penance without complaint, recognising it as an important feature of her Little Way. The regular penances of the religious life are not for "*les petits*" and though naturally Thérèse performed them according to the rule, she never seems to have attached much importance to them and she would have very little to do with corporal penances that the rule did not require. Once, having injured herself with a sharp cross she had been wearing, she said: "It would not have happened to me for such a trifle if God had not wanted me to realise that the macerations of the saints are not for me, nor for those 'little' souls who will follow the same way of spiritual childhood."

But the cold is a mortification for all, however lowly; indeed it is for many, for most, a penance that must be accepted rather than sought. It is the penance of "*les petits*", of the poor, of the common man. So Thérèse endured it for nine winters without complaint. As a child she had loved the snow. "What a delicate attention!" she cried when it fell unexpectedly on the day of her clothing. But as the years wore on and her health wore down under the fierce rule, she felt the cold more and more until it became a thing of absolute dread. Yet it was not till she lay dying of its effects that she protested.

She did not protest in vain. Authority has since intervened and ordered that at least the corridors of a Carmel shall be heated where the climate requires it. But for her, and for others, the concession came too late. No doubt it was a divine inspiration that made her endure in silence till the enemy had done its work, for Thérèse's effective ministry did not begin till she had left this earth. If she had not died in 1897 she would possibly now be still alive, for she would not yet have reached

the age of eighty, an unknown nun in the Carmel of an unknown town in France. How much of her Little Way would
she have been able to carry through a long life? Might not the
inevitable changes of growth and experience have removed
at least some of the bloom of her "spiritual childhood"?
These are idle questions, for obviously no one can answer them.
But if it was heaven's will that she should die young in order
that her life and teaching should become effective, we can see
in her uncomplaining endurance of an almost intolerable
situation the weapon which our weak human nature is sometimes allowed to put into the hand of God.

13

Thérèse's attitude to death is that of the saints. Just as St.
Catherine of Genoa loved everything that reminded her of
death, so Thérèse rejoiced when a sudden haemorrhage
announced the presence of a disease that might be fatal. Such
an attitude is entirely logical in one to whom death is not
the closing but the opening of a door. She did not see death as
the end of all she had accomplished and enjoyed in life, but
as the introduction to new powers and sweeter joys.

From material things she was completely detached, though
not with the negative detachment that comes of renunciation.
She is a glowing example of St. John of the Cross's "Spiritual
Man", who "has greater joy and comfort in creatures if he
detaches himself from them; and he can have no joy in them
if he considers them as his. He . . . rejoices in their truth . . . .
in their best conditions . . . . in their substantial worth." So
Thérèse, living in a strictly enclosed convent, continued to
love her family, to appreciate her food, to draw and paint and
write verses and letters to her friends, remaining all the while
not only detached from these things but from those far more
subtle attachments of the religious life which can be just as

strong and just as dangerous as the attachments of the most hardened sensualist.

Her attachments were not of this earth, and death meant nothing but her removal to where her treasure was. She had always thought that she would die young, and "the hope of going to heaven gave me transports of happiness". But it was no selfish happiness, for just as she foretold her early death— "I will die soon," she had said in the April of 1895, while still in perfect health, "I don't mean in a few months, but in two or three years at the most; I know it by what is happening in my soul"—so she foretold her intention to spend her time in heaven doing good upon earth. The conviction of this post-mortem activity is one of the most remarkable aspects of her last illness. "I feel that my mission is about to begin, my mission to make God loved as I love Him, to give my Little Way to souls . . . . No, I could not take any rest until the end of the world."

The simplicity and directness of this belief robs it of any shade of presumption. Thérèse spoke as she *knew*, and there is something of a child's trust and innocence in her "*vous verrez —tout le monde m'aimera*". Her conviction that she was going to heaven by a very humble way, that because she was too small to walk up so many stairs she had to be picked up and carried, would prevent any feelings of pride. Hers is a very humble boast, which as such has been abundantly fulfilled.

Nor did her readiness to die make her either morbid or insensitive in the face of death. She collaborated joyfully with all the efforts, both medical and spiritual, made towards her recovery. Indeed, during a period when summer and a more generous diet had greatly improved her health, she was filled with the hope that she might be well enough to go out to the Carmel at Hanoi, for she had always longed to be actually in the mission field. But when a novena to the venerable Théophane Vénard (the missionary priest and martyr to whom she had a special devotion) ended only in a relapse she became convinced that a longer journey lay ahead of her than the trip to China.

It was while thus poised between earth and heaven that she gave her novices the doctrine of her Little Way. For some time now she had been novice mistress, a post that would normally be given to a mature and seasoned nun. Her holiness and strength of character had at last removed the reproach of her youth. She was no longer the child who did not even know how to sweep a floor, but one sufficiently grown in wisdom to be trusted with the training of others in the most difficult of all lives.

She must have been a welcome guide during those first testing months. Not only had she herself suffered as a novice, but her natural sweetness of manner would be honey for the bitterest pill of rebuke. Not for her the scolding of Mère Marie de Gonzague, but a delicate, unobtrusive study of her pupil's character. Nor had she any unstretchable rules or insatiable ideals. She aimed at the sanctification rather than the renunciation of natural tendencies and affections. "I do not understand saints who do not love their families" was a pronouncement which must have been balm to many a homesick girl half-ashamed of the agonies of her first separation.

She is also one of the few saints who have shown definite signs of a sense of humour. To a novice who was always melting into tears, she suddenly held out the little mussel-shell which is part of the equipment of a Carmelite drawing-table. "There!—if you must cry, cry into that." The girl began to laugh, but Thérèse continued: "In future I allow you to cry as much as you like, as long as you catch all your tears in that shell." A week before her death, almost unable to speak, she managed to gasp out to this same novice: "You've been crying —*was it into the shell?*" The joke was also sound psychology, for the girl found that the business of moving "*l'impitoyable instrument*" from one eye to the other quickly enough to catch every tear entirely distracted her mind from whatever was making her cry, so that before long she was completely cured of her weakness.

The matter as well as the manner of Thérèse's instructions must also have been a surprise to many. No doubt some of her novices had entered Carmel tensed for a life of holiness on the grand scale, and to such the homely diet she offered may have been something in the nature of a disappointment. It was no doubt to such as these that she said very shortly before her death: "If I have led you into error with my Little Way, I shall soon appear to tell you to take another road; but if I don't come back believe in the truth of my words."

14

What is this Little Way that is now known to thousands outside the novitiate at Lisieux? Thérèse herself calls it "the way of spiritual childhood, the path of confidence and total surrender". As always with the child of Louis Martin, the father conception of God is the strongest. Like St. Catherine she can talk of her Love and like St. Rose of her Bridegroom, but it is a secondary and specialised image. First of all she is God's child, dependent on him for everything and trusting him in everything, unable to repay his goodness except with her love, but comforted by the thought that ultimately that is all he asks of anyone.

The wives of Giuliano Adorno and Pierce Connelly, the daughters of Maria de Flores and Louis Martin . . . . My shadow quartet has played its part in making saints, but there is only one whom I can confidently picture as sharing the glory he has made. The holiness of Caterina Adorna, of Cornelia Connelly, of Rosa de Flores, is like a spark struck from the hard flint of their relatives' insensibility. Monsieur Martin alone has offered the kindling flame that sets another soul alight. It was as his child that Thérèse learned to be the child of God.

A child cannot run very fast, take long strides or overcome great obstacles. In order to please its elders, it depends on their loving kindness rather than anything really useful and effective that it is able to do. So "small souls" can take only small steps on the way to heaven and do small things to please *"papa le bon Dieu"* whose earthly model is not far to seek. "I want to show them little ways of pleasing God that have been completely successful in my case. . . . In my Little Way there are only very ordinary things."

Elsewhere she elaborates the nature of those ordinary things. They are indeed so small as often to be invisible to all save God. At the same time they are not without their cost. Who does not know the strain of performing some tiresome task that a little intelligence would have made unnecessary? But, "there is no merit in doing what is reasonable." And how many of us have enough heroism to endure a bore? Yet, "if you are telling one of your sisters what seems to you an interesting story and she interrupts you to tell you something else, listen to her with interest, even though she does not interest you in the least, and do not try to go on with what you were first saying." One may well believe her when she tells her novices that at recreation above all they will find occasion to practise virtue.

She had a Frenchwoman's sensitive palate and almost moral appreciation of good cooking, yet she not only accepted the worst food without complaint, but ate with every appearance of grateful enjoyment dishes prepared by another sister who wished specially to please her but had in doing so consulted only her own taste. We may feel sure that if Thérèse had ever been in the same situation as St. Rose she would not have rubbed pepper on her eyelids to save herself from paying visits with her mother. On the contrary, we can see her going through the whole boring process with gentleness and gaiety. Every bit as much as St. Rose she would rather have stayed at home, but she would have seen no intrinsic virtue in silence and solitude if they were the states that she herself preferred. Her

virtue would have lain in helping to give a pleasant morning to her mother and her mother's friends, never showing
how the stiffness, stodginess and fatuity of it all bored and
exhausted her very soul.

Yet Thérèse never criticises another saint's way of holiness.
On the contrary, her attitude towards all *"ces belles âmes"* as
she calls the saints in the grand manner, is one of admiration
and humility. In recommending her small wine as more likely
to agree with the average digestion than the great vintages, she
is certainly not belittling or decrying the latter. They are the
fine and the right thing for those who can stomach them, but
she cannot; nor can most people. Yet God must be loved, and
it would be sad indeed if anyone were to be prevented from
loving him because they think they cannot love him enough.

The paradox of this saint is that though she taught the way of
spiritual childhood she herself is neither mentally nor emotion-
ally a child. Hence the special significance of her conversion—
"le petit miracle" of the Christmas Grace. For by virtue of it
she did not change suddenly from a sinner to a saint, but from
a child to a grown-up person. She uses the language and analo-
gies of childhood and there is a deceptive artlessness about her
writing which conceals a mind and judgment essentially mature.
A psychologist faced with St. Thérèse and St. Rose would not
be long in deciding which of the two was the child. Thérèse's
objective view of her own character, her honest and clear
appraisal of the faults and the virtues of others, her delicate
sense of balance between the important and the unimportant
in the spiritual life (so conspicuous in St. Catherine, so lacking
in St. Rose) are all gifts of maturity and take her far from childhood except in her relation to God.

St. Rose could not understand those who were unlike
herself, and her attitude towards evil resembles a child's
shapeless fear of the dark. St. Thérèse saw her way to heaven
as only one, and that the humblest, among many, while though
she acknowledges that at one time she dreaded evil, that was

because she knew very little about it. "I had not experienced that . . . the simple and upright soul sees evil in nothing, since evil exists only in unclean hearts and not in things (*objets insensibles*)."

In her balance and integration of character she resembles Cornelia Connelly. Like her, too, she had a very low threshold of consciousness, so that her Little Way, like the *Book of Studies*, does not come as a "revelation", but through the sober medium of her own conscious thought.

In one respect, however, she is unlike her, indeed unlike any other member of our quartet. It may have been because in her own family she could always find sympathy and advice in spiritual matters that throughout her life she depended so little on priestly direction. We cannot even compare her with St. Catherine, for though for many years this saint was without a director and went only very rarely to confession, during the last period of her life she was glad to turn and find rest in the comforting simplicity of Don Marabotto. Cornelia Connelly, we know, never took any important step without consulting her confessor, while St. Rose had no less than eleven directors in the course of her life.

Thérèse is perfectly frank. She found but little comfort or encouragement in the counsels of those who should have advised and supported her. "The keepers have taken my cloak" is her sorrowful commentary on this side of her spiritual life. She practised confession, of course, at regular intervals, according to the rule of Carmel, and received sacramental grace, but for direction she had learned (no doubt painfully) not to depend on man. "But here I suffer no lack, for Our Lord himself is my director."

Wise indeed were those who appointed her to guide young souls in their first steps along the difficult ways of the religious life. It is notable that her wisdom was all spiritually acquired. She had spent the first part of her life in a small, confined circle, and the rest in a strictly enclosed community, yet she shows a depth of wisdom that has not been equalled by many who have ranged the world. It is a depth which forcibly makes good any lack of breadth there may be. Indeed breadth is only too often associated with shallowness and stagnation. But depth without breadth can call to other deeps and enlarge itself among the hidden rocks. . . . "Deep calleth on deep, at the noise of thy flood-gates. All thy heights and thy billows have passed over me."

There is in the Bernese Oberland, at the end of the Lauterbrünnen Valley, a narrow subterranean stream called the Trummelbach. It runs or rather roars through the towering darkness of cliffs thousands of feet high, to the base of which through countless millenniums it has carved its way. It has cut a bed so deep that the sky is hidden as in a cave and so narrow that the sides are never more than a few feet apart. No voice can be heard "because of the noise of thy flood-gates", as the torrent hurtles on, its cascades springing rather than falling from the angles of the rock, while the pools thunder with the current roaring through them.

If these waters had been wider they would not have cut through the solid rock like cheese, even in ten thousand times ten thousand years. It was their constriction that made them a knife to carve a mountain. There must always be narrowness in the lives of the saints. We may deplore it, we may regard it as one of the effects of Adam's fall which, like the cold Carmel, God allows but does not approve. But we shall almost always find it, even if in some cases, such as St. Francis de Sales, only in part. In Thérèse the enclosure is complete, "a garden enclosed is my sister, my spouse. . . ." Yet I prefer the analogy of the rushing torrent, for the whole nature of narrowness in the lives of the saints is dynamic—as dynamic as dynamite, since it dissolves the rock. Take away this compelling force and the stream is only a gutter where things decay.

A question naturally arises. Why did Thérèse teach her Little Way, her low road to heaven, from the high road—

indeed for most of us the inaccessible heights—of Carmel? The drinkers of small wine surely have no rights in that exalted vineyard. Not only are the majority of ordinary men and women without a vocation to the religious life, but where vocations occur they are likely to be to orders that are less rigorous, less aspiring. Surely to live the life and keep the rule of Carmel is to proclaim oneself a "*belle âme*" and to belong no more to the legion of "*les petits*".

Her answer to this, I think, would be that her doctrine of spiritual childhood is even more necessary in the cloister than in the world. In convents no doubt there are many "*belles âmes*", but there is also a place for "*les petits*". The call to perfection in the religious life is "leave all and follow me," and it is comparatively unimportant whether that all be much or little. When the bridegroom says to the bride "with all my worldly goods I thee endow" he may be speaking of many thousands a year or only of this week's wages. So it is with those who enter even Carmel, and doubtless Thérèse was aware that vocations have been lost through a mistaken idea that more will be required of the soul than it has to give. Hence she taught her Little Way first of all to her novices. There is a place for children in the cloister as well as by the hearth.

Another reason, which is not however one that I believe she herself would give, is the same as that which sets the dancing mistress on a platform in front of her pupils. She must be in a certain degree beyond them and above them so that they can hear her voice and observe her steps more clearly. To drop all similes—how much should we have heard of Thérèse and her Little Way if she had not entered Carmel but had spent her life either as Mademoiselle Martin, given to good works in the parish, or as the busy wife of some citizen of Lisieux? We cannot picture her setting the town alight, like St. Rose, from a cell in her father's garden, nor is it likely that she would have thought of writing the story of her soul. She might have just been as holy, just as dear to God, she might have taught her Little Way to her catechism class or to her own children. But we ourselves would probably have been none the wiser nor the better for it.

She wrote *Histoire d'une Âme* at the order of her religious superiors, and it was they who published it after her death. I will not say that but for that book she would have been unknown, for the scenes at her funeral, decorous as they were compared with those at St. Rose's, suggest that the rumour of her holiness had spread into the town. But it was her book that carried it like a forest fire through the whole land of France and finally throughout the world.

Thérèse, in spite of her obscure life and early death, was canonised by popular acclamation. The decree of Pope Urban VIII which has been haunting us all through this book was set aside in her favour. Fifty years is the decreed minimum, but Thérèse was canonised in 1925, less than thirty years after her death of pulmonary tuberculosis in the Carmel of Lisieux.

The special time concession made in her case was no doubt partly due to the war of 1914-18, which established her firmly as a wonder-worker. When we think of this little girl, and remember the sheltered obscurity of her life, it is difficult not to smile when we realise that the most vocal, indeed vociferous, of her clients were the rank and file of the French army, whose protector through innumerable dangers, whose adviser in situations well beyond her earthly ken, or indeed imagination, she became—"*petite Soeur Thérèse*," the *poilu's* friend.

But it was not only the army. From convents throughout the world, from the mission field, from the hospitals, from countless families came the tale of her favours. "After my death I will let fall a shower of roses." Those words were spoken in sober conviction and have been fulfilled in sober fact. There is no doubt whatever that the dying Thérèse was convinced that she had a mission in the world which could be carried out only after her death. She was completely and innocently confident. "In heaven God will do everything I wish." There with her last breath speaks the loving, trustful child of Louis Martin.

Her reputation as a wonder-worker might well have brought her into that dim, unhealthy borderland where religion fringes off into superstition. She herself would seem to be aware of this and to protect herself (and her clients) by bestowing favours that are mainly spiritual. It is true that many remarkable cures are said to be due to her intercession, also escapes from danger and death. But the fish in her net are mostly those whose lives have been changed either by her doctrine or by some more personal contact with her power, converts from heresy and schism, from paganism, from sin, from indifference, wandering souls brought by her into the Father's house. She herself while on earth had not much patience with those who indulged in spiritual sensation. Once when a rapturous novice told her that "the most beautiful angels clothed in white robes, with shining joyful faces" would carry her soul to heaven, she tartly reminded her that "God and the angels are pure spirit and no one can see them with bodily eyes". She would, one feels sure, have very little sympathy with Christians who regard heaven as a departmental store and the saints as universal providers; and already it has been rumoured that if asked too persistently for material benefits she will bestow instead what amounts to a sharp rap.

In another respect, too, she has protected herself. *Histoire d'une Âme*, besides being both a spiritual and a human document, is also a defence against the hagiographers. Impossible for them to distort or emasculate the human base on which divine grace has worked its wonders or to exaggerate or solidify that grace's spiritual effects. Admittedly the work has been edited here and there, but that is mainly for reasons of discretion, since so recent was her earthly life that even now it involves the names of many people still living. We have her own story, every word of which bears the stamp of modesty and truth.

I wish I could say the same of the illustrations. Obviously, whether photographs or reproductions of paintings, they have been worked upon and "improved" out of accuracy if not veracity. "The Servant of God," we are told, "would when posing sometimes lose the natural repose of her features." This very human characteristic has, unfortunately, been made good by a most unnatural repose, indeed by a "very conscientious synthesis" of the "best elements" of all the photographs. Those who have the good fortune to possess an untouched photograph of St. Thérèse will turn with relief from the smooth, simpering smugness of the synthesis to the cheerful little round French face with its dark laughing eyes and only just not laughing mouth. As for the statues . . . . we can only say that the hagiographers having lost their chance in prose, have seized it in plaster.

But none of this really matters, and for the sake of Thérèse's spirit and her word we will gladly face all the horrors of her cultus. She comes with a special message for an age that badly needs new inspiration. It is an age that has lost its aristocracy, its kings, its geniuses, its great men. It is an age of mass production, of mediocrity, of democracy, the rank and file, the common man. Submerging equally the depths and the heights spreads the great ocean of the average. But even on the face of those dreary waters the Spirit of God can move and call forth life. Thérèse's call is to the average man, who in our day exists for the first time as a real person instead of a statistical calculation. She calls even him to be a saint.

Some Notes on the Nature of Sanctity

IT is significant that the word "holiness" derives from
the same root as "wholeness", the Anglo-Saxon
halig, whole or healthy, leaving us with the conception of the
holy man as the only whole man, the perfect man of God's
creative idea. Following that tendency which we have to twist
words off their roots, holiness has come to mean for most of us
almost the opposite of wholeness or completeness. It suggests
rather a man of one idea, a single-track mind, an outlook
narrowed by religion till it excludes half the activities of normal
humanity. Whereas the holy man is really the only kind of
man in which the type is fully realised.

As we look down the scale of life we see what appears to
be an ever-increasing wastefulness, so that in order to produce the perfect type of, say, a fish, millions of incomplete,
imperfect types are made and rejected by what we call Nature.
In the birds and animals the waste is much less, and in man
the tendency of science and civilisation has been to reduce
it to almost nothing. But the question arises: Would a whole
nation of healthy, intelligent men and women realise the idea
in the mind of God when he said "Let us make man in our own
image"?

The answer which Christianity gives to this question is
unhesitatingly: No. Apart from the consideration that few
human beings really enjoy perfect health in mind and body,
the central fact of Christian teaching is the fall of man in Adam
from God's idea of him and his restoration in the second Adam
to at least the potentialities of that idea.

Treading warily and restraining our words lest we should babble, we pause to contemplate the first man lifting up his eyes to heaven. In that upward look is his whole significance as man. Mentally and spiritually, Adam is a child—a child at ease as children are with forms of life below him, yet looking with desire and expectation to forms of life above, forms of which his vision, though remote, is unclouded, for he is the truly clean of heart who can see God.

Adam is the primal innocent. But as the oak is in the acorn, so in him is the complete, full-grown man of God's desire. Growing up directly under the hand of God, in a world of ordered tranquillity, human nature should have attained its fulfilment in the supernatural as simply and painlessly as the acorn attains fulfilment in the oak. But the process was deflected by a will seduced in its turn by pride and the love of things-in-themselves, so that the natural lost its power of growth and harmony with the supernatural, and can attain it only in conflict, in harshness, in hammering. The tree has become the cross.

This is the cross which no human soul can escape, no matter how he blasphemes it or denies it. The impenitent thief hung on the cross as long and as agonisedly as the good Dismas. The rift between the natural and the supernatural is one that affects us all. The merely natural man cannot take his ease comfortably and happily in the natural, because of that supernatural cross-beam to which willy-nilly his hands are raised. While the natural holds fast by the feet the supernatural man who longs to escape and tread the sky. This is the bed that we have made, and we must lie on it because we are nailed to it. Only the fact that the Son of Man who is also the Son of God was also nailed to this antinomy gives us the hope that one day we may be with him in paradise, where the cross once more becomes the tree—the Tree of Life.

2

The word supernatural as I use it here does not necessarily involve the preternatural. It is a word which common use has shrivelled into a fragment of its true meaning. If we were to see the title *Tales of the Supernatural*, most of us would expect a volume of ghost stories rather than lives of the saints. Now a ghost can rightly be called preternatural or beyond the ordinary course of nature, but it is not likely to be supernatural or above it. Whereas a saint is a human being raised to a supernatural level by the grace of God. He may also have certain preternatural powers, but such powers are not the inevitable accompaniment of sanctity and can in fact exist where it is not, or even apart from Christianity itself. Their appearance in some of the saints is part of an individual reaction to spiritual contacts which in a different human being would find a different expression.

We have seen how even in the supposed darkness of the sixteenth century, the committee of theologians appointed to investigate the spiritual life of St. Rose told her that her visions were "imaginary", that is projections of that image-making faculty which we all possess, but which in most of us functions only in our dreams. In saying this they cast no doubt on the reality of the experience which the image more or less symbolically (as in a dream) expressed. It was only the translation of that experience into visual terms which was the work of her own special mind and temperament.

The mind naturally takes and shapes in its own colours an experience which is properly speaking incommunicable in any shape or colour. Even the words, the message, of the vision can be edited by the transmitting mind, hence the Church's refusal to guarantee the supernatural origin of any "private revelation".

"We certainly are and contain far more than we can

deliberately become aware of at any given moment. Is it possible that among these presentations which we cannot recapture
in reflex knowledge there are flashes of the infinite? That we
cannot recapture them does not prove that they have not come
to us. On the other hand, they can hardly come without leaving
some traces behind. Other presentations will have been
affected; something deeper than the activity of reflex knowledge
will have been modified in such a way as to qualify the whole
content of reflex knowledge; if there has been indeed a divine
touch our sinew will have shrunk."

I quote this passage from Mr. Algar Thordd's introduction
to *Readings from Friedrich von Hügel*, because it expresses this
double experience—the divine touch which is supernatural
and its human transmission which may be preternatural but
more often is entirely natural. We are bound to realise that the
realm of nature is steadily enlarging itself. Much that was
thought to be outside it is now known to be well within, and
it is possible that our not very remote descendants may see the
swallowing up by nature of a whole realm which we have
hitherto considered beyond it.

The state of mind which is responsible for having loaded up
the miraculous with so much that is merely abnormal cannot
be attributed entirely to religious obscurantism. Science has
been to blame in its refusal in investigate alleged preternatural
happenings on the simple assumption that they do not happen.
The rank and file of nineteenth-century scientists (though certain of their leaders were less dogmatic) rejected out of hand
such phenomena as telepathy and even hypnotism. As a result
there was nothing for those who had direct personal experience
of them to do, if they did not attribute them to fraud or doubt
the evidence of their senses, but regard them as miraculous.

It is not till quite recently that Dr. J. B. Rhine's experiments
at Duke University, North Carolina, have made not only
telepathy but clairvoyance and prevision scientifically respectable. They have proved that extra-sensory perceptions exist

in most people, probably in all. Certainly the field investi-
gated is very narrow, but it is no longer possible to deny
out of hand that human beings have been able to foretell the
future, know what is happening at distance, or even produce
certain visible effects on inanimate objects.

It is however just as difficult to maintain that these powers
are supernatural. They seem to be latent in us all; and it is
merely a question as to whether they are newly-discovered
faculties awaiting development or atrophying vestiges of powers
we have lost. Dr. Rhine inclines to the former view. Certainly
many of the saints have displayed remarkable gifts of extra-
sensory perception, and though the possession of such gifts
does not make them saints, I do not think we can say they
have no connection with sanctity. Indeed we may well believe
that certain spiritual impacts have such a stimulating and
enlarging effect that the whole man, including these latent
natural powers, is brought into action. In this way we come
back to the idea of the holy man as the whole man, and may
speculate as to whether the loss or rather latency of our extra-
sensory powers is not just another of the effects of the Fall.
But even so we must not regard these powers as in themselves
supernatural or indeed more capable of being supernatural
than our so ordinary powers of eating and drinking and
growing and loving which God has made the basis of his
sacraments.

Another direction in which the natural has enlarged itself
and swallowed the preternatural is in psychology. Here it has
made rapid progress and even if it may be said to have gobbled
its fare and will have later on to disgorge some of it, the fact
remains that many things which used to be considered supernatural must now be regarded as unusual but perfectly natural
activities of the human mind. We have no cause to feel superior
to those who with the limited means of investigation at their
disposal were misled by certain appearances; on the other hand
it would be unpardonable of us to be misled in the same way.

We can no longer regard, for instance, the appearance of stigmata as miraculous, since we now know that similar phenomena can be produced apparently at will by certain hysteric subjects. There still remains all the difference in heaven and earth between St. Francis of Assisi and a patient at the Salpetrière, but that difference must now be looked for in causes rather than in effects.

We cannot altogether withhold our sympathy from the popular craving for the miraculous. A God shut up in his own creation as in a box is not really "large enough to wear the garment of the universe". Nevertheless that credulous, avid, and (as Von Hügel calls it) unethical acceptance of miracle stories can be just as shocking as the closed mind that insists on equally poor evidence that miracles do not happen. It is certainly contrary to the mind of the Church, which declares as "of faith" only the miracles of Scripture and the canonisation miracles of the saints. The latter are post-mortem signals from another world—Holy Church knows only too well the tricks our minds and bodies can play us in this.

For we must face the fact that a certain type of holiness is often, indeed usually, associated with some kind of psycho-physical disturbance. Is it possible to imagine that the perfectly fitting, smoothly running mind responds less readily to inspirations of a certain order than one which is a little out of gear? "Unhinged" we say . . . . and we can picture the Divine Thief passing down the street between all the snug, sleeping, shuttered houses, till he comes to one where a window is broken or a door swinging loose, so that he can effect an entry. There we must drop the simile, for he comes not to take but to give.

Von Hügel offers the alternative suggestion that certain impacts of the supernatural are too weighty for the delicately adjusted mechanisms of the human mind, and that "those who have enjoyed a full mystical experience, i.e. a direct experience of God's presence, have also suffered from some kind of nervous or mental illness".* This certainly applies to our two mystics, St. Catherine and St. Rose, neither of whom can be considered psychologically normal, while our two non-mystical subjects, Cornelia Connelly and St. Thérèse, are not only without pathological symptoms but would seem to have minds of exceptional integrity and stability. Perhaps it is the directness of the mystical contact which overbalances the psyche; the supernatural is not mediated through the natural, but pours straight into the unconscious mind, and there it may create various disturbances before it enters the narrower channels of consciousness.

It must be remembered, however, that both St. Catherine and St. Rose showed abnormal symptoms apart from religion. Indeed St. Catherine had lived twenty-seven years before her first mystical experience, during which time her mental condition had steadily deteriorated, so that the supernatural impact was in her case not an overbalancing but the recovery of a balance lost. But for it she might have become a hopeless neurotic. St. Rose too shows throughout her life the spiritualising of abnormal impulses which without religion might have become unhealthy and repulsive.

It is remarkable that both our mystics were women who apart from their visions, fasts and ecstasies, led lives full of active works of charity. Catherine was for years the matron of a large hospital, and risked her life nursing the plague-stricken, while Rose not only nursed the sick in her own home and visited them in theirs but worked hard to support her family. The mystical element seems to demand its own active expression in the outer material world, which makes an important difference between the genuine mystic and the psychopath whose impulses not only arise but end within the self.

Comparing the mystical and non-mystical types of holiness, it would be presumptuous to say which more nearly approaches the whole man of God's intention. The mystic would seem to

★ *The Life of Friedrich von Hügel* by Michael de la Bedoyere, p. 109.

have powers which the non-mystical saint has not, but he pays the price in psycho-physical imperfections. The non-mystical saint, on the other hand, usually shows exceptional depth and stability of mind, while he is without those more impressive manifestations which attract while they also discourage the ordinary Christian. There is not, of course, always the clear-cut division between the types that we have in my quartet. Had I included, for instance, St. Francis of Assisi or St. John Vianney, or St. John Bosco or St. Frances of Rome, outlines would have been more blurred.

One might indeed imagine that the perfect realisation of the type is not the work of any one saint. Our human nature has perhaps been too badly damaged in its fall to be able to fulfil God's purpose individually. So the Whole Man becomes the corporate effect of a corporate holiness, of the Communion of Saints, and our hope lies in that fullness which the virtues and merits and intercessions of the saints, together with the best impulses, thoughts, words and works of every one of us, the body of the Head, shall build up one day into the measure of the stature of the fullness of Christ.

3

It may still be possible, however, to make out of all the multiplicity and variety of holiness which has accompanied the history of the Church, at least a rough sketch of that whole man of God's intention. We have hazarded the guess that with such a man the supernatural instead of being a disruptive, crucifying force would be a normal part of his daily life, like Adam's walk with God in "the afternoon air".

In turn we may guess at a very different relation with the natural, created world from the struggling uneasiness which is our portion now. This would include our relation to our own bodies, which is obviously not that of paradise. Sickness and pain, like death, are the fruit of "man's first disobedience": and the lack of harmony between soul and body, the warfare of the spirit and the flesh, is another example of the tree become the cross.

It is a cross which the greatest, the most spiritual, of the saints have had to bear. But every now and then we find among them glimpses of the tree—of a soul asserting its power not only to subdue but to strengthen and vivify the body. The fasts undertaken by St. Catherine of Genoa and St. Rose of Lima not only exceeded the powers of average humanity, but instead of reducing them to weakness increased their vitality and physical health. St. Francis of Assisi, too, was able to follow the example of Our Lord's perfect human nature and fast throughout the forty days of Lent, though out of humility he broke the fast midway, in case he should seem presumptuously to emulate his Master. And if we should think such instances belong only to an earlier, tougher generation, there is the recent case of Father Kolbe, a victim of chronic lung disease, whom nevertheless the Nazis failed to starve in a concentration camp but had to slaughter with an injection. It would seem as if much of the slowness and stumbling of Brother Ass were due to insufficient practice and skill on the part of his rider.

Another extension of the soul's power over the body is the gift of healing. No matter how much we may wish to avoid sensationalism and miracle-mongering, we cannot deny its existence, though we may think that healing would have had no place in a world where sickness and suffering did not exist, and that the gift of healing must be the diversion of a power originally intended for another purpose—for the maintenance, let us say, of our physical integrity rather than of its restoration. It is as it were a little model of redemption, and in Our Lord's constant, compassionate use of it we can see the reflected image of that far greater act by which he restored the world from death to life.

He promised his followers that they too should have this power: "These signs shall follow them that believe . . . . they shall lay hands on the sick and they shall recover"; and the history of the Church, from the earliest times down to the present day, is full of instances of natural health restored by supernatural grace and the body made whole by the spirit. The circumstances may vary from personal contacts during their earthly lives with such saints as Rose of Lima or Pope Pius X, to power transmitted from another world in the after-death miracles of innumerable saints and *beati* or manifested at certain shrines of Our Lady, such as Lourdes. I am writing of cures that are far removed from ordinary faith-healing, cures of organic disease that have stood the test of medical examination. It would not be profitable here to enter into the physical mechanics of spiritual healing, but it is interesting to note that the cures seem to depart no whit from the normal, natural course—the site of an ulcer, for instance, will be marked by "scar tissue"—except in the matter of time, which is enormously expedited. There is nothing abnormal in the cures (to choose modern examples) of the Abbé Fiammia's varicose veins and Madame Augault's fibroid tumour except the suddenness with which they took place. It is also worth noting that a cure of this nature seems first to happen in the mind, which becomes overwhelmingly convinced of the body's well-being and indeed sometimes (as in the case of Jack Trayner) temporarily forgets the illness that had incapacitated it for years. Once again we find that the supernatural touch is on the unconscious, where it possibly organises resources that later are passed into consciousness and finally into action. It was Mr. C. S. Lewis who suggested that but for the Fall the whole of our unconscious would be available to us at will, instead of being shut off in subliminal darkness, from which it often frightens us with ghostly noises.

Another, rarer, aspect of the saint's relation to the natural world, one with which it would seem that the unconscious has little to do, is the terms on which he lives with those whom God put there before him. Adam entered a world already well-furnished and well-organised. It was like arriving at a house which the servants had made ready for comfortable occupation. There is a passage in Jane Austen's *Sense and Sensibility* which describes the servants' delight when the long-expected family at last arrives at the cottage they have been preparing for them. Is it fanciful to picture a similar feeling of joyful relief throughout the world when at long last, after all the successive ages of its history, the master of the house appeared?

Alas! events did not bear out the promise of that coming. If the master of the house did not actually, like the bad steward in the parable, beat the manservants and the maidservants, he nevertheless failed to give them the help and comfort they looked for. We are of course only groping our way through dark sayings, but it seems possible, indeed probable, that God gave man a task to perform for the "other ranks" of nature, a task which he has not fulfilled. We are told that God "gave" Adam the plants and beasts and birds, and we cannot imagine that such a gift would have been for his selfish enjoyment only. His perfection according to God's plan would also have included theirs, for though none but man is made in God's immortal image, the supernatural order is not for him alone. But man has denied Nature her baptism, leaving her "with his salt in her mouth to thirst after him".

This primal guilt is upon us as well as our many later conscious abuses of creatures and breaches of natural law, so it is not surprising that the world around us, apart from certain individuals that we have tamed, seems aloof and indifferent to our joys and sorrows. The friendship of Nature is one of the joys of heaven, a part of the doctrine of the resurrection of the body, just as her undying resentment is one of the pains of hell, so it is fitting that those whose lives are heavenly should have a foretaste of this joy. We do not find, perhaps, so many instances of it in the lives of the saints as we find of preternatural happenings, but this may be partly due to the relative unimportance such a relationship would have in the eyes of their chroniclers. St. Francis of Assisi is of course the classic example, but in our quartet we have another just as impressive in St. Rose. Indeed her communion with Nature had a wider base than his since it included not only conscious living creatures but unconscious plants and flowers. She loved trees and bushes and flowers as she loved all things God had made, even mosquitoes, and had over them the power of love. With them she blessed God for their life: "O all ye green things upon the earth, bless ye the Lord—all ye birds of the air, all ye wild beasts and tame, bless ye the Lord, praise and exalt Him above all for ever."

At a first glance no other member of our quartet seems to feel the same closeness with humble created things. Then we recall a sentence from *Histoire d'une Âme* and realise that St. Thérèse too felt their kinship, and felt it with that most independent and least sympathetic of all natural manifestations, the weather. "In all the circumstances of my life, Nature was the reflection of my soul. When I cried the heavens cried with me, when I rejoiced not a cloud would darken the blue sky." Then as if she heard us murmur "the pathetic fallacy", she tells how for the whole of three days, when her hopes of Carmel were in suspense because of her uncle's opposition, "the sun did not show a single gleam and the rain fell in torrents". But when at last she had won Monsieur Guérin's consent, "I walked back to Les Buissonets under a blue sky from which the clouds had totally disappeared". And yet again, after her appeal to the Pope had apparently failed, "the sun did not dare to shine and the beautiful Italian sky, burdened with heavy clouds, did not cease to weep for me".

A cynic might suggest that this meteorological sympathy was in gratitude for the pleasure she took in kinds of weather which are not generally found pleasing. As a child she had delighted in thunderstorms that scared her elders, and there is:

"Mother, did I ever tell you of my predilection for the snow?"
She attributed this to her being born in winter and having the
snow among her very first impressions of the world. We have
already seen the fall of snow that graced the day of her clothing.
Like her birthday it was in winter and she had wanted to see
Nature clothed like herself in white. But through January the
weather was mild, and she gave up all hope of a snowfall until,
on entering the enclosure after the ceremony, she looked round
and saw the courtyard of the convent white with snow. "O ye
ice and snow, bless ye the Lord . . . O ye cold and winter, bless
ye the Lord. . . ." It was winter's icy sword that pierced her
lungs and brought her where even the weather and the seasons
have their share in the redemption of our body.

It is not only piety or poetry which calls upon the whole
order of created things, including the winds and the rain and
the frost and the snow and the thunder, to join in the priest's
thanksgiving after Mass. The benefits of calvary are not for
man alone, and in the perpetuation of that sacrifice Nature
has already ceased her groaning and has entered with us into
the paradise of the Second Adam. "*Benedicite omnia opera*. . . .
O all ye works of the Lord, bless ye the Lord, praise him and
magnify him for ever." The three Young Men in the furnace
sang their song of unity and kinship in the heart of man's
greatest natural enemy, devouring fire, which as they walked
to and fro in its midst with the Son of God, had been transformed into the friendly likeness of "a wind that bringeth
dew".

4

So far we have considered those qualities which are as it
were scattered among the saints but are by no means to be
found in all of them. Preternatural powers and a new relationship with the created world are not essential to sanctity, since

many saints are without one or the other or either, and we have suggested that the Whole Man of holiness may indeed be a composite figure, represented by the entire Communion of Saints rather than by any individual.

But there are certain fundamental qualities which no saint can be without, because it is they which make him a saint. The others are indeed more than decorations, but they are not indispensable; that is they are not indispensable in this world—they may be gifts that will be supplied later. But none of us can get to heaven at all without at least a pinch of two qualities which in the saints are present to a heroic degree—the qualities of love and suffering.

There has, of course, never been a saint who has not loved God. "The good man without God" has existed in the past and doubtless still does so to a diminishing extent, but his title is a misnomer, for however consciously or conscientiously he may ally himself with unbelief, his goodness, if not the after-glow of a Christian upbringing, is at least the reflection of a Christian civilisation. As it is possible to receive the Baptism of Desire without even having heard of the Sacrament, so it is possible to love God without consciously believing in him. But such a love is not likely to exist in the heroic degree demanded by sanctity. The saint's love of God is not the tranquil adaptation that passes for love with so many Christians, but a complete self-giving, a consuming passion that makes a holocaust of the entire life.

That is why such a vast proportion of saints have either joined or founded religious orders, parting with all they possessed and loved on earth in order to follow Our Lord more closely in a life wholly given to perfection. Others who for various reasons have not entered the cloister, have like St. Catherine of Genoa lived a life of voluntary poverty and chastity in their own homes. Others, yet again, like St. Turribius, St. Francis Xavier and many more heroic missionaries, have braved exile and sickness and danger to carry God's name to regions where it is unknown; and many have offered the supreme sacrifice of life itself for the sake of his truth and his glory.

All these acts of renunciation, whether of goods or love or freedom or of life, are changed from negative to positive by the consuming love that offers them. The entering of little Thérèse Martin into Carmel at fifteen can never be seen as a negative act of withdrawal, because it is so obviously the expression of a love which cannot wait till it has given all. Little Rose de Flores, of a more fearful disposition, seems at first to have taken a negative flight from sin into her garden; but love has changed flight to fight with deeds of heroic penance, by which she makes reparation for the sins of the New World. Cornelia Connelly's cry of love in that other garden at Gracemere, "Oh God, if all this happiness be not for thy glory, take it from me," starts a life not of mere passive endurance but of heroic achievement crowned by that mysterious *magnum opus* (the spiritual fulfilment of the alchemists' age-long quest) by which the base metal of sin itself is transformed into the pure gold of God's glory.

But love is a two-edged sword and no man who ever loved God did not love his neighbour. Most of us find one easier than the other, but each is meaningless without the other. In the saints the love of God has produced an overflowing measure of love for man. The history of their service and affection would run into almost endless lists of good works. St. Vincent de Paul, St. Jerome Aemilian, St. Peter Nolasco, St. John Baptist de la Salle, St. Peter Claver, St. John Bosco, to say nothing of Santa Claus (St. Nicholas of Myra) . . . one could go on adding to these till the list of philanthropists is nearly as long as the list of martyrs. These founded schools, hospitals, and orphanages, started societies for the redemption of captives for the support of foundlings, for the care of the dying, and so on and so on till almost every need of man is covered, as well as ministering with their own hands to slaves, to the sick and plague-stricken, to the old, to the lonely and the poor.

In our own quartet we find a saint even as solitary and withdrawn as St. Catherine becoming the active heart of a large hospital, working long hours in the wards with her prayers upon her like a veil, ready for the dying with a kiss. St. Rose comes straight from her visions of the sinless Son of God and his ever-virgin Mother to minister to the diseased bodies and souls of prostitutes. Cornelia Connelly enlarged her love of her own lost family into the love of countless children from other homes, to whom she brought the gift of a wise and enlightened education. The last member of our quartet might seem at first to have done no work in her neighbour's house. But in order to see the fullness of St. Thérèse's love for mankind we must look beyond her death into that heavenly life which she declared she would spend in doing good upon earth. Seen from that angle she is certainly not among the least of the servants of mankind.

5

The quality of love is one which all men, even those for whom religion has no special meaning, expect to find in sanctity. The average man may appreciate it most when it is expressed in good works for the neighbour, but none would ever imagine a saint without some form of it. The presence of suffering in a saint's life is something quite different, for it is a state which the mass of humanity regards as evil, as a thing to be shunned, or if present to be at once removed. If it cannot be removed it often becomes a stumbling block to faith.

The saints, says the average man, should be joyful. The Church says the same, and it might surprise the average man to know that a saint cannot be canonised without having shown

in his life the quality of joy. Apparently one can achieve beatification without a smile, but the saint must positively rejoice.
The point, however, is not that he rejoices when things go
well with him (he would be an ungrateful churl if he did not)
but that he does so at those probably more frequent times when
they go badly. I am not of course thinking here of that dismal
cheeriness which sails over troubles on the floating planks of
clichés and forced smiles, and is as much out of place in a saint's
life as the grin-and-bear-it of the stoics, but of that deep-
keeled joy which leaves its wake upon waters that can never
overwhelm it and are indeed its stormy way to heaven.

Suffering is a part of the mystery of evil and any attempt
to explain it is to risk the fate of those who rush in where
angels fear to tread. All we dare say for certain is that it is due
to sin and therefore in its present form makes no part of that
Whole Man of God's intention. I say "in its present form",
because Von Hügel has suggested that something akin to suffering, though profoundly different from it as we know it now,
may have been a part of God's creative plan and *may* be present
even in heaven.

Père Louis Bouyer in his most exciting book *Le Mystère
Pascal* makes it clear that the immolation of a victim is not
an essential part of sacrifice and is made necessary only by sin.
The sacrifice that God originally intended was a sacrifice of praise
and thanksgiving from all his creatures, a eucharist of joy. It is
this sacrifice which finds its liturgical fulfilment in the Sanctus
of the Mass. "Therefore with angels and archangels, thrones
and dominations and all the warriors of the heavenly array,
we sing an endless hymn in praise of thee, saying: Holy, Holy,
Holy Lord God of Hosts. Thy glory fills all heaven and earth.
Hosanna in high heaven!"

It was man's sin and God's mercy which wrote between them
the *Qui pridie* and all that follows. Without sin there would have
been no immolation, no death on Calvary, such as are re-pre-
sented bloodlessly on our altars and bloodily foreshadowed in

the holocausts of the Jewish Law. Sin requires death, so sacrifice has come to imply the destruction of the victim, and the human life which should have been a natural-supernatural act of love and joy, becomes instead an immolation, and the closer the union of the man with God the greater his share in the sufferings of Christ.

"What would be the use?" asked St. Rose of those who begged her to invoke her powerful patron St. Catherine of Siena to relieve her sufferings, "she'd only ask me if I imagined I could get to heaven any other way."

The cross is as it were the skeleton of sanctity, the hard frame hidden in the kindness, the love and the power; and suffering is not merely important but essential in the lives of all the saints, though its prominence varies according to the particular build and constitution of the man or woman concerned. In our own quartet we find that with two it is cushioned under softer qualities, while in the other two it is the very shape of their lives. St. Catherine may be said to have suffered more *before* her conversion than afterwards, because then her suffering was hopeless and fruitless, whereas later she was to make it an instrument of penitence and a source of ever-growing purification. However, when her four years of penance and reparation were at an end, she continued to practise poverty and self-denial and to endure conditions of mind and body that must have been a humiliation to her soaring spirit. Nevertheless both she and St. Thérèse are less striking examples in this field than St. Rose and Mother Connelly; she because she seems to be living already half in another world, Thérèse because in keeping with her vocation as the saint of "*les petits*", she suffered as it were in a small way from afflictions that are common to us all, instead of treading the high ground of anguish, either of self-inflicted penance with St. Rose or of Mother Connelly's devoted endurance of another's scourge.

But the sufferings of the saints are only leading us straight into the thickets of another wood, another mystery. They show us suffering as a vicarious condition in which the innocent suffer for the guilty. This may not be so difficult to accept in a case like that of St. Rose (with her male counterpart, St. Aloysius of Gonzaga), where a creature almost without sin is impelled by her horror of it to inflict suffering on herself. The stumbling block lies in the involuntary, unsought sufferings of the innocent, of children and animals, and of good men who have deserved nothing but good. But, just as the victim of the Mosaic holocaust had to be "without blemish", so there is a mysterious efficacy in unmerited pain. The agonies of the impenitent thief brought no one, not even himself, any spiritual good, while those of St. Dismas may well have done penance only for his own sins. The supreme alliance between suffering and innocence is once again to be found in the sinless figure on the central cross, the immaculate Lamb of God whose death has taken away the sins of the whole world.

One may picture suffering as, potentially at least, a force existing to repair the ravages of sin, just as there are bodily forces whose function is to repair bodily injury—phagocytes that the bloodstream carries to the site of the damage to conflict with invading microbes and injurious substances, setting up conditions of resistance and cure that involve pain and inflammation. Where the blood is itself impure in any way the cure will not be so swift or so certain as where it is healthy. So the blood of the living organism, the Body of Christ, carries the repairing force to the seat of the infection. . . . But we had better extricate ourselves from this analogy before it has involved us any further, and take one which is an analogy God himself has used.

Throughout the scriptures we constantly find suffering symbolised by wine, either in its drinking or making, the chalice or the wine-press. The prophet sees the Beautiful One on his way from Edom "with garments deep dyed", and asks, "Why dost thou go clad like the men who tread out the wine-press?" to be answered: "None other has trodden the wine-press but I only." Our Lord cries to his apostles: "Can ye drink of the cup that I shall drink of?" and to his Father he cries: "Father, if it be possible, let this chalice pass from me." While at the very end and sealing of the scriptures, among the clouds of the Apocalypse, the champion of Edom rides out again, faithful and true, clothed with a garment dipped in blood, to tread the wine-press of the wrath of God Almighty.

The process of wine-making, by which the grape is trodden underfoot or crushed in the press until its juice runs out like blood suggests the expiatory aspect of suffering, the amends made to God's justice, the shedding of blood without which there is no remission of sin. No doubt the resemblance of wine to blood inspired this symbolism, and according to Hebrew doctrine "the blood is the life". But the life-blood of the grape, even after all the waste matter of crushed skin and pips has been strained away, has not yet become the draught in the chalice. Suffering in itself can achieve nothing and it is only when it as it were ferments within the soul that the cup can be filled. A period of mysterious but intense activity has followed that of passivity in the wine-press, the nature of the thing is changing —disintegrating, re-forming. In wine-growing districts it is possible even to hear the murmuring movements of the wine in the vats as it changes into itself. So in the minds and hearts of the saints and all who would be like them suffering is an activity that in the end produces a new creature. The crushed and beaten fruit has become wine and the chalice is full of that which is mysteriously the symbol not only of pain and sorrow but of health and joy. This is the final mystery and paradox.

6

Before ending these notes on the saintly character it might be interesting to consider two qualities that seem to be absent from it, as if, much as we value them in human nature, they form no essential part of that whole, supernatural man of God's intention. The saints generally speaking (there are, of course, exceptions) seem to be lacking in a sense of humour and in a sense of artistic beauty.

The first need not perhaps surprise us. A sense of humour as we understand it now in the ability to laugh at ourselves and in the light handling of our daily lives in general and particularly of awkward and dangerous situations, the laughter of the air-raid shelter and the battle-field, is a comparatively recent growth. The early humour of a civilisation is not unlike the early humour of the individual, an affair of clowning and noisy laughter at the misfortunes of other people, the antics of the tumblers, the jesters, the coloured comics, Shakespeare's clowns and the broker's men in pantomime. There is a softened, Christianised version of all this in the *Fioretti* of St. Francis, where Brother Juniper becomes as it were the jester of the little court of friars, but we can well believe that buffoonery has no part in the lives of the saints. The Renaissance brought wit to courts and universities and gave us at least one witty saint in St. Thomas More, but public laughter still remained noisy, vulgar and often cruel. So it is not surprising to find that only the two more modern of our quartet can smile.

Von Hügel laments that St. Catherine had not a vestige of humour, and in St. Rose its presence is doubtful, though I am inclined to believe that her instructions to those visitors who objected to being stung by her pet mosquitoes are not entirely "straight". Cornelia Connelly on the other hand considered gaiety indispensable to holiness, and blamed herself for "misplaced gravity" during those first dreary days at the Trinità dei Monti; and though gaiety is not necessarily humour there is certainly a humorous strength in her face as the photographer has given it to us—humour in the wide, expressive mouth and even in the pleading eyes. But I would be prepared to say that it was a quality that came to her comparatively late in life, and born, as humour so often is, of her sorrows. Had she had it in any effectual abundance during the early years of her marriage, would she have allowed Pierce to dominate her so heavily? I think that he, as well as herself, would have escaped much suffering had he in his younger days sometimes been laughed at. Instead of which he was always deferred to and obeyed from a bleeding heart. A more practised sense of humour in his wife might have spared him the consequences of its total absence in himself.

Indeed the only one of my quartet who truly and obviously has this useful gift is little Thérèse. It is not of a particularly brilliant or subtle kind, but only someone with a sense of humour would have held a mussel-shell under the eyes of a weeping novice to catch her silly tears. I also suspect humour in her appraisement of the convent's cookery when, on being given a thoroughly bad dinner, she abandoned her custom of offering the various dishes to the different members of the Holy Family, saying instead: "*Aujourd'hui, ma petite fille, tout cela c'est pour toi.*"

But on the whole we must acknowledge that humour is not prominent in the lives of the saints, nor in spite of the fact that the Church was founded with a pun can we see in it any great affinity with the supernatural. Its main psychological function is the release of inhibitions and it is also a sort of cushion between ourselves and the hard realities of life. Instinctively we laugh at what shocks us—how well we know the loud, nervous laugh that rings through the theatre at a "blue" joke—and this explains the primitive tendency to laugh at other people's misfortunes, as well as the more subtle grace of laughing at our own. But however much we may need it here and now and may suffer from its absence or its loss, we cannot regard it as one of the eternal gifts of God. It is something quite apart from the joy which we know the saints must display if they are to be recognised as such by the Church; indeed it has its roots in frustration and sorrow. It is a this-world quality, a solace on the way, and though no doubt the saints of the modern world will continue to show it increasingly, its absence in others need not disappoint us as if it were the absence of a virtue. All they are without is a comfort they may not need.

But the case is altered when we come to beauty, for here we have no travellers' joy but a value we believe to be eternal, an attribute of God himself. How can it be that so many saints and holy people seem to regard it with indifference, even with distrust. St. Rose hated and defaced her own beauty, and St. Thérèse, wise and alert in most of her appraisements, combines her spiritual efficiency with a most inadequate performance in the fields of poetry and art. No doubt it is only a few who are scandalised by the fact that so many who live close to God in every other way should either ignore his beauty or translate it into the language of the second-rate. But such a scandal exists, and one can only wish to spread it as one sees on every side the degradation of beauty in the very quarters which should exalt it—indeed wherein it was once exalted.

For a period of history religion and beauty seemed to walk hand in hand, as the former expressed itself in the world's masterpieces of architecture, painting and poetry. It was not till the Renaissance that beauty was allowed, like learning, to forget her baptism and become a part, indeed a privilege, of the "profane" world. Since then her relations with holiness have been strained, expressing themselves in little more than repetitions and imitations of the glorious past; she seems to find no spontaneous, new expression. On the other hand her association with secularism and indifferentism has roused in religious circles a certain distrust—a distrust confined by no means to Protestant Puritans.

For even in Catholic circles the idea persists that beauty is of secondary, moreover of secular, importance. Whoever thought of putting sins against beauty in his confession? Yet beauty is, we repeat, an attribute of God, equally with wisdom, love and power. What is more, it has in comparison with morality (which all forms of religion exalt and cherish) the same eternal value as charity in comparison with faith and hope. For the moral law is as it were camp hygiene, a necessity of transit, a law like the law of Moses made necessary by sin. When the wilderness is far behind us and our wills are perfect and sin is no more, there will be no more need for the moral law than there was for the law of Moses once the kingdom of God had come.

We may perhaps conjecture that but for the Fall man would have grown in the knowledge of Divine Beauty as he would have grown in the knowledge of Divine Wisdom and Divine Love. But having broken off his own spiritual education he was left groping for beauty as for other things. Sometimes he has held it in flashes and reflections, but its true nature has always eluded him. Therefore there can be no sin against beauty, since knowledge is lacking. We do not know what beauty really is. Most of us are at least roughly agreed on the subject of natural beauty, but beauty in art is always arguable and changing fashions constantly proclaim its contingency.

At the beginning of this section I qualified the saints' deficiency with the word "artistic", without which it would have been altogether too sweeping. For no doubt all or nearly all the saints have appreciated beauty in nature. St. Rose, though she hated her own lovely face, delighted in flowers and embroidered them so ravishingly on silk and damask that many thought her work was supernatural; while St. Thérèse, who could pass by all the artistic treasures of Rome, Naples, Florence, Venice and Milan without a word of admiration except for the tombstones in the Campo Santo, bursts into eloquence at the sight of the Swiss mountains. Cornelia Connelly and St. Catherine of Genoa, both women of more culture and education than the two unmarried saints, seem to have had besides their love of natural beauty a degree of artistic appreciation.

Mother Connelly studied art in Rome and has left at least some of her own achievement in a picture which perhaps displays more supernatural than natural inspiration. St. Catherine of Genoa, living in an age when art was natural, was in the enviable position of having almost everything she used in daily life an object of simple beauty. That she appreciated and valued these objects is shown by the testamentary care with which she disposed of them in her various wills.

But we shall make out a very poor case for our quartet's sense of beauty if we limit beauty to nature and art. There is another beauty which perhaps the saints did not see, but which they certainly showed. There is surely beauty in Catherine of Genoa's welcome home without reproach of the husband who had caused her so much misery, in the kiss with which she took the plague from the mouth of a dying woman, and in that final going forth in a deep night of stars to join her Love. There is beauty again in the innocence of little Rose de Flores as she plays at penance with a wooden cross and then with a young brother's help builds her garden cell of boughs, to go there every morning through the grey-white dusk to pray and play with the Holy Child and spend her day serving the sick of soul and body and worshipping God with all created things. While who shall say there is no beauty in Cornelia Connelly's love of all God gave her and in that greater love which gave it all back to God? And though the beauty of Thérèse Martin's life may be of the same homely order as the *jolie petite cruche* which she tried not to regret in Carmel, it certainly shines in the love which carried her family right up to heaven and thence brought down the fatherhood of God to countless humble souls.

This beauty in act, in life, in soul, may be a clearer, steadier reflection of beauty itself than all that is loveliest in nature and art. We are probably wrong in identifying beauty with aesthetics; these represent only the phenomenal side of it, the side that passes away, beauty *in via*. They are temporal and partial reflections of an eternal reality. In holiness the image is clearer and more complete, hence the apparent indifference of the saints to its smaller flashes in art. I repeat that we do not know what beauty really is, what man shall find in the day he truly sees it in the Godhead; but when we contemplate its reflection in holiness we have at least some idea of its ultimate reality, beauty *in patria*.